Tony's eagerness at times bordered on obsessiveness and was apparent through his training. It's a trait you see in great sportspeople. In *Screaming at the Sky*, that fine line is investigated with great clarity. It's a book every athlete should read.

Anthony Daly,
former Clare manager

As a boxer, I have experienced success and defeat at the highest level. Tony's story shows that you can always pick yourself up off the canvas. To me, *Screaming at the Sky* is all about overcoming.

Bernard Dunne,
former Super Bantamweight World Champion

Screaming at the Sky demonstrates how Tony and all at the Tony Griffin Foundation brought two countries – Canada and Ireland – together to make a positive contribution in the fight to eradicate cancer. This is an inspirational book that shows the power we all have to make a difference. Tony's honesty displays the potential and vulnerability of human nature and is a beautifully written piece of work. It is the story of us all.

Alexa McDonough,
former leader of the New Democratic Party of Canada and member of parliament for Halifax, Nova Scotia

Tony Griffin is best known in Ireland as a Clare hurler. He represented the county at the highest level from 2000 to 2009 and won an All Star award in 2006. The founder of the Tony Griffin Foundation that has now raised over €1 million for various cancer charities, Griffin took a hiatus from hurling following the All Star year to cycle across Canada and Ireland in memory of his father. Now director of the sports management firm Sports AI, he lives in Killaloe, Ireland.

T. J. Flynn has won awards for his feature writing and sports writing. He is a former Irish Arts Journalist of the Year and co-author of the acclaimed *Princes of Pigskin: A Century of Kerry Footballers*. He is a native of Killarney, Ireland, but is a wanderer at heart. He is also a Bob Dylan fanatic.

SCREAMING AT THE SKY

Tony Griffin

with T. J. Flynn

TRANSWORLD IRELAND

TRANSWORLD IRELAND
an imprint of The Random House Group Limited
20 Vauxhall Bridge Road, London SW1V 2SA
www.rbooks.co.uk

First published in 2010 by Transworld Ireland,
a division of Transworld Publishers

A CIP catalogue record for this book
is available from the British Library.

ISBN 9781848270893

Addresses for Random House Group Ltd companies outside the UK
can be found at: www.randomhouse.co.uk
The Random House Group Ltd Reg. No. 954009

The Random House Group Limited supports the Forest Stewardship
Council (FSC), the leading international forest-certification organization. All
our titles that are printed on Greenpeace-approved FSC-certified paper
carry the FSC logo. Our paper procurement policy can be found at
www.rbooks.co.uk/environment

Typeset in 10/15.5pt Versailles by
Falcon Oast Graphic Art Ltd.
Printed and bound in Great Britain by
CPI Mackays, Chatham, ME5 8TD

2 4 6 8 10 9 7 5 3 1

Every effort has been made to obtain the necessary permissions with
reference to copyright material, both illustrative and quoted. We apologize
for any omissions in this respect and will be pleased to make the appropriate
acknowledgements in any future edition.

Mixed Sources
Product group from well-managed
forests and other controlled sources
www.fsc.org Cert no. TT-COC-2139
© 1996 Forest Stewardship Council
FSC

Fear is choosing the safe course; most of us feel we have 'rational' reasons to avoid taking risks. The brave one is not the one without fear, but the one who does what he must despite being afraid. To succeed, you must be willing to risk total failure; you must learn this. Then you will succeed.

George Bernard Shaw

Foreword

I have great admiration for Tony Griffin. You will, too, after reading his inspiring new book, *Screaming at the Sky*. What first struck me about Tony was his raw energy and drive. I've been fortunate to have had some great success with my teams at the Tour de France, but let me put that in perspective: nine professional bike riders race together as a team alongside 171 other riders for 2,200 miles. Tony rode 7,000 kilometres by himself and raised hundreds of thousands of dollars along the way in the fight against cancer – $225,000 to LiveStrong. Now that's my idea of a cycling champion.

I have to admit that when I first met Tony in Austin – and could get a word in edgewise! – the idea of one man's quest to ride his bike across Canada and Ireland with essentially no cycling experience was a bit of a wild one. I'd been told that he was a great hurling player (Tony was quick to explain the game to me) and once we got on the bike together I knew that the athlete within would be able to rise to the occasion. But it's not the physical aspect of Tony that is so impressive, it's his heart and desire.

We saw this spirit throughout our experience in Ireland in

2009. I raced in the Tour of Ireland and then attended the pre-
miere LiveStrong Global Cancer Summit in Dublin. Wherever
I went, the people of Tony's homeland treated us like long lost
friends, just as he does with everyone he meets. Tony was one
of our delegates, too, working alongside five hundred people
from more than sixty countries to establish the first unified
global movement against cancer.

He summed up the impact that one man and one small
country can make when he laughed and said, 'There are over
three hundred million people in America, and your 4th of July
celebration is certainly a great one, but held for the most part
in your country. There are just over four million people in
Ireland, but everyone around the world celebrates St Patrick's
Day!' And with a wink he was off again on another conversation, making another new friend and out to change the world.

Lance Armstrong
Austin, Texas, May 2010

Preface

This book began as the story of one year. The plan was to document the 2009 hurling season to show what it's like to play for a county on the west coast of Ireland, but very quickly, maybe a month or two down the line, it developed into something else.

When we thought about it, we realized that the story began with my father's passing away in December 2005. Out of the grief that surrounded his death, many things occurred that shaped my life: an All Star, a 7,000-kilometre cycle across Canada, and self-discovery. And that's to name but a few. It was clear that without these things I wouldn't have become the person I was in 2009, and I probably wouldn't have chosen to write a book.

So this story really starts at the beginning of 2006, less than a month after my father died. That year I fulfilled one of my life ambitions by devoting myself completely to the game of hurling. I was studying in Canada at the time but put my college life on hold and moved back home to Ballyea for the season.

When the hurling year finished I jumped back on a plane in the Autumn and resumed my studies, but there was something nagging at me. For reasons that I didn't understand at the time, I needed a challenge. One evening something clicked inside my head. I decided that I would cycle across Canada in the summer of 2007 and raise funds for cancer along the way. This journey on the roads of Canada was to bring highs and lows and, looking back now, it shaped me in ways I could never have expected.

The highs were immense and beautiful, and they remained planted in my head while I completed my studies in 2008. That spring, I chose to move back to Ireland and back to hurling. (There was a lot of travel between those two great countries back then!) But the thing was, I discovered that after enormous highs, difficult periods sometimes follow.

I wasn't ready for much of what 2008 threw at me. After that long cycle my body was unprepared for the demands of hurling and for the first time in my sporting life I played with an injury. On top of this, I hadn't come to terms with my father's passing and the year, inevitably, beat me down. It was challenging and it was tough.

Then, late that year, while running in the Ballycugguran Woods in east Clare, trying to clear my head and make sense of the season and my life, I had the idea to document 2009. Maybe, I thought, through its recording I could begin to understand something more about myself, and so the wheels began to turn and this book started to become a reality.

As it happened, 2009 was a challenging season for everybody involved with our hurling team. But despite this I regained my love and passion for the game: something that had been missing the previous season. And I also came to understand more about the fears and doubts that existed within me.

So this is the story of four very different years and the journey I took through this period of my life. It's the story of many things – of people and places, of sport and of life.

And for the most part, it's been an extremely happy journey.

Many people have guided me over the years covered in this book and all the years before that and I would like to express my sincere thanks to them.

To my family, I would like to say thank you for your invaluable contribution to not only this project, but to all the others. For the support and direction, thank you, Mummy. We are all doing our best, aren't we? I love you for it. To Daddy, I know you are enjoying your well-earned rest and all the 'tracing' with old friends. Thanks for all your quiet support and hurling talk. Most of all, thanks for the example of the best parts of human nature.

My thanks also to TJ: we did it, we wrote it and we did it our way. Your belief in the book was the difference.

To Eoin McHugh at Transworld and copy-editor Dan Balado Lopez for their support and patience – most of all for allowing TJ and me the freedom to write this our way.

To Kieran Shannon and Haley McInnis for their advice and encouragement, and to Angela Griffin, Shane O'Neill, Ivor Flynn and Tom Enright, who offered support and feedback on the manuscript as it evolved.

To Travis, my third brother, thank you for your friendship and all the great laughs, most of all thanks for your faith in me.

To Bruce – again thanks for the belief in the vision. Oh, and you are now officially fired!

To Martin Donnelly. Martin, thanks for listening to my message and deciding to get behind me. You were and remain an inspiration in thinking big.

To Eoin Conroy, thanks for everything, most of all your patience and belief. And yes you were right . . . I probably do think too much.

Thanks, too, to Lance Armstrong for providing the foreword to the book. Much appreciated, Lance.

To Gerard Hartmann, thank you for making an invaluable contribution to my career. Thanks also to Hayden Landry for his many hours of treatment and the good laughs.

For the use of their photographs, my thanks to Seamus O'Reilly, Eamon Ward, Sportsfile and Inpho. And a special thank you to John Kelly for the cover image, taken on a cold winter's day above Lough Derg.

To all of the Irish and Canadian TGF volunteers. Words are inadequate to convey my thanks to you for getting behind the 7,000-kilometre Ride for the Cure – we couldn't have done it without you. You know who each of you are and you know what we all learned and shared through TGF.

To all at Dalhousie University. To president Tom Traves – a special thank you for your support and encouragement. To Dr Stephen Cheung – Coach, you are an evil man to whom I will forever be thankful, and I am glad I dissuaded you from your atheist ways. Also, you owe me a cinnamon bun!

To John McCabe. John, you are a true friend and I am convinced the man above placed you on my path just at the right time. Thanks for the advice, the guidance and most of all the words you often repeated that I could do anything and not to set limits. Also thanks to Cathy for those special dinners and many great laughs.

To all in Ballyea Hurling Club. It was an honour to run out in Thurles, Páirc Uí Chaoimh and Croke Park, knowing I was from this small club with big ambitions. I was honoured to be Ballyea's first All Star and know that I will not be the last.

To all the Clare supporters who kept faith and followed the team all over the country, a sincere thanks. Please continue to do so. Success and great days are not far away.

Finally to Keira, thank God I found you. The cycle was worth every kilometre.

2006

The beach at Spanish Point is short, no more than a mile in length. It faces the light-grey Atlantic and only in summertime, when the ocean turns blue, does it fill with people. In the winter, it is an Irish desert.

From here, like the other little beaches that dot the western coastline, it is difficult to distinguish between sky and sea; the horizon is an indefinite blend of both.

Looking straight out across the Atlantic, the nearest chunk of land is 3,000 miles away in the direction of North America. Maybe it's a big city like New York or Boston or a smaller port town on the coast. Maybe it's the island of Newfoundland.

From here, the world is a great, vast place, and on these seashores that divide continents, you can think big. This is a good thing.

The lack of human traffic on the colder, damper days means Spanish Point is also an ideal place to come and train. Its tight dimensions are perfect for middle-distance runs, the kind that shed the down-season paunch and get the muscles breathing once more.

Even though it is early morning on New Year's Day, the weather has been kind and you know that the sun, however pale, will later pitch itself in a clear sky.

Right now, we are here, thirty-four men, to lay the

foundation for a season ahead, to dream of summer and success, to prepare for those days when heat will once more live in the sunlight.

But this morning I am not entirely focused. I look at the sea and feel a heaviness that has not lifted since we buried my father three weeks ago.

I think of my mother and the rest of my family, probably still asleep in their beds, and the private pain they, too, are going through. I think of next week when I must return to study in Canada and wonder how I will cope with this grief, even make sense of it all.

I try to hunt these thoughts from my head. I focus on the session and decide, after a quick deliberation, to take this morning's training in bare feet.

Up ahead, our physical trainer is walking away from the group with a bunch of poles in his hand. As we stretch lightly on the sand, his are the only footprints we can see. He continues walking for a few minutes, and as he does so, some of the players holler down the beach.

'Hey, Johnny! Far enough, far enough! Good man, Johnny. Don't kill us.'

There's always a giddiness to the first session of the year. You look around at your teammates, wonder who will make the cut for the season, study the lines of their bodies and draw conclusions as to who has looked after themselves over the winter and who has not.

Most are in decent shape. Even in the off-season it's wise to maintain fitness and in winter little training groups emerge. A few runs here and there. A weights session or two. Nobody wants to be the guy left behind on the first day back.

We figure Johnny Glynn, our trainer, must now be 700 metres in the distance and at this point he spikes the sand with five coloured poles, marking the finish line. Our manager, Anthony Daly, arranges us into groups of four. The drill is simple: we are to go out at force, round the poles and maintain our speed to the starting point, the manager and trainer making discreet and subtle judgements on their players' physical well-being.

The drill will continue for ten runs with a brief break between each one and if you're wise, you will aim to win each run while keeping something in reserve for the final two or three, finishing strong. By then the decision to run in bare feet will have paid off. You believe that you're a few ounces lighter without boots to weigh you down. You may be wrong but it's a comforting thought.

For this session Brian Lohan is one of my running partners. Lohan is the silent leader of our team, a peg driven into frozen ground; unshakeable. Before I broke on to the squad I saw him as the public at large did, as the gruff, bearish type. I was wrong. He rarely agrees to newspaper or television interviews, he plays with controlled aggression, he puts the fear of God into the opposition, but I have learned that he is not bearish. Lohan is perceptive and a deep thinker. When he speaks, you record every syllable.

In my early days I gauged my value to the team by him, and among us younger players he had no equal. Everything about him spoke strength – he patrolled inches, he would argue over the result of a sprint.

Lohan did whatever it took to win a ball and if I could surpass him during training and equal his intensity I knew I was making progress.

A few months before, he and Colin Lynch, another leader, had squared up to each other during a vigorous training drill. It had been my job to feed a ball to both in a tight square as they tried to win possession before passing the ball back to me. After a few minutes they began crashing into each other with brute force before ending up grappling on the ground.

There was a reason for the tension that night. Three weeks before this incident, during a challenge game against Kilkenny when we conceded our third or fourth goal, Lynch roared at Lohan, telling him to up his game. Few in the team had the authority to question Lohan's commitment. During the game he refused to respond to Lynch but that night three weeks later he remembered.

These were the men who led our county to glory for the first time in close to a century, men who delivered honour to our territory, to our patch of the world, County Clare. When they came to blows that evening, they resembled two warriors. Pupils dilated, veins throbbing in their arms. I struggled to restrain Lohan, our manager looked after Lynch.

An onlooker could have put this incident down to a usual heated exchange on the training field, but there was something deeper at play. Both were maintaining their status that evening, refusing to back down, and even within a team there are times when you must claim your place as your own. You must stand up for yourself. This is what hurling demands.

Back on the beach, and as we're waiting for yet another whistle to signal the start of yet another run, Lohan turns to me with a question.

'When you going back to Canada?'

'Week on Tuesday.'

We're panting. Hands on hips, trying to quickly catch our breath.

'Listen, would you not think about giving college a break for the year? Concentrate on this, on the hurling?'

He was measured in his words, and for him to say something like that meant he had given it some thought. On top of this, he was coming to the end of his playing career, maybe a season or two left, and this question showed his ambition still burned. He was saying he wanted every player to deliver that season, that he believed something big could happen.

'You might have a point there, Brian.'

For the rest of the session, remaining in Ireland for the year was the only concept that existed.

The pieces seemed to fit. My father had just passed away. Staying at home would keep me close to my family.

As well as that, I'd often thought about committing myself purely to hurling for at least one season, and by now, having spent two years abroad, I knew the schedule that living in Canada and playing for Clare demanded.

Over the course of the previous two seasons I'd recorded the number of aeroplanes I had boarded to get from Halifax, Nova Scotia, to Ireland in order to play for Clare. The total was eighty-four.

A Sunday game in Ireland brought a familiar routine of airports and waiting lounges and check-in desks, always beginning on a Friday night.

Halifax to Newfoundland. Change planes. Newfoundland to Heathrow. Change planes. Heathrow to Dublin. Change planes. Dublin to Shannon. Sleep.

When I reversed the trip and arrived back on campus the

following Tuesday morning, I sat in lecture halls surrounded by students discussing their weekends.

'So, what did you get up to?'

'Partied Friday, studied Saturday, then caught a movie, chilled on Sunday.'

Had they asked, I could have told them I'd travelled more than 6,000 miles across the ocean to play a seventy-minute game, that my manager, Anthony Daly, went eyeball to eyeball with the opposing coach, that I logged every single play in my memory and that for the rest of the week my immediate world would be determined by how well I'd played.

I could have told them I lived a different reality.

A good seventy minutes meant I was at peace, that I wouldn't scratch at the doubts and regrets. It was a beautiful world where we as a team had the potential to win an All Ireland championship.

A few mistakes and I analysed not only my game but also my self-worth and visited the dark places of my mind. During those weeks after a poor performance I lived beneath an imagined fog and trained and trained and waited for the next game to come and cleanse me.

Maybe staying at home would not only help keep me close to my family, it would allow me to train harder and play better and steer clear of those shadows, at least for one season.

So Lohan's question was backed by the beauty of good timing.

My thoughts were clearing. Around me, training was coming to an end and the morning was turning into one of those sunny days when you forget it is winter. There was a lovely air of anticipation.

Up on the road, I noticed a small crowd had gathered to watch as we warmed down. Couples out walking their dogs, teenagers still making their way home from New Year's Eve celebrations. They must have wondered what had brought this group of men to the beach at 8.30 on the first morning of the year.

As the session finished we gathered round the manager. Behind us, the empty beach looked as though a stampede of horses had galloped through the sand.

Aside from a few encouraging shouts, Anthony Daly had remained quiet for the entire morning. Now he spoke. It was his third year as manager of the team and when he preached, he never failed to deliver a sermon illuminated by his own character. Into the simplest of talks he poured his soul. His eyebrows bounced and his head bobbed.

He spoke of the upcoming season, of the potential that existed to create something great in the months ahead.

The previous August, we had lost the All Ireland semi-final to a strong Cork team that went on to win the championship. We had come close but there was a gap, he said. We only had to find the bridge.

This morning he was talking within himself, simply stirring the embers of belief. It was too early in the year to catch fire.

I believed in everything he said because with Daly you always knew where you stood. There was a transparency to his words, and as he spoke I was coming closer and closer to remaining in Ireland.

To leave for Canada the following Tuesday would mean two months of training on my own. Training in the dark.

Training in the snow. I could picture the eight weeks in front of me. When I returned to Clare for the season opener I would be welcomed by the lads, accepted into the team, but they would know and I would know that I hadn't suffered with them during the bleak nights of January and February when players are doubled over with exhaustion and pain, locked in a crucible only a teammate can understand. These are moments that give you a voice in the summer, a right to air your opinion. The previous two years had taught me that without this I wouldn't be part of the daily grind and so I would consider myself as being outside the circle.

At Spanish Point I could feel momentum gathering as Daly spoke, momentum I would have lost had I returned to Canada.

His talk ended. Players dispersed.

I looked up past a thick harvest of beach grass that swayed in the wind, high above us on the sand dunes. Light drenching the beach. The slap of waves against the shore.

Lohan had asked a question but for all the world it felt as though a higher power had also spoken.

My decision was made.

John McCabe, walking that quiet, slightly shy walk of his, comes trundling into class, throws his soft blue eyes towards the seats in front of him. Professor John McCabe to his students.

This is my first day on the 2004 kinesiology programme at Dalhousie University. The course is a study of human move-ment with a focus on sports performance. Graduates work in medicine, physiotherapy, sports psychology. One of the guys in the year ahead is now working as a golf club designer for Nike.

So it's diverse and it appeals to me, and it's also a passport to a new world.

John facilitated my move to Nova Scotia.

We met through a mutual friend one rainy Wednesday in a restaurant in Clare. John was in Ireland researching his familial links to County Cavan; I was looking for a new direction in my life.

For the previous two years I had worked as a sales representative for a medical company, playing golf with clients, picking up the tab after we shared fine dinners. Towards the end the job didn't float my boat, didn't even put it in the water. It didn't fulfil the part of my mind that wished to wander.

For a while I searched for a new challenge, and the science of sport had always fascinated me. I also thought that maybe through its understanding I could unlock the secrets of the perfect performance.

Study options existed in Ireland and England but I chose Canada because of John, because it was far away and because it represented adventure.

There were stumbling blocks, always are to a gut decision. I would need $16,000 to enrol – a very significant chunk of money – but I had faith I could find it and already I knew that the *how* wouldn't matter if the *why* was strong enough.

I would have to juggle my emerging hurling career with living in Canada. That, too, was an obstacle I would learn to navigate because I was determined to make Canada work.

When I arrived in Halifax for the first time I did have

mixed feelings. I loved the sense of freedom a new city brought. Back home, a hurler is simply that, a hurler. To most, he doesn't exist outside the confines of the lines on the playing field. It's a frustration and it can become limiting. Because you are a hurler you feel an obligation to eat and sleep the game, but I wanted to fill my head with other sports, other thoughts, new horizons, travel.

Those first days in Halifax I walked around wearing a white woolly hat that my sister had bought me and a big pair of shades. Anonymous. Loving it. This, I felt, I could not have done at home on the streets of Ennis.

Shocker: County Hurler Struts with Strange Hat and Dark Glasses!

Because I was born with a restless mind, I've wanted to push beyond hurling and explore new territories and at times that has driven me outside the invisible stereotypes of an Irish hurler. Once, at a post-match meal, a waitress from overseas was serving us. Out of pure curiosity I asked where she was from. Venezuela. 'Interesting,' I said. 'That's Hugo Chavez country, isn't it? What are things like there these days?'

So we shoot the breeze for a minute or two as she lands mountains of food on the table, and as soon as she's gone, one of the lads pipes up.

'Ah Griff, you're full of it!'

'What?'

'Chatting up a pensioner! You should be ashamed of yourself!'

The lads were in stitches. I was the punchline.

I knew the drill though, knew it was coming. It would have been easier to keep my head down, stay quiet, drink some water as my friend from Venezuela gave us our meal, but I am curious, and my curiosity is there to be satisfied.

It's not that those comments don't register. They do, and on occasion they will win but the trick is to push past them because they will always exist.

This year, 2006, I realize that I must drown out the voices of others to live life according to my own commandments, but sometimes that's still difficult.

Sometimes I don't feel like a typical hurler, or at least a typical hurler defined by the public, by tradition and by some of those who play the game.

It's like this. Hurling is a world where a new pair of shoes in a dressing room is a big deal. Too flash and you must be on the market for a boyfriend; too plain and you're a dullard with no taste.

So the anonymity and tolerance of Canada were welcomed, and these were currencies I valued.

After a short time I came to fall in love with the place. Halifax is a friendly maritime city whose sloping streets fall gently to the water. As the largest city in Nova Scotia, I was struck by how relaxed and easy-going it was, and whenever I left, like others who leave Halifax, I found that I missed the smell of the sea, the salt in the air.

Then there were the girls – the beautiful, head-turning, neck-straining girls on campus. Behind my shades, I was bug-eyed as they floated by.

But it did take some time to settle. My first phone call home was made the first Sunday after I landed at a beat-up phone box on the way to John McCabe's for a turkey dinner cooked by his wife Cathy. Back home the whole family were having an end-of-summer barbecue. There was a familiar hum in the background, the noise of any family on a Sunday, and being one of seven kids, the chatter made that phone box a lonely place.

After the call ended there was a deep pang in my stomach, then the thought: What have I done?

John made it easier to cope with the rhythm of this new life and lifted me from the folds of homesickness. He picked me up from the airport every single time I flew in, found me my first apartment in Halifax, loaned me his bike. He took me on little trips around the city, pointed things out, told me the history of the place. Most of all, he encouraged me to stick by my decision to come to Canada and regardless of his age and status as a professor, John and I became close friends.

John McCabe was a character. When he spoke, he sounded like some hero out of a Luke Kelly song and you sensed he hadn't just flowed through life but tasted it. Little details captivated him.

He was born to an Irish family and lived for a while just out-side Boston. As a youngster, maybe when he was fourteen or fifteen, he had the hots for an Irish girl. It was innocent stuff. He took her to the movies, brought her on dates. Being young and apparently in love, he suddenly got it into his head that he wanted to marry her. But there was a hitch. She told him straight up that her father wouldn't approve because John was second-generation Irish. Her father wanted to return home to Ireland one day, his fortune made, and no way could his daughter bring back a second-generation companion. She had to find herself a first-generation boyfriend, so she and John were forced to part. He cursed his second-generation luck.

14

In his chronicle of stories, this is one that always makes him smile. John holds memories as personal treasures and endears himself to others because he recalls tales most would label as meaningless, yet this illuminates him.

During that first day in class he had his game face on but deep down he's a joker and he can't resist an opportunity.

So he's going round the lecture hall, picking out some students from a list of names on the desk in front of him, randomly asking people to introduce themselves.

When I walked into the hall I had looked around and noticed everybody was a few years younger. At the back sat an older guy, around my own age, and I figured that in a room of eighteen- and nineteen-year-olds I wouldn't stand out beside somebody of twenty-three or twenty-four.

Also, the seat was in a good location. Easy access. In. Out. Head down and stay anonymous.

As John is calling out names I'm hoping he will not pick me out and embarrass me, but sure enough, he gives me my moment in the limelight.

'Do we have a Tony Griffin in the class?'

I stand up.

'Tony, says here in my notes you're from Ireland.'

The whole class turns round. Ireland?

'From a place whose name I can't pronounce.'

Of course John McCabe knew how to pronounce Ballyea, my little parish just outside Ennis. He had written many letters to my home, but that day he was having fun with me and in the process my anonymity was being eroded.

I was from Ireland. A faraway place. Others were interested in hearing about my country.

After class, my seating companion stuck out his hand and had a question or two about why I'd chosen to study in Canada.

He was interesting. His name was Richard Ashton and he was about to take part in an Ultimate Fighter event. I figured I could learn some new sports techniques from this guy so we arranged to train together later that week.

In the autumn of 1968 Richard Nixon was preparing to become President of the United States, the Vietnam War was wall-papered on people's minds and my father drove from London to Falkirk, in the heart of Scotland.

He was working in England's capital at the time, putting funds together to return to Clare in order to purchase a farm and live off the land. That September he and a neighbour from home took the 700-mile round trip to visit another Clare native who had married and settled in Falkirk.

It was there, in Falkirk, that he met my mother as well as her sister, Brigetta, who had married the Clare native my father was visiting.

'Maria, Jerome would be a smashing fella for you,' Brigetta told her.

'Go away, he's far too quiet for me!'

The following day my father returned to London and on the way out of Falkirk stopped by my mother's workplace.

The way she tells it, with her accent that's still tinged with Scottish tones, she can bring you right back to the moment.

'I was working in a big office with a winding staircase and Jerome and his friend, this fella Hanrahan, stopped by

Monday morning to say cheerio. Hanrahan's car had one of these musical hooters; he was a real character. So they hooted from below and I came down to wave them off. Well, the bould Hanrahan grabbed me and planted a kiss on my cheek. Jerome told me later that if he did, then Jerome wasn't going to be out-done! It wouldn't be his style to do something like that because he was reserved but he grabbed me too and I got two kisses that day!'

My father travelled back to London and the two remained in contact, regularly writing to each other.

Something blossomed between them and just four months later, in the final week of January 1969, my father was packing his belongings and moving to Falkirk.

He stayed with my aunt, Brigetta, and her husband and for the next nine months he and my mother went out together every night, finding places that catered for folk music and going to the pictures.

The first evening they missed on the town was the night of their wedding, 13 September.

They remained for eight years in Falkirk, where five of their seven children were born, and during that time my father worked a lot in Plymouth, right at the bottom end of England. It was a long journey down, nine hours on the train, but he was saving up, like many of the Irish community in Britain at the time, to move back home.

Work in Plymouth was tough and my father was away from Falkirk and his family for three or four weeks at a time. Down there he worked underground on the gas tunnels. Regulations were unheard of at the time and at some stage he came into contact with asbestos.

After eight years, my parents and the five eldest children left their house that overlooked Falkirk and relocated to Clare, settling in Ballyea.

Our home sits on an old and narrow country road that forms part of a cobweb of other old and narrow country roads. If you are unfamiliar with the area, it is easy to get lost. Our home is enveloped on all sides by green fields and close by, my father farmed some land in the evenings and went to work during the day.

If you ask my mother about her husband one of the first things she will say is that he was ever so quietly determined. One of her favourite stories happened a few years back, shortly before Dad became ill as a result of the exposure to that asbestos.

As is the wont of most mothers, she had always been conscious of over-spending. 'Old habits die hard,' she will say.

My father had always been fond of cutting timber to stock the fire for winter, but as it happened his chainsaw gave up on life. He brought it to Ennis to have it repaired and was told the machine was beyond saving. He returned home to relay the news to my mother, saying he would have to buy a new chainsaw as soon as he could because the winter was approaching. 'Ah,' said my mother, with her accountant's hat on, 'we won't be needing it, Jerome. We have the oil to keep the house warm. We don't need any more timber.'

My father nodded.

Many men find chopping wood a peaceful and soothing process, and in this my father was probably no different.

But unknown to her he saved some money and a few weeks later came walking up the road outside our house. My mother was in the kitchen and from the window could see he was concealing something beneath a coat. A couple of minutes passed before the hum of the chainsaw started in one of the nearby fields.

She deduced what had happened. As the chainsaw continued to hum, she boiled the kettle, made some sandwiches and filled a flask full of tea.

She wandered out into the fields and walked up to where he had cut down a large tree. He said nothing, just continued to split the timber, cutting one log as a bench for my mother and one as a bench for himself. In the middle of the two seats he placed the biggest log of all, as a table.

They sat down and ate their picnic.

As John McCabe and I were driving through Halifax on one of those early trips, my eyes were drawn to a curious green incline in the middle of the city. Citadel Hill.

From the top there are sweeping views and you can see Halifax Harbour, where, John says, in 1917, the world's largest man-made explosion prior to Hiroshima took place when a Belgian relief vessel, the *Imo*, and a French munitions carrier, the *Mont Blanc*, collided.

It's a sad story from a beautiful place.

John and I walk to the peak of Citadel Hill and before we reach the top I have found my first Halifax training camp. The incline is tailor-made for long, hard uphill sprints. Back home I know the team will push themselves to the limit before the season starts. I choose not only to do the same but to compensate for my absence by going beyond the line.

I flog my body. I force it to places it has never been. I gorge on the training possibilities presented to me.

Citadel Hill became my private crucible.

From my apartment on College Street I jog the ten minutes to the base of the hill three evenings each week. For the following hour, relentlessly, I sprint to the top, panting, gasping, not caring about the panorama from the peak, ignoring the twinkling lights of the city, oblivious to John McCabe's harbour story.

I see the lads at home, bent over in pain. I jog to the bottom of Citadel Hill and start again.

In a room beneath the Dalhousie swimming complex I spar with Richard Ashton.

Richard is a tough guy, an angry guy. For him, boxing is a way of letting it out. For me, it is a way of allowing my body to become acquainted once more with the sensation of being hit and knocked to the ground.

When I first joined the Clare squad in 2000, one of our physiotherapists, Colum Flynn, a boxing trainer, arranged for me to join Chick Gillen's famous boxing gym in Galway, where I was studying economics at the city's university. The first night Chick threw me into the ring with a big, solemn Russian. I looked at my brush-handle arms. Looked across at the Russian, all muscle and ripples and quivering torso. I shuddered.

The bell sounded.

I pictured *Rocky IV* – Balboa v. Drago – and was quietly petrified.

Chick told me to work the jab, and as his words rang in my ears I couldn't even figure what a jab looked like; I simply concentrated on staying upright as Drago pounded away at my head and body.

The bell sounded once more. Chick put his arm around me and said maybe I was born to be a hurler, not a boxer and Rocky quietly left Chick's gym in defeat.

I joined the Dalhousie varsity track squad, one of the best collegiate outfits in Canada, and trained with their second team. I was shown how to squat properly, how to sprint more efficiently. We had to run tied to a sled loaded down with weights. This was structured training, something to do on Tuesday and Thursday nights, and it also meant I was part of a team again. The track work fed my obsession with improving my speed, which would thereby, I felt, improve me as a hurler.

That first year in Halifax the snow came in November. I was surprised by its enormity. The city turned white beneath thick, heavy snow, snow that crunched under your feet and went up to your waist, snow that arrived in furry blankets and remained for months. The temperature dropped to minus 40 Celsius. I was unprepared, but I refused to relent.

On the university soccer field I continued to take my hurley out to hit some ball on the astro turf. Flanked by the bare trees and grey skies of South Street, I would shoot at the soccer goals, imagine I was playing in Croke Park on a warm August afternoon. I would provide a loud, spirited commentary, always saving the game from the jaws of defeat.

It was difficult to run on the snow and my supply of balls was dwindling. Every long-range shot brought the possibility of losing a ball, having it buried in an avalanche.

Whenever one went missing, I would try to retrieve it,

searching a 10-foot radius in a freezing rage. I rarely found joy. Gave up with numb hands, icicles for fingers, the ball lost until the thawing of springtime.

In the winter I continued to run the cold, snow-covered Citadel. I questioned my sanity but a t'ai chi group was not disturbed by the weather and continued to show up every day. That was enough to propel me forward.

But there were times when I chose not to train, when I was defeated by the conditions or seduced by a college party. Later, I would beat myself up over my decision and vow to go even harder tomorrow.

Those winter evenings, after an hour on the hill, my feet became blocks of ice. I would reach the top and look back at the slushy trail I'd worn through the snow, and as I inhaled, my nostrils would flare and scorch.

Any time I tired or wavered I would focus on the team training in Clare. 'They're doing so much more than you,' I'd tell myself. So I'd overcompensate.

This happened regularly. In 2005, during the lead-up to a league game against Waterford, I once more convinced myself I had not done enough. In Canada I upped my regime in the four weeks before I travelled home, loading the training schedule I had pinned to my bedroom wall with extra sessions – weights, plyometrics, stamina work, core sessions, striking drills. I would train three times every day when my college timetable allowed.

I did this because I doubted myself. Doubted my ability to produce. I worried what people at home would say if I returned and didn't perform.

Ah. Griffin. Not up to it.

Over in Canada. Should be living here like the rest of the team.

I allowed the outside voices to seep into the crevices of my imagination.

I came back to play that Waterford game and scored a goal and two points. I had done my job and the 1–2 would keep the gremlins and their voices off my shoulder. That week, the world I returned to in Halifax would be beautiful once more, and in my head I could clearly visualize Clare winning the All Ireland.

But I should have paid more heed to my body. During that Waterford game my muscles were tired. My legs creaked. My calves cramped. Having trained on the snow of Halifax I wasn't used to running on grass. The unfamiliar sensation of mud and soft ground in Waterford, on top of my overtraining, meant my body simply couldn't last the game. Five minutes before the end I had to come off, shattered, replaced by my good friend Barry Nugent.

The compulsion to improve had always been there. After my first championship season for Clare, 2002 – a year when we made the All Ireland final and a year when I should have been content with my contribution – I vowed to bring my game to the next level.

One of the things I chose to work on was my goalscoring. I sought the advice of some of the best goalkeepers in the county and they gave me an inside line, told me the trademark of great goalscorers is their unpredictability and that, logically, a goalkeeper is unable to plan for something he cannot foresee. Because of the shape of my body when I struck the ball, goalkeepers could guess my target, so instead of aiming for the top corner of the net with most of my shots at goal, I would carry the ball a few steps further and unleash it with power. Or, I would hop the ball in front of goal instead of choosing a clean shot.

In Halifax, I persuaded a conditioning professor to help with my striking. He recorded my movement as I struck the ball and this was broken down into a detailed analysis. As a result, we found I was leaning back too far and was prone to hitting under the ball as opposed to striking through it.

I fixated on his advice and it seems like it's always been that way. I would take little nuggets of information from any nook or cranny. When I was treated by the renowned physical therapist Ger Hartmann at his clinic in Limerick I would lie on his treatment table and plague him with questions about other athletes he worked with. I asked him what Tiger Woods ate for breakfast, what kind of training Paula Radcliffe did to ensure she didn't burn out late in a race, my eyes popping out with whatever scrap he threw my way to keep me quiet.

If I felt I could achieve a half per cent improvement to my game, I would do whatever was necessary. It's a common theme with athletes, but sometimes this compulsion can drag you under. Sometimes you need to step back.

Another classroom scene. Sports Psychology. A lazy Friday afternoon, warmth outside, lecturer and students drifting for the comfort of the weekend.

I'm called on to help demonstrate how athletes should deal with pressure. I'm asked how many people I play in front of when I hurl for Clare. 'A few hundred?' the lecturer enquired. 'Or does the crowd ever reach to one thousand?'

I could have kept quiet, cradled my anonymity, but I decided against downplaying the truth.

'Well,' I said, 'the last game I played at home was five weeks back and fifty-six thousand people showed up to see that one.'

I knew I would get a reaction and there were distinct, audible gasps. The class snapped to attention and questions were thrown at me.

What is this sport? Who plays it? What the hell, man, you train five days a week, play in front of those huge crowds and you don't get paid? You do this and get up next morning to work? Holy shit!

It was the first time I was asked to speak about hurling to an audience who hadn't grown up with the game, but since that day I have been asked hundreds of times, What is hurling? I would refer to it as the fastest field game in the world, cite rules, say that each team has fifteen players, describe it as a hybrid between ice-hockey on grass, rugby and Scottish shinty, but only when I explained *why* Irish people played hurling did the enquirers understand.

First, I had to explain that it isn't just a sport. That we don't really choose to play it, we are reared with it. We are born into it in the way that we are born into our religion; it is part of our biological fabric. We travel to school at five years of age with a hurley in our hands, which we place under our desks each morning and retrieve each lunchtime.

We become so familiar with holding this stick from such a young age that it morphs into an extension of our own arm. We chase cows with it, hack at ditches with it, we search brambles and briars for lost balls with it, like small pirates on the prowl for buried treasure.

As a kid, the game consumed me. With my brothers and a handful of friends I would play in the field at the side of our house, beneath sycamore and ash trees, just like kids would play hockey on frozen ponds near Saskatoon, or soccer on the beaches of Rio, or basketball under streetlights in Indiana. They were Gretzky, Pelé, Jordan; I was D. J. Carey. I hummed commentary in my own head. I dodged cowdung like it was an opposing defender.

In the darkness, I answered my mother's calls for bedtime by begging for five more minutes, time to score just one more goal, and even though that field no longer resembles Croke Park, even though it has shrunk in size, those echoes have never left me.

Hurling presses against all of us. In the complex and hushed relationships between your average Irish father and your average Irish son, conversations about sport are the one line of communication that remains open. You can discuss the form of a team, an upcoming game, and not feel awkward.

A father will express his emotion and love through hurling. Before a game, my own father would tell me to mind my hands, not to allow them to get broken by the hurleys of opponents. I read between the lines and understood what he meant.

And because the place you are born becomes the team you represent, there is an ancient, almost allegorical quality to the sport. It is like going to war without treading on the battlefield, and it's a throwback to old Irish history when the men and women who played hurling were depicted as brave and courageous.

Way back then they played in clans, and though we no longer organize ourselves into battling tribes, we must still acknowledge that aggressive DNA we have inherited. Hurling fills this role.

Canadians understood the game without ever seeing it, not simply because they have the game of hockey, but because through hockey they relate to hurling's core value: the field is the only place where your gladiatorial ancestry is given free expression, where you can address certain questions about your true self.

There's a macho element of course, an ego-feeding element that exists. But there is also an element that goes deeper than feeding off the thousands watching in the stadium, beyond the clusters of girls who choose to follow hurlers from bar to bar after a championship game.

Because you live among the people who watch and judge your play, everything you do on the field is magnified.

For some, and for me in particular, hurling is a high-wire trick played out in front of family, friends, neighbours, coaches. It's a tightrope walk with no apparent safety net.

Make the tackle, score the goal, and you're a hero. You have answered those questions about your character, and con-gratulations, you are now a true man.

But there's a flip side, and this was the one I dwelled upon. When a game hung in the balance, with seconds on the clock and my body tired and weary, could I pull a win out of the bag?

If I slipped up, I was weak. I lacked mental strength because my brain could not master my body. My self-worth plummeted. That's when the fog really came in.

A bad game was like a nightmare lived out before those

whose opinions I respected most, and because the game has always been so intertwined with who I am and where I am from, at some point the lines blurred and it became difficult to separate the hurler from the person.

The darkest night arrived after we lost to Wexford in the league of 2006. I sat on my bed and looked down at my feet. Little blisters had gathered on the soles. My muscles twitched and a boiling rage grew within me.

Our defeat that afternoon should have been packaged and filed away simply as a February game best forgotten, but I couldn't let it go.

The previous week, in the league opener, we had pre-dictably beaten a below-par Down side by a big score and had yet to be tested. An away game against Wexford would indicate how my eight weeks had been advancing, but if there was any personal progress test that day, then I failed it miserably.

Afterwards I searched for answers, replayed the day scene by scene and concluded that even before we reached the stadium, I hadn't been focused. I was sitting close to the front of the bus, chatting more than usual. The atmosphere was relaxed and easy. Even the management were taking things in their stride, joking around.

Part of what endeared me to Anthony Daly was his ability to communicate, to laugh with the players, and the ease with which he would switch to game mode always amazed and impressed me. An hour before throw-in there would be a transformation, like a priest putting on the collar; but for me there was a risk I couldn't shake that casual tone if I became too immersed in it.

Wexford was one of those days.

Climbing off the bus, I hadn't flipped channels – I couldn't – and on the field it showed. The day was freezing and overcast. All over the pitch Wexford were tuned in and sharp while I played without confidence or conviction. I created some chances to score but in those crucial split seconds I made the wrong decisions and chances slipped by. We lost by eight points.

The drive back to Clare was one long funeral song. The bus was quiet, which was usual after a defeat, but I was bogged down in my own head, grieving over our lack of passion and belief, worrying about my own lethargy. Then, as if by reflex, I began to pick at any sore I could find.

In the first half I had charged in on goal, ball in hand, and found myself in a prime position to strike. I hesitated. Shoot or pass?

I was half-blocked and the ball trickled wide.

Did this mean I was lazy, that I didn't have it? This was to be my year. I had given up everything. I was living like a hermit, financially broke, spending my days training, resting and preparing for games, and for what? To play like this?

By the time I reached Ballyea I was boxed in by anxiety. It didn't matter that there was a fire burning or the house smelled of a hot meal cooking. I didn't care about the usual kind words of 'hard luck', 'next time' from my family.

This night stood by itself. I had invested so much of myself in the league, thought I was going somewhere with my preparations, but Wexford seemed like a dam in the river.

My head throbbed with thoughts, and without ever deciding, I found my fingers lacing a pair of runners, my eyes searching for some training gear, and my feet walking out the front door.

I turned left up the hill and ran past farm buildings and sleeping houses. I ran to quieten my mind, to drop from fatigue, to wash the dirt from my body. I pounded hard on the ground. I longed to feel pain.

The game played over and over in tiny fragments and flashbacks like one of those black-and-white movie reels. I ran faster, climbing to the top of the hill, where in the light you can see the River Fergus glitter in the valley below.

I kept going, kept running in the dark. I felt the lactic acid seep through my blood and mingle with the stiffness of the game and the journey home. For some reason this felt good and somewhere on that grassy lane I began to see things clearly.

When I reached the main road to Ennis, I stopped. Looked up.

This wasn't healthy. I wanted perspective. I wanted to play without fear, and under a clearing sky I decided I could not play and live tied up by these shackles of self-doubt and over-analysis. It was a decision half-made but I was moving in the right direction.

My legs and feet ached. I jogged back home, back to bed, pain spreading from my ankles, the blisters beneath my feet already beginning to form.

That night was a small breakthrough and afterwards I chose to play things smarter. Dedicating every single day to the game for eight months meant, effectively, I had become the first full-time hurler in the modern era, and this brought its own pressures, internally and from the outside.

One afternoon in the spring, I was drinking coffee in Ennis and picked up a newspaper. In the sports pages, the 1996 All Ireland-winning Wexford manager Liam Griffin was address-ing my so-called 'professionalism'. He said it was worrying for hurling that I had gone full-time and I interpreted this as Liam Griffin saying I was leading the game in the wrong direction, moving it away from its amateur ethos – the foundation on which the game was built and continues to thrive.

But all I wanted to do was spend a year hurling, focused on the game that had come to define me. It now clicked that analysts and supporters were expecting bigger things of me, and for a few days I allowed this to weigh me down. I won-dered what would happen if I collapsed that season; would people look upon me as a hurling failure? The stakes were higher.

I needed a break, a release. I felt I had crossed the line and stepped into a destructive state of mind immediately after the Wexford defeat. The unvaried nature of the Clare routine was getting to me and I craved the stimulation of Canada, the sight of a new girl in class, the target of getting to know her before the week finished.

Hurling had become my sole focus for a couple of months and I was in a trough. I needed to see the White Caps. I woke one Thursday morning and decided to book the next flight to Halifax for the weekend. If purchasing a ticket meant I tumbled further into debt, then I didn't care.

John McCabe picked me up when I landed and deposited

me at my friends' house. I met some old buddies. Drank some beer. Once more I caught a glimpse of life's other side.

When I embraced John at Halifax airport four days later for the return journey, I had a longing to stay in Canada, but once I arrived back in Clare I knew I had returned with the perspective I was looking for. Hurling was becoming part of the bigger picture.

I sensed I was developing into the fittest player on the team. Brian O'Connell – athletic and strong – had burst on to the squad a few years earlier and was the barometer when it came to measuring the shape you were in. The whole team was given a fitness test of sorts one evening. We had to go through endless sit-ups and this torture was followed by a press-ups challenge. Johnny Glynn lined us up in a row under the lights of St Flannan's College. Last man pushing got the glory.

When we made it to sixty, bodies started to drop. Slowly, past eighty and ninety, only a handful remained and I knew only Brian and I would be left pushing. I refused to give in. We passed a hundred, just the two of us, Johnny counting aloud, the other players looking on. By now we could just about hold ourselves off the floor. Our legs and arms were buckling. It took every unit of energy just to slightly bend our elbows. When Johnny counted 108, we collapsed simultaneously.

I was also beginning to make my voice heard. At the Temple Gate Hotel in Ennis that January, the team was introduced to video analysis for the first time. After the address from the analysis expert, I was first to speak. This was significant. Surrounded by big characters, All Ireland winners like Sean McMahon, Lohan, Lynch, I was making my own statement, saying I was ready to assume some leadership and I was slowly chipping away at the uncertainties I'd allowed to live within me.

I put any free time to use. I wrote down my goals. Win an All Ireland. Win an All Star.

Most of all, I wanted to rid myself of the self-doubt that crept in. I faced up to some things. I acknowledged that I always had a warped sense of my own ability, that in terms of hurling I would rarely allow myself to appreciate my better qualities.

Even as a teenager it was there. When I was twelve, I was chosen on a Clare Under-14 squad. After a couple of practice sessions the group was cut to twenty-two. I analysed each player. I took out a copybook the night before the cut, wrote all forty names down and ranked each player according to their strengths and weaknesses as I saw them. I was sure I wouldn't make the grade. Though looking back now I was one of the stronger players on the squad, I picked myself as number twenty-two, right on the bubble.

More than ten years on and a similar lack of confidence had followed me. Again, it was tangled up in hurling. In a game, I could contribute positively ten times but I would focus on the one blunder. While I was working for the medical company, driving to and from the office for days after a game, I would dwell on that mistake. 'Could I have won that ball?' 'Does the fact that I fumbled it mean I don't have the right stuff?' The radio would hum with music but I wouldn't hear it. I couldn't focus on the outside world, and my job suffered.

I was also putting too much stock in the words of others. I had to start thinking for myself.

I had forever felt the need to impress the manager, the coach, the person in the crowd. I wanted them to think, 'Tony Griffin is great.' More importantly, I wanted to realize this myself through positive feedback.

But 2006 was the year I had to learn that I owed nothing to the world.

I thought a lot about my father and I knew he was his own man, that he really didn't care what people would think. It's a great ability to have because you can do so much more with your life if you're your own man, if you own yourself.

I remembered a particular summer evening in Galway when I was fifteen. At the time my sister Angela had started her first job, which was in Donegal, right at the northern tip of Ireland. On Sundays we would drive to Galway where she would board the bus. It was a day out.

This one warm evening, she had chosen a seat at the very back and we waited outside to wave her off. My father disappeared. A few minutes later, he passed us by with an ice-cream cone in his hand. He walked on to the bus like a man stepping on to an ocean liner. The seats were packed with people but he continued, proudly, to the very back where he handed Angela the cone.

That moment stayed with me.

He didn't care. He had that great ability to remove himself from the opinions of others.

Changing my approach didn't happen overnight but I found that you could teach your brain to think in a certain way. That you have a choice and you can evolve. You can return to your older habit or you can reinforce your improved behaviour, which, over time, becomes your automatic decision. I had to make and re-make my decision to focus on the positive, to remain aware that life was bigger than hurling and bigger than Clare. I vowed to throw off the shackles.

I conditioned myself to play with no fear and therefore to have no fear. If things were not going well on the field, I would overcome this. My doubts and insecurities could be conquered. If I was playing well, I could play even better.

For games, I continued with a pre-match strategy that had served me reasonably well but promised that I would adhere to its targets in a stricter way.

Prior to every game, I recorded what I had to do. In the middle of a page I circled the opposition and the date of the game. I drew arrows around the circle and listed a dozen or so specific things I felt I had to do during the game. 'Stay in the moment.' 'Use speed to run at opponent.' 'You always play well against Offaly.' 'Meet tackle with tackle.' 'You are a patient goalscorer.'

Things like that.

Aside from these specifics, I had a general concept: never panic and always retain your focus.

I would picture that page and recall the plan during a game. If I was marking a wing-back and he picked up a loose ball and fired over a point from 70 yards, stirring the crowd into a frenzy, I could say to myself, 'Okay, fair enough. He scored. Move on. Things don't change. The plan stays the same.'

At the time I had finished reading *Winning Every Day*, the book by the former Notre Dame football coach Lou Holtz. He had come up with the term W-I-N: What's Important Now, and that stuck in my head because you can apply it to any situation.

What's important for, say, a parent bringing up two kids alone? Is it to fill your weekend by sitting on a barstool or is it to be there, always, for your children?

On the field, what was important? To spend mental energy fixating over a missed opportunity or to focus on the next challenge the game will throw at me?

When each game was finished, I would return to my page and provide a short written assessment of how well I had done. So, after the championship game against Wexford on 23 July, beneath my arrowed instruction 'When taking on marker, do so aggressively' I concluded, 'Could have been better, will be better.'

As the 2006 season developed, so too did this new mental approach, but it would take time to kick in fully.

I adapted to the slower beat of Ballyea after moving back, but in the early weeks there were times when I questioned the decision I made at Spanish Point.

Three weeks into the year I was missing Halifax, finding Clare to be more confining than ever.

On the street in Ennis I bumped into a neighbour and hurling man, Michael Keane. He asked how I was keeping. I told him I was unsure if I had chosen the right thing to do for the year.

His answer was astute; it lifted the cloak of doubt from my back.

'Well Tony, when you're doing something, just do it. From today on, don't think of the "what ifs" or the "should haves". You're on this path now. Just go after it.'

Sometimes people walk the same streets as you for some unknown reason. After that, I never looked behind.

In the morning I would lie in bed and stare at the mist falling on an ash tree across the fields. I watched the leaves change colour as the weeks went by, getting greener and fuller, and I tried to preserve the image.

I had a whole season ahead of me but I already realized my time would pass in the blink of an eye. In the silence I saw beauty and God in many things and became increasingly aware of a higher power.

I stacked a pillar of books – sports books, books about Che Guevara and Muhammad Ali, literary works by Kerouac and Hemingway – on the floor of my small bedroom in Ballyea and vowed to finish each one.

From time to time I took an individual session with Jamesie O'Connor, a former Player of the Year, and he provided additional coaching on how to attack effectively. Jamesie had been my economics teacher at school and a hero to every aspiring hurler who walked the halls at St Flannan's. When I first joined the Clare panel in 2000, his commitment stood out. In the middle of a winter training session in Crusheen, we were doing a drill that involved sprinting and press-ups. Sprint for a few seconds, then down into press-ups. At one point Jamesie noticed I wasn't doing a full press-up. He roared at me, 'You're not doing it properly! Go down the whole way!' He was entering the latter period of his career at that stage but he was still hungry, still putting his face into the mud and muck of Crusheen, still demanding more from himself and others.

Aside from Jamesie's occasional sessions in 2006, I found a routine that worked for me and so the weeks had a familiar timetable. Usually, I woke at 7.45, I ate Weetabix and an orange, then went outside to feed the calves. After that I returned to bed for an hour, got up once more, cooked porridge, ate a tangerine and two slices of brown bread with peanut butter.

That pre-season, rest was also becoming part of my arsenal. A practice game on Sunday meant I could recover all day Monday before a light training session in the evening. On top of the three scheduled collective training sessions each week, I would go to the handball alleys on Tuesday to practise my striking and to keep my wrists strong. Later on I would puck some ball under the grey slate of St Flannan's College with my teammate Diarmuid McMahon. There, we could leave off whatever steam was building and that in itself was a welcome bonus compared with the days and nights of training by myself in Halifax.

Wednesday was the big session of the week. We met at 5.45 in the evening for a weights programme at the gym then we travelled together to the field for sprint coaching, reaction work and running intervals, which began at seven.

Thursday I would swim, loosen out, stretch.

On Friday, my routine was to jog 5 miles in the dark to St Flannan's. There, I would lift weights for forty-five minutes with an album by the Irish band The Frames playing continuously in the background, then jog back home again.

My worries were few. I had a quiet, warm place to live. My dinners were prepared at home by my mother and my training gear was looked after.

I didn't flog myself to the extent that I had done in Halifax and I could visualize my body growing in strength and laying down little capillaries into the muscles so they could be fed with more oxygen.

On the odd occasion people poked fun because I refused to get even a part-time job, but I wanted to immerse myself in this lifestyle and I knew other players would give anything to be in my position, even for the chance to recover fully from a training session or game without having to rise and go to work or college the following morning.

The previous season, 2005, had ended with a semi-final defeat to Cork on an August Sunday. It would be five months before Clare played again.

During that vacuum I spent hours in lectures, travelling to class, in bank queues and coffee shops swirling the Cork game around in my head, concluding that I hadn't contested honestly for loose possession and I hadn't run at their defence in the closing minutes of the game.

These thoughts added to my longing to get back on the field.

The opportunity came with the pre-league tournament the Waterford Crystal Cup and a low-key game deep in winter against University College Cork. For most it was low key. For me this was my first game as a full-time hurler. It had significance.

The night before, my mother and I spoke about my father. I could see that his death was weighing heavily with her.

I would win an All Ireland medal this year and believed

this would ease the pain. Other years, this idea was a concept that existed out there, somewhere on the horizon.

This year it was different. Belief had replaced hope.

I scored four points the following day, rated myself as a six out of ten, but that day's significance lay in the fact that this was the first game of my Clare hurling career my father did not attend. Once, in the first half, I looked at the small crowd and was certain I had seen him. After the game, with my head down and jogging for the dressing room, I glanced up and expected to see his face. He was not there.

Later on, when I had to sort out some of my father's things, I came to realize a lot. In his top drawer I found a trove of faded hurling articles and match programmes. I was struck by his huge regard for the game and how he had traced my hurling life from the day it had begun.

In mid-December 1999, while I was still studying in Galway, I'd got a phone call from Cyril Lyons, one of the Clare senior selectors, to say I had been called up for Clare training. My heart pumped. The phone in our flat could receive incoming calls but we couldn't call out, so I raced to a phone box down the street to call my father and let him know the news. The glass on the phone box was smashed, the night was blustery and a wind gushed across the phone, but I could hear the delight in his tone.

A few days later, Sean McMahon – the same Sean McMahon I'd emulated as a youngster in the field beside my house – picked me up for training. He was working in Galway at the time and as I waited by a car dealership for him to collect me, I wondered what in the world I would speak to him about on the eighty-minute drive to training. Inevitably, I tapped him for information, wondered how often he trained, did he lift weights, what weights did he lift.

Those trips to and from training with Sean helped break down a lot of barriers. We began to gently slag one another, and through Sean I became comfortable in the company of guys like Lynch, Lohan and Davy Fitzgerald.

Three nights a week that winter Sean would drop me to my door in Galway, the conversation never fading, always arriving back at 11.45.

And so the journey began.

I recalled my first game for Clare in the hurling outpost of North Kerry. That day in February 2000 the field at Ballyheigue was bleak and windswept but while the world was oblivious and spinning normally, for me it rotated a beat or two quicker. I was fulfilling a dream, wearing a Clare senior jersey.

I was introduced in the second half for the All Star Fergus Tuohy, and after a few minutes I registered my first score. My father happened to be standing behind the goalposts. After I struck the ball, it went into an adjoining field, but my father had watched its flight and afterwards located it. At home he wrote the score of the game and the date on the sliotar. He placed it in his cupboard.

As I looked at the clippings that night, I was surprised by his custom of recording games. At times I had wondered if he had taken the required interest in my career, but this was proof. He'd remained silent so I could follow my own journey.

Those clippings were also a reminder that games pass. Games won, games lost, games thrown away. They become memories.

But still, I craved an All Ireland medal, believed it would

arrive, convinced myself it would lift the cloud. And secretly I promised my father I would win one for him.

The season tumbled on. January, February. The middle of March. By now some flickers of light were poking through.

I religiously documented my training schedule so I could glean some confidence from my toil later in the season when the chips were down. I spoke to my legs as I trained, told them to remember the cold nights on the warm days of summer.

One evening stands out. A Saturday.

I'm running by myself at the Fair Green in Ennis, the town's grassy park. I recall being tired, fighting my laziness, longing for convenience and a comfortable chair.

But suddenly I found another tempo. It was extraordinary. I could see myself almost from above, as though I existed outside my body. A silhouette in the streetlights, blowing cloudbanks of air into the evening.

I rounded a curve and noticed everybody was moving, going home, going out, caught up in their own voyage. It seemed like I was standing still. There was a monotony to everything and I lost myself in the numbness of the evening. I realized I could switch off my thoughts and exist only in the flow of the moment, and this was a new feeling.

An energy vibrated from the ground below. It was unmistakable. The scent of mud and potential. Springtime had arrived and balmy evenings were around the corner.

I wanted to shout out, tell people I was on a path and tell them why I was here, why I was running. I wanted to let people know I was breaking through. That on the other side lay the goal, achieved.

I thought of the last ten minutes of a game when you have to win the ball even though you are jaded. I wanted to go through a game and not question how tired I was and push my body to the outer limits.

At the time I was wrapped up in a book, *Tour de Force* by Dan Coyle. In it, Coyle mapped out a cycling season, allowed the reader to trace the contours of a professional cyclist. I was mesmerized by their stories.

Coyle followed the peloton in 2004, the year Lance Armstrong was aiming to win his sixth Tour de France. One cyclist stood out. Iban Mayo, the Basque.

His story really made me think. In spring and early summer, Mayo was flying. He won the Dauphiné Libéré, considered the most accurate barometer for the Tour de France, and during the Dauphiné Mayo had taken two minutes out of Armstrong on one stage alone, a time trial on the demanding Mont Ventoux. Two minutes is huge, the Grand Canyon in cycling terms.

After that, Mayo was regarded as a major challenge to Armstrong in the Tour, but he never did challenge. He lost time in the mountains of France later that summer and quit in the middle of the race. The lesson was that Armstrong had timed his season to perfection; Mayo had peaked too soon. I vowed this would not happen to me.

The real wallop of lightning arrived in Cusack Park at the end of March, a home game against Offaly, the fourth of the league.

As a team we were still finding our feet in the season. A

hurling year is split into two components, beginning with the league, which is followed by the championship. You are judged by your performance in the latter – it's the World Series and Super Bowl of the Gaelic Athletic Association – and to most onlookers, the league merely provides an opportunity to assess the quality of a team. For players, it's slightly different. When you're encased in any competition it becomes all you can see, and more importantly, it's an indicator of personal form. As you evolve and mature as a player you learn to treat the league with a little more detachment because it's possible to peak in the league and bonk in the championship – in much the same way as the cyclist Mayo did – but you never disregard it completely.

Two weeks before that Offaly game in 2006 we had beaten Waterford and the result had placed us second in the table. Offaly were top. It meant that this game was going to define our league because a win would put Clare ahead of Offaly and provide us with the opportunity of making the semi-final; lose, and the league was essentially finished.

Five minutes before half-time, Offaly had pulled back a two-point deficit and it looked like they were gaining momentum.

A crossfield ball came to me, I won possession and, just as I had done in the Wexford game earlier in the season, I broke through the defence to a goalscoring position. This time I didn't recoil. I struck, and the netting billowed. My goal put us back in the lead and the Offaly charge had been halted.

We pressed on and led by two at the break, having played well against the league leaders, but in the dressing room the management took our performance to pieces. I felt they were being unjust and maybe I should have said this, but I was trying to make sense of my own world, and with my back to a cold dressing-room wall, I found some clarity.

In my interpretation, Anthony Daly and his assistant coach Ollie Baker, two hurlers I'd looked up to as a kid, two double All Ireland winners, had read the game incorrectly. I was convinced of this.

Things became clear to me that even men you respect can get things totally wrong, and I felt I should begin to trust my own intuition and gut, not rely on external affirmation. When you are so used to thinking one way, the idea of a new outlook can seem monumental.

That episode was a fleeting moment but a decisive one all the same. For the first time I really questioned the sanity of placing so much stock in the words of others when in reality I was the only person who had to face myself in the mirror at night. If Daly and Baker could get it wrong, why not live only by my own expectations? I had feared being substituted, feared missing a shot at goal, but I began to realize that life would go on.

In six years playing for Clare I had always felt I had to prove myself to the public, managers, supporters, but in that dressing room that sense of fear began to leave me in the way an ache can leave your stomach. It was liberating.

We went back out, won by eight points and topped the table. Two weeks later we travelled to play Cork and returned to Clare with two more league points. We had made the semi-final, setting up a duel with Limerick. Confidence and enthusiasm were high. We were playing with courage and spirit. After the Cork game Clare were installed as second favourites behind Kilkenny to win the competition. Anthony Daly went public and said he felt the county could take down a league title for the first time in twenty-eight years. We believed him.

When Clare won the All Ireland in 1995 it seemed like a great tree had sprung up.

Just like the Red Sox in Boston, a so-called curse had settled in the mist above Clare. In Boston they had lived under the Curse of the Bambino, said to have begun when the Red Sox offloaded Babe Ruth – known as the Bambino – to the New York Yankees. After Babe's departure it took eighty-six years for the city to welcome home another World Series. In Clare we were told we were operating beneath the Curse of Biddy Early, a local healer who, when described as a witch by a nearby clergyman, was said to have cursed Clare hurling. It was a dubious but quirky story and the media filled previews of Clare's voyage to success with reference to Biddy.

Curse or not, it took eighty-one years – an entire lifetime – for Clare to recapture the national championship, and the summer of '95 had become a countywide procession to Croke Park.

I was fourteen, open to influence, ready to have my imagination sprayed with new heroes. My brothers, my father and I followed the team across the province, and unbelievably Clare won the Munster title that July. That afternoon the county ignored the constraints of history and the tradition of defeat. Even before the game was over, masses of Clare men and women began to swarm the field at Semple Stadium and some Clare players later said they were worried the onrushing fans might jeopardize the win, that somehow fate would intervene to take away this glorious moment. That was the mindset Clare lived by back then.

When the game was finished, the field was dressed with a blanket of saffron and blue. Supporters were overjoyed and everybody clambered to get on to the grass. At the final whistle a wave of bodies pressed against the barriers on the terrace. My father helped ease the pressure by holding open a barbed-wire fence, allowing supporters on to the field. I looked down and saw blood dripping from his hands. In his euphoria he hadn't noticed that the wire was cutting through his skin.

That summer we drove all the way to Dublin to see Clare play on the lush grass of Croke Park and, majestically, we beat Offaly in the final.

Afterwards, the captain, Anthony Daly, provided one of Ireland's great speeches. There was eloquence in what he said, great delivery, and his words penetrated straight to the gut. 'Down through the years we were told to stick to our traditional music. Well in Clare, we love our traditional music but we love our hurling as well. I think of the many great Clare players down through the years who were never as fortunate as we are. Now we accept this Liam McCarthy Cup on behalf of all those teams.'

In the space of three minutes he captured several generations' worth of pain and defeat. Clare had always been the whipping boys, a county of tradition and music, a county looked down upon in hurling terms, but now we were taking our place among the giants of the game.

He addressed the team manager, Ger Loughnane. By now Loughnane had earned mythical status not because of his methods but because his methods worked. It was common knowledge that he had forced players to new places in terms of preparation; word had escaped that he was relentlessly running players up steep hills, gathering them for training before the sun had risen, verbally abusing them in order to wring out the last measure of effort. What went on during his training sessions would not be tolerated in general society, but Loughnane's players looked upon him as a powerful zealot.

In the great scheme of things Daly was his general, the conduit between him and the other players, and his final words as he spoke to the world with the Liam McCarthy Cup in his hands were fittingly reserved for Loughnane.

Standing on the railing below Daly, Loughnane remained stoic, and this was the only time he raised his head in recognition. But you could see that the day moved him immensely. The veins on Loughnane's temples bulged as Daly spoke, his chest lifted and dropped and his breathing sped up.

It was a pure moment.

In 1997 Clare won again, and later Loughnane would say that year surpassed 1995, that it proved Clare were a force to be reckoned with.

Loughnane and his players still fill hurling conversations. Their achievements look down on us from some holy, untouchable perch, and in order for the county to move on, to retire those glory years to the past, we need to win further silverware.

Anthony Daly is seen as the man to lead us. Three years after he finished hurling for Clare he was offered the job of manager, and though many of the guys he would preside over were former playing colleagues, his passion for the county meant he couldn't refuse.

Daly is one of life's special people. When he walks into a room, it's like a light being turned on in the dark. He was unlike any other manager I have played for. He reeled you into his way of thinking.

We're sitting down for a post-match dinner. In comes Daly, full of life and devilment, claps his hands together, scans the room. 'Jaysus, lads! Waitress is a cracker, isn't she?' He communicates directly to players and allows each player to relax in his company.

Early in the 2006 season he talked to me and said he believed I would win an All Star. It was only the second time anybody had verbalized this goal I had first written down when I was thirteen years old. He told me I was as good as Henry Shefflin or D. J. Carey. I didn't believe him. He would follow this up with a text message at eleven o'clock on a Friday night: 'Griff, you are better than Shefflin this year. Trust me. You are playing out of your skin.' He reinforced this opinion so often that I had no option but to trust him and believe in myself.

During my first handful of training games after coming into the squad, Daly marked me. He was a man who had presented me with medals when I was a kid coming through the club ranks and here I was directly opposed to him, trying to stake a claim on the first team. In the middle of my very first session I noticed he was pulling me and dragging me whenever the ball was at the other side of the field. He was looking for a reaction and I refused to retaliate. Loughnane was the referee and I'd learned quickly that unless somebody had been beheaded on the turf of Cusack Park he left his whistle in his pocket.

The second session the process was repeated, and I came away deciding that if this happened again, I couldn't bow down. So, third night, a high ball drops between the two of us, Daly holding on to my jersey, stalling my jump. I swung back with my elbow and caught him hard on the shoulder. Almost in unison, Daly and Loughnane bawled, 'That's more like it, Griffin!'

It's now Daly's third season as manager and the time to deliver has arrived. Under Daly we are on the cusp of a break-through having lost the previous year's semi-final by a point to the eventual winners but a top-four finish this year won't suf-fice, personally and collectively. It is time to gather the harvest, time to rip the grapes from the vine.

Two years back, in 2004, Daly began his championship career as a manager with one of the heaviest defeats in the history of Clare hurling when we lost by nineteen points to Waterford. It was shocking and humiliating. Questions over Daly's ability to manage rumbled across the county. The players never questioned him though. As a group we knew we were pathetic that day. Brian 'Bull' Phelan roasted me. Brian O'Connell was making his debut and John Mullane ran him ragged. We were caught on the hop; all over the field we were putting out bonfires with water canisters.

Daly could have panicked after a defeat like that. He could have hung his head, but he didn't. Through his reaction we saw he had character and we rolled on to an All Ireland quarter-final, drawing against Kilkenny before losing the replay.

The previous year, 2005, our season ended at the semi-final stage once more when we went under to Cork. Daly refers to that day as the lowest point of his management career. The morning of the game, we went for a light jog on the golf course beside the Stillorgan Hotel. In the pre-match team meeting we spoke confidently of how we were going to win.

With under quarter of an hour remaining we led by six but we were beginning to tire and we failed to protect our lead. We played eyeballs out, all-attack. Afterwards, I privately questioned our tactics and felt we should have defended our six-point lead instead of trying to build it. Perhaps we should have withdrawn two forwards into the midfield area to close down space. Daly did shuffle players around but the options he chose didn't work. He was still a new manager, raw and learning.

Late in that game, our wing-back Gerry Quinn and I closed down Brian Murphy, who was in possession of the ball, and chased him to the Cork corner of the field. I shouldered Brian over the line and we had possession.

I looked up the field, towards the opposite corner where my marker was standing, and failed to see how I could run the 150 yards.

'Long way back,' I thought. 'Long way back.'

My legs were buckling. Other players were running on empty and it brought home that our panel wasn't deep enough to win an All Ireland that year. Cork were hardened by seasons of competing at this stage of the championship and had a bench with three or four players who would start for most counties.

They began to chip away at our lead and breasted the tape just ahead, by a single point. After losing to Tipperary in our championship opener that June we had been written off by most critics, and even though we had proved them wrong, it was a devastating loss.

It took some time to get the memory out of my system. I was walking the beach in Lahinch the following week and still it whirled around my head. My brother sent a text message wondering had I got over the defeat. I told him I was still low.

A few years earlier we had watched the film *The Field*, which at one point explores an old Irish patriarch's relationship with his wife. The thing is, this patriarch, Bull McCabe, and his wife don't speak. Late in the film when their son dies, the Bull takes it really hard and is on the edge. His wife finally shatters the silence. 'Don't break, Bull,' she tells him. She hadn't said much, but she had said everything.

After I texted my brother and told him I was still getting over the game, the phone beeped back a few seconds later. 'Don't break, Bull.'

The Cork defeat was torture because we were so close and had allowed the game to slip from our grasp. The morning after, Anthony Daly woke up and felt sick. The following Monday he woke up again and felt worse. The previous afternoon, Galway had beaten Kilkenny in the other semi-final and he was convinced we would have beaten Galway in the final.

What 2005 showed us was that we were one win away from success, and 2006 could lead to something big. Unknown to us players, one Saturday morning a few weeks after that defeat to Cork in the semi-final of '05, Daly, Brian Lohan and Sean McMahon played a game of golf. Lohan was thirty-four; McMahon, probably the greatest centre-back the game has seen, was thirty-two. Both could have retired after Cork. Daly could have walked away to safeguard his prospects of managing the county in the future. Playing it safe wasn't their style.

That morning on the golf course they spoke about 2006. Lohan and McMahon were willing to push it to the limit for one more year. Daly felt an All Ireland was within Clare's grasp. They looked at it objectively and figured Clare were third in the pecking order behind Cork and Kilkenny and it could take just one massive performance to win in September. They looked at the second wave of players that were maturing, players like me, Gerry Quinn, Diarmuid McMahon, and reckoned we wanted to taste an All Ireland final occasion once more having been beaten in 2002 by Kilkenny. So everybody stepped on to the ship for 2006, certain that Daly was steering us to a new world.

The league semi-final against Limerick came and went in late spring. We lost, but it didn't bother us greatly. In the second half it seemed like we didn't even want to win, as though there were better things to come, that we were working on a grander masterpiece. We got careless. With the game still open I beat Seamus Hickey to the ball, flicked it over his head, picked up the ball again and ran through on goal. I struck it wide. I had done the difficult thing right but was casual with the finish. Things like that were happening to us all over the field. Had it been Cork or Kilkenny who played Limerick that day they would have closed out the game, but when we spoke afterwards, we said we believed we would beat Limerick if we met them later that summer in the championship.

The focus shifted to Cork. The first round of the provincial championship. May and Thurles and a sun-streaked afternoon. Our aim was to conquer our province by winning Munster, undefeated, which would propel us through the competition, avoiding the doubts that can linger on the qualifier route to Croke Park.

We were back on the tightrope once more. Under Daly, Clare had yet to win a game in Munster and this was used as an insult to throw at us from time to time. We had fallen the previous two years, that embarrassing day against Waterford and in 2005 against Tipperary in the rain when we missed five goal chances, conceding two with terrible sloppiness.

Cork in '06 was an opportunity to atone.

By now I had given myself completely to the season. Halifax rarely entered my mind. Self-belief had risen and at last, ironically, considering it arrived during a year when I was playing full-time, I viewed hurling with a healthy perspective. My father's death, my life in Canada, the reality that the world was vast, that everybody makes mistakes – all of these contributed to that attitude. I still clung to the dream of an All Ireland as though to a lifeboat but it was becoming part of a broader dream.

A week before the championship I sat at home, at the kitchen table, eating breakfast by myself, and replayed my personal reel of training sessions in my head. I talked once more to my legs, telling them they'd worked hard, that they had hundreds of miles in reserve. The hard work of winter and spring gave me confidence. For the first time in three seasons I had played a full league campaign and each game had brought me on an extra two or three per cent. I had a full tank to call upon. At the table I pictured us chopping Cork down with majestic hurling.

Two weeks before showdown we played Galway in a challenge game in Cusack Park. Everything clicked. Even the setting was perfect. To many, Cusack Park is a ramshackle old place, a throwback to a grey generation. Those people only see the creaking stand, the tin-covered shed, a couple of bald terraces. I feel the bounce of the soil beneath my studs. I see Ennis Abbey stand solemn and ceremonial to the back of the goal. I hear the hum of a drowsy summer training session and the crash of hurleys breaking, always followed by the sense of achievement as you walk off the field, training over, job done. To me it's a special place. I found that when I was in Canada, this was one of the snapshots of Ireland I constantly returned to.

That night against Galway I was picked to play midfield, which I found odd. I went out and ran the length of the pitch, scoring five points, and felt positive about the week ahead.

When the team for Cork was named, I was chosen at mid-field to partner Colin Lynch. In the previous year's semi-final, the management thought Ben O'Connor and Tom Kenny had dictated too much; they felt I could add power and stamina. It wasn't a position I had great familiarity with but my approach didn't change.

Preparation for the game was perfect, and under Daly we had a ritual when we played in Thurles. On the way to Semple Stadium we would stop at a beautiful Victorian home a few miles outside town. It was set on luscious, rambling acreage, cornfields in the background, and we were served great food.

It was early afternoon, a couple of hours before the game, and the sense of anticipation was swathing us. We stretched among the gardens, and as we warmed up I was hit by the thought that my touch had never been as good. The ball just stuck to my hurley.

Then, on to the bus. The slow parade to Semple Stadium. A CD was loaded into the player, the same CD we had used during the winter nights when we lifted weights together in the gym. Each player had chosen one song for inclusion. Mine was Weezer's 'Only In Dreams', which rises and falls before eventually building to a stirring guitar solo. David Hoey had gone with a Paul Oakenfold track, Lynch and Conor Plunkett had doubled up on a couple of loud AC/DC anthems. The music added to the anticipation on the bus and energy was rising from my stomach into my mouth and out of my lips.

We snake through the thousands on the streets, bypassing the traffic. The theme tune from 'Remember the Titans' builds up, finishes with an impressive crescendo, and we're almost within sight of the players' entrance where a flock of Clare supporters has gathered to see us into the ground. I look around the bus; faces are serious and switched on. The CD player jumps to the next track. It starts with a low beat and some heavy breathing, that are both immediately recognizable and clearly out of place: 'What you gonna do with all that junk, all that junk inside your trunk? I'm a get, get, get, get you drunk, get you love drunk off my hump.' 'My Humps' by the Black Eyed Peas has descended upon us like some alien. It's Gerry Quinn's selection and knots of laughter escape through-out the bus. For good or ill, that moment of focus is snapped.

The game. For the first ten minutes I try to rough Jerry O'Connor up as much as I can but figure I'm wasting my time, using up too much energy. We start well. I hit the ball into

Barry Nugent and he's winning possession. Players are linking up throughout the field. Even when I need to find my second wind early on I don't panic. I know it will arrive.

At one stage I see Lohan emerge from the full-back position, legs spinning. He wins the ball, bursting through tackles with savage power. 'Shit!' I'm thinking. 'I never realized he was so quick!'

The ball is travelling like a speedboat up and down a small lake. We have settled surprisingly quickly and we realize we are better than Cork, but this isn't something we have planned for.

It's also the fastest day of hurling I have experienced. Savage pace. Action, action, action.

We get on top but never stretch too far ahead. Cork have guile. They steady, the game evolves into a lightning battle, and with a quarter of the game remaining Cork have pushed eight ahead and are almost out of sight.

The defeat is crushing. Our third first-round loss under Daly, and like before, if we are to make Croke Park we have to go through the qualifier system. Seven points. I didn't dwell too much on the score because when a quality team like Cork forge ahead late in the game they can quickly turn a two-point lead into a seven-point gulf.

In the dressing room, Johnny Glynn stood staring at the corner for five minutes while I placed my hands behind my head and wondered how we could face the return to Clare later that evening.

In his own time, Anthony Daly examined his approach to the Cork game. He wondered if he had over-analysed Cork and failed to allow us to unleash ourselves on the game.

That's what a defeat like that does. Everybody asks questions of themselves. But it was clear that Cork had travelled to prove a point. Clare, a team aiming to break into a higher atmosphere and compete for glory, had got too close to Cork the previous year so in return they decided to make a statement to Kilkenny and the rest of the country that the All Ireland champions were going to reclaim their crown.

We boarded the bus in silence, and Daly was the last to climb on. He looked around, exasperated. 'My humps,' he said. 'My fuckin' humps! Whose song was that?'

We rolled out of Thurles and about an hour later arrived at a hotel for an arranged meal. The Clare hurling team? Sorry, no booking.

Back on to the bus, hunger now replacing distress, driving into the dimming night with no idea of where we were going. I didn't care if we kept on moving, further away from Ballyea and the punch of reality that would hit, as it always did after a hard defeat, when you opened your eyes in your own bed to greet another black Monday morning.

We made the outskirts of Limerick, the shuffle of suburban lights, car dealerships, take-away joints.

Daly turned his head back in our direction. 'Lads. A pint?' Nobody disagreed.

We found a small pub and scattered about inside. The game was being analysed on TV. It was hours since we had eaten and the meagre menu we found before us wouldn't satisfy our appetites or refuel our bodies. We loaded up on crisps and soup and toasted sandwiches and sat beneath the television screen on barstools looking up at the dissection of our sorrowful day, eating crap, drinking beer, wondering how we were going to drag ourselves out of the mire.

You could say we went on because there was nothing else to do and continued hurling because that's what we did, but there was more to it.

We slowly came round. The defeat to Cork was an ugly one but Anthony Daly had created a system that cushioned us against situations like this. Above all else, Daly was honest and passionate. He let you know he was human, that he wasn't infallible. When he made a mistake he put his hand up and you trusted him more because of that. After that disaster against Waterford in his first championship game in 2004, he'd walked into the dressing room with a pale complexion. He was demolished inside but he still had the strength to address the players to say he'd had us too psyched up for the game but he would improve as a manager and we would improve as a team.

When he appointed Fr Harry Bohan to the management team there were whispers and quiet criticisms around our county. Fr Harry was Clare manager in the late 1970s and guided a fabled side to the brink of success but that team seemed to hit the wall every time it reached a watershed game.

Over two decades had passed since The Priest, as we referred to him, was involved at the coalface of inter-county hurling. People wondered if he could read the modern game and notice the fresh nuances that had developed since his time as boss, but Daly dismissed this argument. He took a more astute viewpoint.

When The Priest came on board there was an understanding

that team selection and match-day issues wouldn't be his concern. He wasn't a dogmatic hurling selector. Instead, he lived in the background, away from the crowds and the sprint sessions, in a place where seasons, not games, are shaped and crafted.

Harry's is a wide view of the world and he exudes a respect and a love for people. The first time we spoke one to one was at a training camp in Portugal. He asked my opinion on several things, none of them relating to hurling. I wondered about his life as a priest and he said that at times he found it lonely but he loved God and would serve Him throughout his life.

When it came to people, The Priest was perceptive and sharp, a physician of the soul. He understood the complexities of human nature and his addition was essential because every player goes through moments of crisis.

Early in the year I was unloading my gear from the back of the car for a training session, feeling bothered about my first touch and how I was playing generally, when Harry appeared behind me.

'Anything up, Griff?'

I could confide in The Priest in a way that I couldn't confide in Daly, and something he said to me that evening really registered.

'I know that nobody likes to doubt themselves or have anxiety or nerves,' he said, 'because you don't think anybody else suffers from this. But I know they do.'

When your manager wonders if you're going through a rough patch you will do everything to plaster over the cracks. No player will admit a loss of playing form to his manager for fear his position on the starting team will be threatened.

It was different with The Priest, and Daly's intuition also came into play here. If he heard a player was having girlfriend problems or experiencing other difficulties outside hurling he would send The Priest to seek them out, sit down with them and chat over a pot of tea. From Daly's perspective, this ensured he maintained a certain distance from his players.

Our trainer, Johnny Glynn, added something else to the mix. He was prepared, looked at every angle and ensured he was covered for all possibilities. At times, Daly and he rammed heads. If Daly felt a player was going through a particularly hard time and felt the need to pull him back into the loop, he might bring him for a pint and coax him back on board. Word of this would seep out and Johnny would become exasperated that Daly had shared a drink with a player, but he came to understand this was Daly's man-management skills coming to the fore.

There was a further layer to what Daly had created. A performance coach, Liam Moggan, worked regularly with us, and he provided an outside perspective. Our analyst, Denise Martin, provided us with regular individual stats and prepared individual DVDs of each player's best career moments, with a personalized soundtrack. Whenever I needed a boost I would load that DVD and watch as a guitar solo from *The Last of the Mohicans* soared and lifted my heart rate.

Then there was Gazzy. The familiar face of Gazzy, the man in charge of our kit and auxiliary items, was a gush of positivity. Gazzy was christened Michael Collins and spent his life working as a barman at Shannon and Dubai airports. He has served US presidents with Irish coffees and has poured whiskeys for sheikhs. At Clare, he looks after the players with the presence of an adoring uncle, always paying attention to detail, and when Gazzy is happy, the players are happy.

It's a subtle but crucial element, so Daly would make sure Gazzy always carried a smile. If Gazzy wanted an ice machine after a training session, it was there. If he sought the latest isotonic drink, a crate was ordered.

The pieces of Daly's jigsaw fitted seamlessly, and this allowed us to move on from Cork. If a player was still depressed three days after a defeat, Daly sent The Priest. If we needed additional work on our tackling, Johnny Glynn devised the perfect physical training drill. Alan Cunningham, our hurling coach, came up with unique reaction drills.

The older players were also vital. Lohan, Lynch, Sean McMahon, Davy Fitzgerald. These men had experienced bleak days and heavy defeats when the world must have seemed a dark place but they bounced back and tasted success. Because of this, they helped lift the younger players and put things into perspective.

Then we got a break when the draw for the All Ireland qualifiers group was made. On 18 June, three weeks after Cork, we would play Limerick in Cusack Park in front of a capacity crowd of over twenty-five thousand, followed by Offaly then Dublin. If we topped the group we would play the losers of the Leinster championship, probably Wexford. Croke Park was back in our line of sight. There, we believed we would beat Cork or Kilkenny. There, we would excel in the heat.

Just as June was catching fire, a letter from Dalhousie dropped in the letterbox like a dispatch from some other universe.

Halifax was now a million miles away but the letter reminded me that in order to continue my studies when college resumed in late autumn I would need the equivalent of €12,000. It may as well have been €100,000. I wasn't working and I had no savings, but the extra time on my hands had equipped me with a strong sense of spirituality and a belief in the impossible.

The hours I spent reading altered my outlook. The semesters in Canada had been spent immersed in physics textbooks or science papers. My schooldays in Ennis had been all about end-of-year exams. But now I not only had time to choose my own material, but space to develop my thoughts.

Learning about people like Che Guevara and Lance Armstrong affected me.

Che had given up his life as a doctor in Buenos Aires, put this to one side to search for something greater. It took him on a journey that led to the book *The Motorcycle Diaries*. He joined the Cuban Revolution and fought for a belief. Once, in the woods, when his raggle-taggle band of soldiers was on an ambush, somebody turned to him and asked, 'Che, why are you always reading?' He replied, 'Because I am preparing myself.' Nobody could have known the political life he would subsequently lead.

Armstrong's chances of beating cancer were darkly described as being less than a coin toss, but he fought it, beat it and came back to dominate his sport.

I dwelled on these people for weeks and their achievements showed me that I should have faith in my own journey even if there was no certainty on the road ahead. I saw that if you put action behind a dream, you could make anything happen, despite what the world might tell you or despite its attempts to knock the life out of your dreams.

My dream was to get to Croke Park that autumn as the greatest hurler I could be. Finding a job for the remainder of my time in Ireland would not allow me to do that, and I couldn't compromise.

I had to return to university that September or I might never go back, so I would get the €12,000 from somewhere. I sat at the kitchen table and considered my options. I wasn't looking for alchemic shortcuts but I had to think outside the box, focus on the possibility, not the problem.

The four most prominent business people I knew came to mind. I wrote each a letter and explained my predicament.

The morning of the Limerick game came upon us with a great billowing wind. I looked out the window, across the field, and the ash trees shook. I had been chosen to play in my familiar surrounds on the full-forward line, and a day such as this can be nightmarish for a scoring forward: the wind can push long-distance shots askew and mess with your mind for an entire afternoon. But I refused to linger on the conditions.

I ate Weetabix and some fruit; drank a litre of water; fed the cattle; checked my boots; packed my gear. I focused only on the aspects of the day I could control.

During our last meaningful training session a few days earlier, Sean McMahon stood on the grass of Cusack Park and conveyed to us the importance of the weekend's game. Limerick had beaten us in the league semi-final but in our own heads we were better. Now was the time to prove that, he said. We knew that one more defeat and our season was as good as dead. Limerick were coming, he said, to bury us on our own ground. Would we let this happen, would we die in front of our own people?

It is a theme that all hurling players and managers touch on with regularity. Sometimes it works. That blood-and-guts element of hurling can stir my adrenalin even though it's a motivational device I've heard ever since I was a kid. Essentially, for me, it depends on who delivers those lines and how they are delivered, and that evening McMahon executed his speech to perfection. When a warrior speaks, you take in what he says. McMahon led from the front, the first man out of the trench, and players tend to follow the fearless. On game day, though, I had learned I couldn't entertain a battle cry like that. I would lose control and my energy would taper on the field. But coming three days before a game it would serve to supplement my focus.

We had a new routine for championship games in Ennis. The team met three hours before the game, then travelled by bus to a hotel a few miles from Cusack Park.

I was reading *A Farewell to Arms* by Hemingway for the first time and finished it on the journey to the hotel. The book brought me to another world. My mind was removed from the game and in the hours before throw-in I experienced a deep sense of relaxation. At the hotel we ate and went for a light run.

All day the sky was bloated with clouds, and just as we began our warm-up rain spread over Cusack Park in heavy sheets. I looked up and the drops hit my face. 'Come on,' I thought. 'Come on. Let it lash down on top of me.'

We ate Limerick up. Destroyed them.

After twelve minutes, Tony Carmody picked me out with an 80-yard pass. I caught the dropping ball, moved wide past the Limerick defender, then cut towards the 14-yard line. I shot with pace and accuracy into the left corner of the net. We had our first goal of the game.

Shortly after, I moved out from the goal area, collected another ball, shot and scored. A minute later I was at the other side of the field, winning ball and scoring again.

'Jesus,' I said to myself. 'It's like you're somebody else today.'

The comedian Tommy Tiernan tells a joke about Cian O'Connor, the Irish showjumper who won gold at the 2004 Olympics, but whose horse, Waterford Crystal, was later found to have been doped. 'Who else but the Irish would drug their horse?' Tiernan asks. 'That day in Athens the horse is there, souped up, and he must have said to O'Connor, "Cian, you don't have to do a thing this afternoon. Just sit on my back and don't get in my way."'

That's how I felt. I just had to keep out of my own way and let the game flow. It's a beautiful thing to get to that level, when you do things on autopilot.

Late in the game you're not questioning your stamina and your ability to finish strong. You know it's there. You can concentrate on the next ball and you're not merely trying to get to the final whistle.

Limerick had been weakened before the game when they shuffled key positions on the team, but despite that we had swatted away a team that had beaten us earlier in the summer. That's what we took from the game. We had a phenomenal seventeen points to spare at the end. I scored 1–5 and picked up the Man of the Match award afterwards.

The win and performance were essential for the team. We had bounced back with a savage display.

And for me, the work of the winter and spring had materialized into something tangible. I continued to believe, nurtured my confidence for what was yet to come.

There was one flip side to the Limerick game. I damaged my groin, an injury known as osteitis pubis. It's an inflammation of the area where the pelvis joins the groin and it can end a lot of careers.

I kept the injury quiet, not wanting word to leak outside the team that I had been hurt. The media never knew and the public at large never knew, so it never became an issue. I wasn't forced to answer questions about my injury in the lead-up to the next game and this helped me remain positive.

I had to manage the injury because it flared up the more I trained and there were times when I had to ring Daly and say I couldn't make a session. 'Right, Griff. Rest it.' That flexibility and trust helped greatly and he knew I wouldn't abuse any free pass from group training.

Before games and any heavy sessions my lower body had to be strapped with a tight layer of gauze in a way that made it appear as though I was wearing a corset. Between the proper medical care and the lack of pressure to push the injury in training, my performances for the rest of the summer remained unaffected.

Together we pushed on, comfortably beating Dublin and Offaly in early July, setting up a quarter-final against Wexford.

It wasn't the route we had planned to take but the first mount had been crested. We were back in Croke Park.

Summer was peaking. Long evenings. The light unwilling to fall away beyond the cliffs of West Clare. I made it a priority to make the most of my time. I travelled to the beach at Lahinch or Spanish Point and sometimes thought about the hurling season we were going through.

I thought about how each one is unique and condensed, how our championship season is unlike baseball or basketball – sports with lengthy seasons and endless games and averages and winning percentages and player transfers. Ours is simpler. More passionate, more primal. It's a high-risk season that can tumble at your feet if you make more than one mistake. It's kamikaze stuff. Spend six months preparing, then lose twice and your year is over, logged away as another failure for the historians and analysts to dissect. But it's that fleeting nature, that mortal sadness, that lends beauty and distinction to each Irish summer.

I thought about Anthony Daly. He was the highest-profile man in our county yet he walked beside and conversed with the very people who would judge him as a man for the decisions he made on a hurling sideline. He made his living from his sports shop in the heart of Ennis and his bottom line surely ebbed and flowed with the form of the team.

My own season was also something of a big-stakes wager. The tag of the professional hurler that followed me all summer seemed to give supporters a right to demand more. For the first time people were telling me, to my face, I had to begin to lead the team and drive the attack. These were no longer comments from the crowd or lines in a newspaper. I had earned a reputation as a powerful, self-sufficient scoring forward, but now greater demands were being placed on me, by myself and by others.

So Wexford loomed and my increasing faith in my ability and my belief in our management meant the game didn't completely devour my thoughts.

I enjoyed games in Dublin, and that brought comfort. I enjoyed them not only because they brought the opportunity to play in Croke Park, I also savoured the whole routine. So much of a player's happiness is based on how he will conform to a pre-determined routine: training routine, pre-match routine, warm-up routine.

We stayed in the plush seaside town of Portmarnock, away from the noise of the city, at the Portmarnock Hotel and Golf Links, a two-minute walk from the beach. This gave us a window to walk the strand or hit some ball or go for a swim. The location was perfect.

When there were championship games in Croke Park the day before our own, we had the option to travel to these outings as a team and watch the action. The thinking was it would introduce us to the atmosphere of Croke Park but would also take our minds off our own game.

That Saturday I passed. Brian Lohan's brother, Frank, and I walked into the village to have coffee. I enjoyed his company and had huge admiration for him as a person. Frank was the first player I had told in 2004 that I was moving to Canada and was one of the few players I kept in constant touch with. He had varying interests and shared his brother's fierce competitiveness, but carried it more lightly.

The day was warm and carefree as we strolled back to the hotel. I slept for an hour, happy that I had skipped the traffic and crowds of game day in Croke Park.

I woke early evening and joined the puck-around on the beach that had become a ritual on the eve of Croke Park games.

Afterwards, there was still some warmth left in the day. A handful of players took a dip in the bay and Tony Carmody and I waded out towards Brian Lohan, who was alone. The water was cooling. We had been taking in the silence for a little while when Lohan hit me with a question.

'Who're you marking tomorrow?'

'Doc O'Connor.'

'He's a good player, boy. A right good player.'

I misinterpreted what he said, thought he was pronouncing Doc a better player, thought he was wondering if I would survive in Croke Park going head to head with Doc.

Poor Griff. He's going to get roasted tomorrow.

Even though I believed I was overcoming my own doubts during the season, I didn't have the security to realize that Lohan was saying Clare had put faith in me to shackle a player like Doc O'Connor.

I gave Lohan a glance he could have designed himself, beat the water with my hand and roared at him, 'I'm a fuckin' good player as well!'

I tried to storm out of the sea but the water was up to my waist and making progress was difficult. I splashed my way to the shore, half in slow-motion, and left Lohan, bemused, in the water. It was a comical scene, but I was fuming. I went to my bedroom and ignored the full-back for the rest of the evening, and all of match day.

I shared a room with Niall Gilligan. In a droll routine the night before a game, Gilly would ask me the same question: 'Right, Griff, what positive shite do you have for me tonight?'

That evening I told him I was scraping to find something positive myself when he pulled out a little book Liam Moggan had given him. Sports psychology was something Gilly hadn't really come on board with but he was an advocate of this book and his opinion on mental preparation was changing. I banished the Lohan incident from my brain and drifted off with Gilly flicking through the psychology book.

I woke, as I usually did, a few hours before our scheduled ten o'clock breakfast. I went to the dining room and loaded up on porridge and fruit, went back to bed for two more hours, then joined the rest of the team for more food.

Back to the beach, a few pucks, a light jog, and then on to the bus.

Each player has a favourite seat. Conor Plunkett, Gerry Quinn and Gilly are towards the back, nonchalant and mellow. Lynch is at the very back corner, quiet. Davy Fitzgerald is at the front left, bathing in the rising atmosphere. Daly is behind the bus driver.

I'm a few seats from the front. Players differ on the trip to Croke Park. For some it's filled with tension, but I love the sense that we're moving towards destiny so I take in the match-day postcards outside the window. A father and son walking, holding hands, wearing Clare jerseys. The police escort at the front. A mingle of kids waving at our bus.

What gave the day added significance was that at its core

this team had the potential to make a county feel good about itself.

Croke Park soared above the skyline for miles, the crowds on the streets turning to thousands as we sped closer.

We reach the players' entrance, into the fluorescent light of the tunnel, and walk straight for the dressing room.

Inside, the strapping to my groin is applied, players get their wrists taped, and then Daly speaks to us in the warm-up area beside the dressing room. We know our jobs, we know our roles. He says nothing we're not already familiar with.

I'm handed my jersey. That year I ordered a size smaller to make it more difficult for a defender to grab on to me.

We're now slaves to the clock. My challenge is managing my arousal levels. I don't want to be pumped to the point where I flatline ten minutes in and I don't want to joke around to the point where I can't switch my focus back on.

Davy and Lynch speak emotionally, hit hurleys off the floor, say we have to go out and die for Clare. By the time they're in full flight I'm in the adjacent bathroom. I can't allow my adrenalin to take charge. It's their way of preparing for what lies ahead just as much as it's their way of communicating the importance of the game. I always thought that even if they were cyclists, they would have to pump themselves up verbally before a big race.

It's rare for Lohan to speak. He simply changes into his gear and sits there as everybody else mills about. His eyes stir from side to side but he seldom moves. He has his red helmet in one hand, a big John Torpey hurley in the other. No tape on the hurley, just a long stretch of wood. It looks like a weapon.

As a group we had yet to be successful in any tangible way. We had been beaten in finals and semi-finals, but that day I sensed I was part of a special team. I was playing for my county among men who had achieved everything in the game but I was also playing among men who had won nothing but who could drive Clare back to the top rung.

The first ball I contested that day was dropping a few yards in front of me. I had read the path of the ball perfectly and was quick to push forward, but Doc grabbed a handful of my jersey from behind, out of the referee's line of sight, and used the momentum to propel himself ahead of me. He gathered the ball and cleared it down the field.

It didn't take long for the situation to repeat itself, Doc stretching the jersey again and flying past me. This time his clearance found Michael Jacob. It was Lohan's job to curb Jacob's influence that day, but Jacob scored directly from the possession.

Whenever Lohan concedes a score the opposition will feed from it. It has significance. Shouts from the Wexford crowd rose to the heavens, and I was now under pressure. I had been beaten twice for possession, one of those had led to a Wexford score, and it felt like the stadium's eyes were on my back. I thought of the previous day's incident with Lohan. I could have caved; instead I went back to my pre-match sheet of paper. 'Stay in the moment.'

I also thought of something Daly had been preaching to me privately all year: 'Try and play it smart, Griff.'

So I looked for the alternative option. Rather than lose concentration by lashing out at Doc the next time he pulled me back, I jogged calmly to the umpire beside the goal. 'Umpire, you see what he's doing. If you don't call the ref the next time, I'll take action myself.'

Suddenly a voice in the crowd, just behind the goal, caught my attention. 'Griffin! Griffin! Give up that shit! Fight your own corner now, Griffin!'

It was a Clare supporter in his fifties with the saffron and blue jersey on his back and his daughter by his side. In a stadium of fifty thousand people this one man, from my own county, had got to me. I wanted to jump the hoarding and thump him. In a split second numerous thoughts competed in my head. 'I'm putting myself through so much shit for you,' I thought, 'I'm running to St Flannan's in the dark, lifting weights. And you're the man I've been trying to please since I started to play for Clare? You're the man whose opinion I used to gauge my own worth?' I had to choose to remain unaffected by this voice from the crowd. This thought was significant, like another brick in the wall was being removed and more light was shining in.

I jogged up the field and got a mouthful from Doc, who felt I'd snitched on a classmate.

I didn't respond but decided to stay with the Daly approach. The next ball we contested was a diagonal pass from Gerry Quinn. I allowed Doc a second to get in front of me, yanked his jersey back, sprang forward, collected the ball and scored my first point of the day.

Another ball rained down on us. I won it, shot. My second point. I began to take pleasure in the open acreage of Croke Park, scoring from long range and difficult angles, helping Clare to a dozen-point victory, ending the game with 0–5 to my name and picking up my second Man of the Match award of the season.

When the game was finished, Doc came over to shake my hand. 'Sorry about those few words, Tony. Heat of the battle.'

I respected his sentiment. 'No worries.'

If the Limerick game was decisive in copper-fastening the confidence of the team, then my own performance against Wexford was important for my personal development. Other years, having lost the first two balls in a game like that, I would have replayed those mistakes in my head and been unable to move on. My focus was on what had just happened rather than what was about to come. Wexford showed me that a negative thought doesn't have to destroy you if you focus on the wide angle, if you learn to adapt your behaviour to reframe the negative.

When a game didn't go my way, in the past I would have wondered if players like Colin Lynch, who always gave 100 per cent, questioned me. I now knew I couldn't stay in that reality because it would ultimately diminish my performance. I had to accept that I had prepared and would play to the best of my ability.

The end result was we had made an All Ireland semi-final. We were two wins away from the dream, the moment that would right whatever wrongs lived within me. Two wins from fulfilling my promise to my father.

It took a while to get beyond the thousands from Clare who lined the tunnel leading to the quiet dressing room. I was one of the first back, and seconds later in walked Lohan, panting. He scanned the room looking for me.

'You're a fuckin' good player too, boy.'

*

At best, our year had two games left and the basic profile of the season had already been shaped. We would face Kilkenny in an All Ireland semi-final with the winners most likely set to meet Cork in the final.

Even though I was still in the midst of it, I felt the season had developed into something for me personally. Aside from the first round against Cork when I started midfield, I had been Clare's highest scorer from open play in every game and I knew I was contributing to the direction of the team.

When Daly met with Lohan and McMahon on the golf course that previous autumn to discuss their futures, their assumption that guys like me – guys who had played in only one All Ireland final – craved another showdown was completely accurate.

After tasting a final, I wanted an opportunity to walk on to the big stage once more. That 2002 season had been my first full hurling year and it had begun and ended like a crazy fantasy. I was twenty-one years old and had waited two seasons to make my championship debut.

We played Tipperary in the first championship game of that summer and I was named at centre-forward. At half-time, Daly was asked to speak to the players. His inter-county playing career was over but his value to Clare was not forgotten – he could still contribute from the periphery. The entire team was huddled together in the dark, old dressing room of Páirc Uí Chaoimh. As the noise of the crowd shuddered around us, Daly moved from player to player, addressing them individually, speaking about the importance of the championship.

In full flow, and to emphasize a point, he would jab his

finger repeatedly, as if prodding a doorbell that wouldn't work. He looked each player in the eye, jabbing furiously, hitting the right notes.

He walked in front of me and put his finger to my chest. He told me that this was a day I had dreamed about since I was a kid, told me I had worked for years to get here and that I was now representing my parish and my family. He wasn't just recycling old-fashioned themes because when you saw him speak you knew he believed in what he was saying.

It had been a good opening half for me. From my first two touches I scored twice and felt as though I had put down roots on the Clare team. But it ended a bittersweet day. I finished with 0–6 from play and we had still been beaten by a couple of points.

The following day, one of the newspapers carried a photo-graph of me on my hands and knees after the game, my head welded to the ground. I remember the shot because Colin Lynch ran towards me as I lay sprawled out, shouting to get up, get up. 'Don't ever let them see you lying down,' he said, and since that moment I've always left the field with my head high, especially after defeat.

Coming off the pitch I knew I had achieved something, and making my way towards the dressing room I was met by a small troupe of supporters offering me congratulations on my performance.

I caught a glimpse of my father, standing quietly away from the commotion. I walked off and almost got emotional. We shook hands.

'Will I take your hurleys for you or are you going back on the bus?' he asked.

I told him I would go to the team hotel for a short while but I would travel home with him.

I shared my sense of achievement with my father. He had been at my side from the day I began hurling, driving me to games and training, never saying he was too busy or had other things to do.

He would listen to the 11.00 p.m. sports bulletin on national radio, the last one of the night, picking up hurling updates and team news, and the week of the Tipperary game, my name was mentioned for the first time. I was asleep in my bed, resting for Sunday, when my father came up the stairs to wake me and tell me the news. This was the same sports bulletin he had listened to when he worked in England and hearing my name was significant.

'You know, Tony is one of the best forwards in the game this year,' he told my sister once.

'Really?' she wondered.

'Definitely.'

It was something he would never tell me. He was proud of what I had achieved but equally stoic, which made conveying this pride to me difficult.

So we lost that day to Tipperary, but despite that early setback we made the All Ireland final. My first season had led to the biggest day in a hurler's career. I was being talked about as a possible All Star for the centre-forward position even though I was moved away from that position from time to time. I didn't mind as long as I kept my place on the team.

We met Kilkenny in the final and I was told so many times not to let the day pass me by that, inevitably, that's exactly what happened. A gale blew into our face in the first half and I already felt I wasn't at the level I needed to be at yet – I felt I had peaked earlier in the season. I finished the year with 0–18 to my name, all from open play, but for me that Kilkenny game left behind unfinished business. I wanted another taste of September hurling, and four years later Kilkenny offered a shot at that salvation.

There's an interesting backstory to the semi-final of 2006. The previous year we had produced our best performance of the season in the semi-final but were still beaten by Cork. We weren't favourites that day and I felt that as a group we weren't good enough to compete with Cork, particularly at critical stages of the game when they effortlessly shifted momentum.

It meant the mindset for Kilkenny in 2006 would have to be different to Cork in 2005, and it would have to be different, also, to Kilkenny in 2004.

That year we bounced back from the Waterford debacle and had Kilkenny on the ropes in the quarter-final. The game ended in a draw and some of us looked on the result as a moral victory.

The following morning we were still in the bar of the Fitzwilliam Hotel. The evening had turned into a drinking session and the early morning had become a farce, practically the entire team drinking pints. In my head and in my heart I knew this wasn't good preparation and I should have said something, but the fraternity was too strong and the fun was rolling over us in waves.

Even though we didn't know it at the time, the replay was six days later, it was now getting towards four a.m., and outside the first fingers of light were poking through the window. Kilkenny, for sure, were not on a drinking spree.

Johnny Glynn came down three times and asked us to go to bed. We told him we were on our last beer, told him to relax, but we stayed drinking because we believed we had achieved something and it deserved the required celebration. Ultimately, though, we were once more accepting defeat.

The fourth time Johnny appeared he was exasperated. 'For fuck's sake, lads. We could be playing next Saturday.' It was enough to break up the gathering.

That night killed our chances of beating Kilkenny. We travelled home on Monday and instead of using the day to recover from the game, we used it to get through a hangover. Mentally we were not fresh for the replay, and late in the game, when the doubts crept in, the Fitzwilliam haunted us. Kilkenny eased past us by five points.

In the week before the 2006 semi-final I continued to keep my mind only on what I could control. Commentators said Clare would win if Tony Carmody and Tony Griffin made a significant scoring contribution. At times we get labelled together. We share a first name and a similar physique and we've been friends since school where we played hurling together in the handball alleys. We couldn't control whether or not we scored freely that Sunday against Kilkenny but we could control our preparation.

I watched the tape of our 2004 clash and repeated a maxim to myself: 'The Tony Griffin Kilkenny saw two years ago is nothing compared to the Tony Griffin they will see on Sunday.

I am stronger mentally and physically and I have dedicated my year to this challenge.'

I planned for every eventuality. That year I worked on a scoring drill I had devised myself. One of our defenders, Conor McMahon, had told me there was one attacking play that was difficult to combat.

When a forward breaks across the field on to a ball with his back to goal he's running for the sideline and his natural instinct is to turn to goal in order to shoot. This narrows the scoring angle significantly. Conor told me that a defender is likely to allow the forward in possession to move away from goal because he is travelling further from the scoring area and is moving against the traffic. I figured if I could perfect an over-the-shoulder shot with my back to goal I would improve my scoring return. I came up with a relevant routine and worked on it for months. In the lead-up to the Kilkenny game I repeatedly simulated that scenario on the training field. If I could score one point as a result of the drill it would be worth the hours of work.

I also drew on any previous incidents I could think of. In the league final of 2004 I was in front of goal about to double on the ball when the Kilkenny goalkeeper James McGarry came from behind me and planted his hurley into my head. It wasn't dirty, he was simply batting the ball clear. I remembered this and decided that if a ball came down on top of me near McGarry's goal I would double on it with everything I had.

I couldn't see the season ending with the Kilkenny game and the entire year was building to that Sunday. For the older players it was a final chance to grace an All Ireland final. For me, a win and a good performance would justify the previous eight months.

The season, quite simply, would have to end in gold.

There would be no fairytale. Under the glow of an August Sunday, Kilkenny beat us with a strong finish. We didn't know it at the time, but that Kilkenny team was on the cusp of establishing itself as the greatest of the modern era, putting together a remarkable unbeaten run that stretched to the end of the decade.

Even with such perspective that wouldn't have mattered. We had failed when the game was at stake, and what's more, for a while it genuinely seemed as though we could get past their challenge.

A few hours before the game I'd stood in the reception area of the hotel in Portmarnock and spoken to a businessman I had come to know. He was aware of the financial predicament I was faced with in relation to returning to university in Halifax. After a few minutes he handed me an envelope.

'Open it when you go back to your room,' he said.

Strangely, for that entire week before the game I had felt certain I would come by the money I required, and by my calculations I knew I still needed €5,000 to continue my studies. When I was alone in my hotel room I opened the envelope and saw a cheque for exactly €5,000. I dropped to my knees and read the attached letter. It stipulated that I had to complete an honours degree, a task I had previously been unsure of taking on, but I became one of six out of the class of 120 to take the honours course.

The second stipulation was that when it was my time to carry out a good deed like this, I would pass it on.

Hours before the Kilkenny showdown, relief swept across me like a desert wind.

As for the game itself, we began with intensity and attacked with venom. I was winning my battle, Niall Gilligan was on top, Tony Carmody had just scored a beautiful point from 85 yards out. The crowd and the players were beginning to believe.

During the game I used another strategy of Daly's. He was celebrated for talking to his opponents and had once told me that if he was beating his marker he would start the winding-up process immediately. 'Listen, lad, there's a forward warming up there. You're going any minute now so be sure and shake my hand when you're going off.' Something like this can get into a player's mind.

I had scored my second point of the day and turned to the nearest Kilkenny man. 'That was nice, wasn't it?'

'Fuck you.'

I looked at the sideline. Two Kilkenny substitutes were jogging up and down.

'They're hardly warming up a substitute so early, are they? Which one is coming on for you?'

'Fuck you.'

He glanced at the two lads warming up just to make sure.

I knew from my early scores that I was causing Kilkenny problems and the elements I'd prepared for were paying off. For that second score, after I picked up possession, Tommy Walsh had allowed me to run away from goal. Before the game I had walked on to the field to memorize the placement of the advertising hoardings around the perimeter of the field. When Tommy allowed me that space, I had my bearings, knew I was within striking distance and nailed the chance.

The game comes back to me in snatches. Under the first dropping ball near the goal, I doubled ferociously, just as I had visualized, beating McGarry and Jackie Tyrrell, and made clean contact with the ball. I turned to see it trickling slowly, slowly for goal. I stopped. McGarry reacted, and for a moment it looked like he would keep it out, but Gilligan suddenly entered my line of sight and scooped the ball over the line. Goal.

At half-time we knew we were in with a chance of causing an upset. We were deadlocked on the scoreboard, 1–10 apiece, and Daly was pumped. 'Now, lads,' he said. 'Now we see.' We no longer needed to prove to ourselves we could compete with Kilkenny. In our minds we had played with more passion and intensity than they had in the first half and now we had to go back to finish the job. But we knew that, like the wind, hurling games change.

Gerry Quinn has the greatest delivery of any defender I have played with and against Kilkenny he had played some wonderful hurling. Seven minutes into the second half he broke his hand and had to be substituted.

Seven minutes after that, Eoin McCormack rifled home a goal to put Kilkenny five ahead. The game was sliding from our grasp but we refused to die and brought it back to a one-point game.

Then, hurling's modern-day great, Henry Shefflin, sprinkled some magic and scored four points without reply. With the minutes slipping by they crowded us out and hemmed us in. Kilkenny squeezed the life out of us, one breath at a time.

When it was clear that the game was up, Shefflin gathered yet another ball. I had drifted deep in search of possession because the supply to the forwards had dried up. I was a yard from Shefflin and he had the chance to shoot to bury us further. Instead, he flicked the ball over my head. I raced after it but he had turned to regain possession and passed to Eddie Brennan. Brennan hit it back to Shefflin and I gave chase. They were toying with me, and part of me thought, 'Fuck it. Let him off. Let him score.' But I overrode that idea, chased Shefflin again, and he drove the ball wide.

I didn't care if they beat us by a dozen points. I decided to push until the very end, to have no regrets.

When it was over, though, there were regrets. The ending of a season is difficult to handle, and I slipped back into old ways. My preparation had been meticulous but in the anger of defeat I punched holes in my approach and reopened the old sores. I'd had one glorious goal opportunity early in the first half. I rose for a dropping ball 14 yards from their goal and caught it over the heads of the defence. When the ball slapped into my hand I had only one thing on my mind, but I reached so high off the ground that as I landed I stumbled, and it took two steps to steady myself. Just two steps, but for weeks I ached over them both.

Because of those two steps I had given Kilkenny's J. J. Delaney the chance to get the slightest of hooks on my shot, I didn't make clean contact, and the ball shuddered off McGarry's body. If I had scored that goal, Clare would have won the All Ireland. That was the theory I rolled around my head for a fortnight after the game. I had reverted to a private world, occupied only by me.

At dinner with my family a few days after the game, I remember being asked a question. Everybody was laughing at the time and I played along, laughed and smiled and fobbed off the answer even though I had no idea what the question was. My mind was still replaying that goal chance.

The questions sprang up again. Was I just not able to do it? Was I weak? Did I somehow stumble because I couldn't step up to the plate? Whenever I applied any logic to this situation and told myself that I couldn't maintain balance because I jumped so high, I had an immediate counter-argument. 'Tony,' I'd say, 'you're making excuses for yourself.'

When I got back to Clare I put my gear on, went to the field at Ballyea and tried to recreate the scene to see if there was anything I could have improved on.

It took some time to see the light, and I learned I had to go through the process of constant reinforcement. Let games go. Don't over-think things. Move on.

We felt Daly was moving on, too. After Kilkenny he told us he wouldn't make any immediate decisions on his future but from his tone you suspected it was his last game as manager, and later that week he officially resigned.

A great year was coming to an end. On the bus from Croke Park our assistant coach Ollie Baker asked what my plans were. I told him I wasn't sure but I would have to continue my studies in Halifax. Then he said something that had deep meaning. He told me hurling had taken up so much of his life that there were times when he wished he could have done other things, seen other places.

I thought about 2007 and wondered how I could continue to live in Canada and play for Clare when I had seen the benefits of doing it the other way. Preparing in Canada and playing in Clare wouldn't work any more. It would feel like running through quicksand.

The night of the Kilkenny game we moved to a Dublin City hotel. I went to bed early but found no rest. I tossed and turned. I got up and sat at the side of the bed, put my face in my hands. I couldn't accept we had been beaten and this was the end of my full-time season. I felt sure there was something we could still do to reverse things.

My body was sore and stiff and there was an eerie silence in the room. I put on my clothes and went downstairs, no September hurling to keep me in Ireland.

The lads were taking in pints. I ordered a beer. A sing-song started up. A lament for the year we had just buried.

When the following morning caught up I still couldn't let the season go. I packed my bags, said goodbye to the team, caught the bus back to the hotel in Portmarnock and checked in by myself. I was trying to recreate the memories and promise of that Saturday and every Saturday we had stayed there under Daly.

I walked the beach and sat with my back against a sand dune. I slept for over an hour and the exhaustion of the previous forty-eight hours poured out of me.

I was shrouded with disappointment and questions still needed answering. I hadn't reached a point where I could find out for sure if I could push beyond the line. I needed a yes or no challenge, an equation to solve, something that I could either fail or pass, and maybe a team sport could never provide that.

Sitting on the beach, it was only a half-baked theory, and I drifted back to sleep.

2007

It was late November 2006, the evening of the All Star awards, for which I had been shortlisted. We were en route to the ceremony, just about to leave County Clare and drive across the border into Tipperary, when there was a lull in conversation. I remember the moment clearly.

Travis is driving, I'm looking out the window with Lough Derg shining away to my left. We're slowly passing over the grey narrow bridge in Killaloe and I know I have to strike.

For years this bridge has had significance in our part of the world. In 1920, on another November night, four local freedom fighters were shot with their hands tied behind their backs on the bridge. They'd been accused by British auxiliaries, deployed by the Crown to suppress the Irish revolt, of attacking a police barracks a few miles up the road and were made an example of. Terror reverberated across the area afterwards.

For me, that story is filled with symbolism and it floats into my head from time to time as I cross that body of water. That evening, on our way to the All Stars function in Dublin, this bridge that joins Clare and Tipperary seemed like a call to action.

So I struck.

'Trav, I have this idea about cycling across Canada.'

Depending on what he said next, things could have gone

one of two ways. If he dismissed the idea, I'd have shelved it there and then; by the time we'd hit Tipperary soil the notion would have been dead. That's the amount of value I put in Travis's opinion.

He didn't take the negative option though.

'Tell me more,' he said.

So I unloaded a few things on the journey. I'd already run the idea past a handful of people in Halifax and they'd been supportive, but coming back home on the plane, for the eight hours in the air, I'd told myself this dream would live or die by Travis's reaction.

He could have said to concentrate on hurling. He could have said the cycle would kill me. He could have told me to stop dreaming. He didn't. He wanted to know more.

For the world, it seemed like the trip to Dublin passed in a few seconds. We were suddenly absorbed by the potential of this cycle, and that was strange. I'd devoted myself to hurling for nine years. It had been an obsession, and the season just finished I'd pushed myself to the limit. I'd made sacrifices. I'd tailored eight months of my life around being the best player I could be and the All Stars night should have been monumental. It should have been vindication.

I was on the cusp of a national award and it should have been the only topic on the agenda during that journey. It wasn't.

I told Travis more about this idea.

My father was central to it. Since he passed away I'd been searching for something to do but I didn't know what. I look back now and see that throughout 2006 I had also been avoiding coming to terms with his death, which was typical of me.

Whenever I was met with something I couldn't change, I got busy. I ran. I trained. I studied. Anything but stay static and deal with my thoughts.

My sisters were constantly talking about Dad and bringing him into the conversation. That was their way of dealing with his death, but I had my own. Block it out. Get busy.

One afternoon when I arrived home from training they asked me, 'Tony, what do you remember most about Dad?'

I became angry and told them to stop talking about him. 'For God's sake, can ye talk about something else?'

It was the wrong reaction but I couldn't help it because I was surrounded by memories. Plagued by them.

At the time I was at home every day and the routine never altered. I'd get up and feed the cattle, his cattle. I'd get his old coat from the shed and wear it while I was working on the farm. I'd use his pitchfork and shovel, and for a few moments things would be fine, but suddenly I'd remember that just a few months ago he was wearing this coat, his hands were working this pitchfork, and everything would come flooding back. The suffering he went through, the disease he fought, the effect his death was having on the family.

Most of all it killed me to see how sad my mother had become. If I was working close to the house there were times when I could hear her crying in the kitchen.

I told Travis all of this but avoided telling him the raw truth, the truth that had the ability to haunt me, and did, particularly as the cycle got closer and journalists were constantly asking me why I was doing it.

I gave them the stock answer: 'To raise funds for cancer.' I told them what they wanted to hear. 'To do something in memory of my father.' It meant I had the hero's headlines, but I wasn't being transparent. I was using those clichés to veil reality. They contained some sincerity but they didn't tell the complete story.

One Saturday afternoon Dad and I had an argument on the farm over something silly and he gave out to me. I had an ash stick in my hand and I flung it into the ditch and stomped off home through the fields. It was your regular father-and-son argument, but in the months after he passed away this incident came to me often.

There's another skeleton in the closet. There was this note I handed to him four weeks before Christmas, just as I was about to leave to go back to college. Again, inevitably, I was gearing up for exams. In the note I told him to stay positive. Told him I had exams to finish and training to endure, that it was going to be tough for both of us but we'd battle through the next month together and have a good Christmas in Ballyea.

Battle through the next month together? How stupid was I, to equate fighting cancer with studying and training? For months after his funeral, whenever I thought about this note I could only shake my head.

And here's the thing. That was also the last time I saw him alive.

For some reason there seemed to be a perfect black symmetry to everything, or at least that was the way I chose to see things.

While I was studying in Halifax for those Christmas exams my sister Rosaleen rang with the news and I was stunned. I made arrangements and booked the next flight home, which meant there was time to kill and action to take in order to block out that stupid note I'd written.

I crossed campus with a sinking feeling, and in the falling haze of that December afternoon I saw the place where I would find some refuge: the Dalhousie gym.

I walked down the stairs and it took a moment to adjust to the brightness of the gym. For the rest of the world it was a regular day. Two girls working out. The sounds of weights crashing. The whirr of the treadmill. Business as usual.

I began to pound aggressively into a workout, but two minutes later, from across the room, 'Hey, Tony, you all set to fly home to the folks for Christmas? You must be excited.' I gave my friend a smile and told her yeah, I was really looking forward to the trip. I couldn't bring myself to let her know I was preparing to fly home that evening to shoulder my father to his place of rest.

A few others passed through the gym and that conversation was replayed three or four times. I never said what had happened because somewhere within me something was telling me this wasn't supposed to happen, and if I uttered those words out loud, then it had to be true.

It did not make sense. My father was supposed to be one of the few who win the battle and his death made me question everything.

I had just come to trust that the power of the mind could override whatever life threw at us, so his death shattered that belief system. It's a cliché, I know, but I began to ask God how he could take away somebody so devoted to Him.

There were just so many different things to come to terms with.

These were things I wasn't prepared to face, and the entire season of 2006 was, in a big way, running to avoid reality. If I trained until I hurt, then trained some more, I knew my mind would be muzzled. Forget the All Star or the All Ireland. In a major way, these were branches of a greater objective – to numb the brain.

So, now that the season was over I needed to do something with 2007 to maintain that detachment from reality. Raising money for cancer was a positive offshoot to the cycle, but looking back now, I wasn't just doing it for my father. I was doing it for myself. It was an attempt to deal with the grief and guilt that surrounded his death.

It was an attempt to make some sense of it all.

My father wasn't a cycling fan by any means. Hurling was his game. He loved it with a fierce and deep passion that he passed down to me, but he could always appreciate an athlete. Before he became ill himself, I told him about Lance Armstrong and how he'd returned to cycling after his illness to dominate his sport. 'He must be a mighty man,' is what Dad said.

For me, I'd always been fascinated by cycling. It's a basic, earthy sport. Push the pedal and you move. Push it harder, faster, and you win. Those are simple principles.

And Armstrong's book, *It's Not About the Bike*, had knocked me out. It wasn't the cycling that put me on the canvas but his determination to pick up the pieces after beating cancer to excel as an athlete. I found that inspirational.

The book fuelled my passion for cycling even more. I wanted to go and watch the Tour de France, mainly to get a closer look at this guy Armstrong, and I promised myself I would.

So after the 2005 qualifier game against Waterford I set my alarm for 2.00 a.m. to drive to Dublin airport. That evening Anthony Daly had arranged a minibus to take the players to West Clare for a drinking session, but I passed on that night of Guinness. Plenty of time for those.

Instead, I caught a flight to Lyon, rented a little silver Corsa and made it to the small city of Grenoble at the foot of the Alps. It was early morning when I arrived there and the lads in Clare were still sinking pints in Doolin, wondering how they'd get home.

I had worries of my own. I had no place to stay so that night the back seat of the car moonlighted as a decent mattress.

I was up before the sun the next morning to find a good spot on one of the world's most notorious ascents, the Courchevel, a 21-kilometre ride into the clouds.

The spectacle of Le Tour surprised me. Even the build-up. As you waited for hours for the cyclists to pass your perch on the mountain, a carnival atmosphere dripped through the air. Sponsors' vehicles would pass up the hill, blaring music and giving out free souvenirs. The climb was wedged with Spaniards, Germans, French and English, and by 2005, thanks to Armstrong, Americans had Tour de France fever as well. All of them were sipping wine and beer, waiting under a beating sun to shout on their men.

When the stream of cyclists finally trickled past it was

scary to see how lean they were. They looked like machines pedalling up the slopes: all sinewy and much thinner than I had ever expected and I wondered how these guys could be so powerful.

I've read a lot about the altered bodies of the Tour and cycling in general since then and it's opened my eyes, but when you're there for the first time you get swept along. It's what all athletes aspire to: being in that peak physical shape, being at the top of your sport.

That day really drove home how torturous sport can be. Pain and suffering were etched on to every cyclist's face, and some of the hard training sessions for Clare were put into perspective.

In a sadistic way, I came back wondering if I could endure those levels of agony. Could I cycle with a picture of pain on my face? It was just a brief curiosity but one that would return and nag at me.

Before I spoke to Travis on that All Star journey to Dublin, I'd told my college roommates and great buddies Matt Bethune and Ben Whidden that I'd been considering doing something different with my summer, but didn't know what. I'd told them this had been an intention of mine for a while, but I hadn't come up with anything concrete just yet. Maybe I just didn't have the courage to jump out of the comfort zone that surrounds you when you're on an inter-county hurling team so I'd kept putting this plan, whatever it might be, on the long finger.

A few days after we spoke, Matt emailed me this video clip of the Hoyt family, Rick and his father Dick.

In Canada and the United States, theirs is a well-known story. Their faces are on billboards and they're referenced on TV programmes. Over there, the Hoyts are recognized as two men who have broken the boundaries of human possibility, but I'd never heard of them.

I clicked the play button on the laptop and within this three-minute clip was the ultimate tale of love and adventure, and its message strengthened my view of life.

Rick had been brain-damaged during birth and was wheelchair-bound for his entire life. When he was ten, his family raised $5,000 for a computer that allowed him to communicate, and three years later he entered public school for the first time.

A little while after this, Rick heard of a school charity run for a kid who had been paralysed in a sports accident. Immediately, he wanted to take part.

How? wondered Dick.

Push me, tapped Rick.

Trouble was, Dick was a middle-aged guy from suburban Massachusetts with a pot-belly and a taste for fast food and soda. But push him Dick did.

Dick's body was aching that night but Rick typed out a message that changed both their lives: 'When we were running, it felt like I wasn't disabled any more.' That was a turning point, and there and then Dick decided to help his son run and compete for the rest of their lives.

They began to take on huge challenges. They tried to run the Boston marathon in 1979 but weren't allowed. They didn't fit the category of solo runner and they didn't fit the label of wheelchair athlete, so a race official booted them out of the field. When the official wasn't looking they came back to the starting line and ran anyway, like a couple of bandits.

Four years later when they were finally allowed to run officially, they finished in the top quarter of the field.

They kept looking for challenges, and somebody suggested a triathlon. Dick couldn't swim, so he learned. He hadn't cycled in years, but he bought a bike.

In total they've competed in over two hundred triathlons, Dick towing his son on a dinghy tied to his waist, pedalling with a fully grown Rick sitting over his front wheel, and pushing his wheelchair for miles to get them both across the line.

Amazing.

When the video clip finished, I noticed my heartbeat had picked up pace. I was sitting in my room on Pepperell Street with the evening falling in, and in the half-light things clicked into place. It was like somebody flicked a switch.

The Hoyts. A cycle. My father. All of it came spilling over me and the idea was born.

I'm going to cycle across Canada. I am going to throw it all in and pedal a bike across the second largest landmass on the planet. Over mountains, across plains, into sniping winds, through cornfields.

It didn't rest easy, though. I told Matt and Ben and they wondered if I'd lost my mind. I woke that night at five, and in the darkness I dismissed the idea. I reckoned it would never come to pass – there would be too many elements to juggle. Studying. Training. The logistics of it. I shook my head, turned over and went back to sleep, but for days afterwards it continued to eat away at me. The idea grew, and before long it demanded attention.

If Travis thought it was worth running with, then this great adventure was no longer an idea, it was now a plan. In true Travis style, he didn't just say to go with it, he prodded the idea along, and by the time we reached the City West Hotel in Dublin for the awards a few things were beginning to take shape.

Travis asked, why just cycle across Canada? He reckoned I'd have to bring in an Irish ingredient, so we decided that once I'd finished the Canadian leg I'd fly home and cycle across the belly of my own country, from Dublin to Ennis, east coast to west.

He said I'd have to set up a foundation and give my name over to it, and this was something I was uncomfortable with.

Putting my name to a foundation? What would people in Ireland think? We're a cynical crowd at the best of times, and for some reason we're particularly cynical in the GAA world. Would people say I was getting notions about myself? Cycling across Canada was going to raise enough eyebrows without having my name up in lights.

But I listened to Travis. 'You got me this far in my hurling career,' I thought. 'You believed in me when I didn't believe in myself.' So I trusted his judgement.

I first met Travis McDonough at the tail end of 2001.

Funnily enough, the first time I'd heard of this Canadian chiropractor I was sitting at the kitchen table at home, eating breakfast with my parents.

They had been in Ennis for a quiet drink the previous night and Travis, who had treated Dad for a back injury he'd picked up while working on a construction site, approached the two of them in a local pub. 'Do you know your husband is the fittest sixty-three-year-old I've ever treated?' he asked my mother.

'Who're you telling?' she whipped back, quick as lightning.

The three of them talked for a while and whatever he said that night, Travis left a lasting impression. The way my mother described him he sounded like he had a huge personality, and I'd pictured him as this big giant of a man, like one of those gods who feasted at Valhalla.

He'd drifted out of my head for a few weeks when one night he appeared out of the blue at a Clare team meeting. Travis was there to talk about nutrition and how the body works, and when he introduced himself I couldn't believe it was the same guy my mother had spoken of. His frame was the first thing that struck me. 'Jeez,' I thought, 'he's no giant anyway.' He was small, slender, well dressed and neat. He spoke fast but precisely and gave a very, very scientific presentation that blew the lads away. He was so specific and detailed and packed in so much information that half of what he said went over the heads of most of us, but I was engrossed.

I approached him afterwards and said I'd like to talk some more, get some more information. At this stage I was just after breaking on to the Clare squad and I was hungry for anything that might give me an edge and push me closer to the starting team.

We arranged to meet at his office a few days later and that's when things took off. That weekend Clare were playing Meath in the league and Travis and I did a ninety-minute physical assessment and treatment the Thursday before the game. I arrived at his clinic, this gangly nineteen-year-old who built his entire confidence and sense of self on the premise that he might be good enough to play for Clare some day.

From a personal point of view the Meath game was a huge success. I went out and scored seven points, and in my own head I'd answered a few questions. Essentially, I knew I had the ability to make the team, and that was significant.

Afterwards, Travis said he could help me improve physically but needed to change the structure of my body. For the slightest improvement, I would undertake whatever he called for.

Back then I was 12st 4lb, thin as a rake, ribs like a broken umbrella, so first off he provided me with an exact weights programme to strengthen my upper body.

This was all new to me. Weights were still considered somewhat exotic in Clare. Our manager at the time, Ger Loughnane, the messiah of the county, had delivered success when many had considered Clare hurling to be dead. His methods became the template for other counties during the mid to late 1990s, but by the time I arrived on the scene, these methods were becoming antiquated. His approach had definitely evolved but his knowledge of weights and how to develop a player's strength was, to my mind, non-existent.

Loughnane gave me a lot. He called me on to the senior squad and supplied me with several national league starts, and under him my confidence began to grow. But weights training was not in his bag of tricks.

One of the first times I was in the squad we were eating lunch after an early-morning training session and I was sitting opposite him. He gave me a puzzled look, threw a glance over my skinny bones and said, 'Tony, you'd want to start doing weights or something.' Ger didn't exactly provide a clear indication of what I should do, but Travis did.

He is a big believer in the value of core strength, in developing the muscle groups that stabilize the spine and pelvis, which are critical for the transfer of energy from large to small body parts during sport. He helped me develop my flexibility and power and devised a training programme specific to hurling. He had me stand on a wobble board with one foot while I mimicked the action of striking a ball, which improved my balance. Because I was tall and skinny, I was round-shouldered; Travis gave me exercises to open up my chest and square my shoulders.

For the previous few years I had simply replicated what I saw in the gym. Big guys lifting big weights. Lift, lift, lift. That's all I did. My biceps and chest were well developed but this didn't relate to hurling in the slightest. Travis's training focused only on the game. He only gave me functional power and muscle endurance.

Working out together, we quickly became close friends, and when I was with the medical company searching for some unknown path, it was Travis who suggested human kinetics. He had studied the same course at Dalhousie, and he was the one who introduced me to John McCabe. When I landed in Halifax for the first time, Travis's network helped me settle.

Within a year I was bringing his engagement ring from Halifax to Clare. Travis had been back visiting his folks in Canada with his then girlfriend Margaret and, unknown to her, he purchased a ring downtown. They were flying home in a couple of days but the thing was, he couldn't risk putting the ring into his check-in luggage in case it got lost. He couldn't take it on the plane, either, because what would happen if he set the metal detector off? He would fish the ring out of his pocket, Margaret would know what was going on and he'd probably be forced to go on bended knee in the security zone of Halifax airport with passengers and staff looking on. Hardly romantic.

So he filled me in on the situation.

'Griff, you're coming back to Ireland next week, right? Can you bring the ring?'

'No problem.'

I was travelling home that Friday for a crucial club game with Ballyea and to arrive on time I had to make a connecting flight at Logan airport in Boston. The problem was, my flight out of Halifax was delayed and it looked like I wouldn't make the Boston connection. I was now in danger of missing the game.

I spoke to the lady at check-in and explained my predicament. I was met by a stone wall.

'Everybody else has a reason to get home too, sir. You'll just have to wait for the next flight out like everybody else.'

'But I have to make the Boston flight.'

'I'm sorry, sir. It just won't happen.'

Then I remembered the ring.

'Listen,' I whispered. 'I'm travelling home to propose to my girlfriend and if I don't get there tomorrow she'll have left for Australia.'

'What?'

'It's true.'

I showed her the ring. Her face lit up.

'Well! Let me see what I can do!'

A minute later she found me a ticket home. I would fly to Toronto and connect for Boston, but there was a catch.

'You'll have to travel first class, sir. It's all we have left.'

'No problem!'

When I plunged into the soft first-class seat, the American beside me looked familiar but I couldn't put a name to him.

We got talking about Ireland and he said it was one of his favourite places, even showed me his claddagh ring.

A while later, when we were in the air, it was still gnawing at me that I didn't know this guy, that I should know him. I got up and asked the hostess if she could throw some light on the subject.

'That's Michael Stipe,' she said. 'The lead singer with REM.'

When I got back to Ennis, Travis lapped up the saga.

Sometimes you meet somebody and they're already on the same page as you. That was the way it was with Travis. The more he and I worked together, the more his obsession with hurling grew. He'd go to every game and revel in it. We would meet afterwards and he'd have recorded every play I was involved in, how many balls I had caught, how many runs I had made, whether or not I had taken any lazy options, if my shooting was off.

He'd study my movement and my striking, but balance was at the centre of his training schedule. His sports background is broad but he excelled at tennis and boxing. He has represented Ireland in the Davis Cup and boxed for years for Canada at a high level. And if you take tennis and boxing, they're two sports where balance is key. If you're not centred, you might miss your return of serve or you might get nailed by that punch coming at your face.

So he broke everything down into a frame-by-frame analysis. How to strike the ball when you're off balance, how to gauge balance, how to ensure the hips are moving with more freedom. This approach was way ahead of its time and the effects were almost immediate. I was playing with more freedom and confidence and my upper body was gaining pounds and strength.

Above all else, his faith in me was astounding. Almost from day one, he told me I could be the best in the country, and as a young hurler who thrived on positive outside influence he provided the genuine endorsement I was seeking.

This little story shows the kind of guy Travis is.

When his boxing career was gaining momentum, he trained at a gym in Halifax's North End, the Citadel Boxing Club. It has since closed down but in its heyday it was populated by some of the nation's top fighters. You could walk in and watch two Olympic medallists spar while four world-ranked boxers waited to get some ring time. The heavyweight Kirk Johnson, the light-middleweight Olympian Ray Downey and the international coach Taylor Gordon operated out of the Citadel at the time.

One day the gym door opened and in walked a kid, six feet six inches, 147lb, thin as can be. He had fresh scars all over his face, arms and back and seemed to be carrying a broken hand.

Travis glanced across the gym and was looking at Dave Defiagbon – the man who would later become known as Dave the Dream.

Defiagbon was already a hero in his native Nigeria having

won Commonwealth and African titles and was from a family of seventeen struggling to survive in the countryside outside Lagos. At international meetings he struck up a friendship with Taylor Gordon, who happened to coach Travis back in Halifax. Defiagbon would plead with Gordon to bring him to Canada, to safety. Gordon was unsure of what Dave was wishing to avoid in Nigeria, but at one tournament, in front of two hundred people, he grabbed the trainer by the ankles and wept openly, begging Gordon to take him under his wing. The trainer sensed the gravity of the situation and agreed, but when Dave attempted to leave Nigeria and defect to Canada, he was beaten and abused by representatives of the government, hence the cuts and injuries to Dave's body when he first entered the Halifax gym.

Gordon introduced Travis and Dave, and Dave found himself living in the McDonough household. In the middle of the night Travis would wake to cupboards in the kitchen opening and closing. Dave would be downstairs shovelling food into his body. Eating was still a novelty to him. The McDonoughs watched as Dave's weight moved from 147lb to 167lb to 187lb, and this is how he came to box in the heavyweight division.

It was 1996 and the Atlanta Olympics were coming up. Dave had a genuine shot at a medal and it was his ambition to box for the Canadian flag but the authorities were stalling. Travis recruited the help of his mother, Alexa, the celebrated politician. With Alexa's help, only days before the final cut for citizenship declaration, Dave officially became a Canadian.

He travelled to Atlanta that July and returned with a silver medal. His story had become the stuff of legend in Canada, hence the nickname 'Dave the Dream'.

Travis helped Dave reach his potential because Travis is a visionary. Where others may turn their back on a concept, he will give it his full attention.

It's that belief that led him to throw the dice and move to Ireland to set up a chiropractic business at a time when the practice was unheard of in the country.

By 2002 we had already begun to set goals for me to hit, and when I started against Tipperary in the championship that summer, I ticked my first box.

The last, as it happened, was getting that All Star in '06, but with the talk of the cycle we lost track of time and arrived late at the City West. Marty Morrissey, a fellow Clareman and one of Ireland's leading sports announcers, was at the door of the hotel waiting for us, pointing at his watch, smiling. He was master of ceremonies for the night, and as I didn't have a mobile phone he was wondering where the hell I was.

'Ah, Jesus, Tony! We're about to go live on TV! Hurry up!'

Travis and I didn't have time to check into the hotel. We jumped out of the car and changed into our tuxedos in the car park.

I had one last chance to gather my thoughts. I thanked God for bringing me this far and repeated to him what I had said previously. The All Star was in His hands, it was His decision. After six years of total devotion to being the best player in my position, here I was, having flown home from Canada, in the car park of the hotel where the awards were about to start and I genuinely knew I would feel no malice if I didn't collect an award I believed I deserved, an award I had focused completely on for the previous eight months. For a time after the 2006 season had finished I'd thought about the All Star on a daily basis, before concluding that I couldn't let the thought own me. That's when I handed it over to God. 'It's yours,' I said. At the time, the cycle was still a vague notion, but I asked that if an All Star could propel the cycle, to let it be. Either way, I was content to relinquish it.

Maybe I was already moving away from hurling, maybe I was finally beginning to answer my own questions, or maybe on some level I was certain I would get the All Star. I didn't have time to figure out which one.

'Griff, c'mon!' Travis roared from the other side of the car.

The two of us ran to catch the start of the ceremony.

It's the first Saturday of January 2007, five weeks since I received the All Star, and it's snowing in Halifax. All morning the sky above the city has had this drained, dull, grey look about it. A little like what you would see most days at home, but with a touch of menace.

After two years in Nova Scotia I can read the winter clouds and these have frostbite scribbled all over them.

Outside it's about minus thirty, and this morning I'm heading out on my first bike ride in preparation for the cycle. The contrast with five weeks back couldn't be sharper. When I received the award in the City West Hotel I was already thinking that the accolade could propel the cycle further, give it a higher profile and bring it to a wider audience.

Since the conversation with Travis I've slowly put the idea out there and a few people have come on board. Bruce and Todd have become two of my right-hand men. They're going to look at the logistics of the cycle and plan it out, but they also want to help me train.

So we arrange to meet outside Perks Coffee House at the end of Oxford Street.

I've got this green mountain bike that John McCabe has loaned me and as I cycle on to Oxford I can see Bruce and Todd waiting for me, jumping up and down beneath the canopy at Perks to stay warm, their bike shoes clicking on the ground, a cloud of fog escaping from their mouths.

The two of them are all kitted out. They've gone and bought top-of-the-range road bikes and they've got every piece of gear you can imagine to keep out the cold. Todd has a facemask, they've both got insulated long-finger gloves, they've even got protective glasses and booties to keep the snow from getting into their cycling shoes. Bruce's yellow windbreaker is stuffed with protein bars and chocolate.

Me? I'm wearing a green woolly jumper, sweat pants and a pair of hiking boots. But it's my hands that grab the attention of the two guys. I've a pair of hurling socks over my paws, and when they see this they look at each other in disbelief.

I've only met Todd once and he turns his head away and says to no one in particular, 'So this is the guy that's going to cycle across Canada?' The two of them burst out laughing and Todd tells me I'll need proper gear if I'm not going to freeze to death.

The thing is, I'm a student. I don't have the bucks for extras. But I'll have to rustle something together.

I met Bruce Mansour by chance that Christmas. I decided to stay in Halifax for the holidays and on St Stephen's night I bumped into him at a party, introduced to him by Travis. His enthusiasm for life hit me immediately. Bruce is in his forties but he looks at the world with the enthusiasm of a teenager; his energy could power small cities. Nothing is impossible to him. He owns a company, Make It Happen, that does exactly what its name suggests.

He's extremely open-hearted, and because of this he has a profound impact on people. I didn't know it then but he influenced the way I looked at the world, and when my energy and enthusiasm fizzled out during a dark period, he helped pick me up.

That night I met him he showed a lot of blind faith in the cycle, which was just about in its infancy. We spoke for a long time. He explained he wanted to help in any way he could and handed me his business card, which I proceeded to mislay.

A few days later, Travis, his father and I were discussing the cycle over a meal downtown. We were putting out the idea of linking up with the Lance Armstrong Foundation to lever exposure for the ride when Bruce passed our table. It was like fate was putting him in my path again.

We spoke once more and arranged to meet that Friday.

I told Bruce about our Armstrong plans but said we didn't have a direct contact route to the organization. Bruce said not to worry, he could make it happen. He had briefly met a guy named Todd McDonald who was friendly with the LAF crew. Over a cigar at a party one night, Bruce and Todd had shot the breeze, exchanged business cards and walked away. Thought no more of the contact. Now, Bruce was flipping his phone open, dialling Todd's number and telling him about this Irish guy's wild idea to cycle across Canada.

When he came off the phone he had arranged a meeting with Todd for later that week, and on the back of that Todd got to work on getting me to Austin, Texas, to see Armstrong.

Our training sessions turn into weekly events, and on one of the first Saturdays Ben joins us for the spin. By now, Ben and I have pooled together to buy a pair of cycling gloves and the deal is that we will alternate their usage.

Ben shows up wearing them. I'm still in the same gear as the first week, and a few miles into the ride Todd cycles by and looks me up and down. 'Tony, my man, you're at least going to have to get gloves.'

'I have a pair,' I tell him. 'Look,' I say, pointing back to Ben. 'He's wearing them. But don't worry. It's my turn to have them next week!'

Todd was right. It was icy and my fingers were cold like meat from the bottom of a deep freezer, but I was so enthusiastic I would have trained with no clothes.

These group training trips really gained momentum. We started off with three that very first day, but within a few weeks we'd attracted a little posse of about ten, going for pancakes afterwards and feeling enthused about the challenge to come.

It was a great release to be out on the road talking with other people because the real hard work was done on my own, on a stationary bike in a tiny room the size of a prison cell. Those sessions were more brutal than any physical training I'd ever done in my life. I had become used to the tough hurling sessions in Crusheen when your body tells your mind to stop. I knew how to negotiate my way past that pain; I'd understood it and learned how to manage it, how to focus on something else. Cycle training was completely different. In that small room I had nothing to occupy my mind, and because I had never really cycled before I was working parts of my body that had been cobwebbed for years, so my muscles tired easily. The only distraction I had was the DVD player in the corner of the room, but there were only two DVDs. The first was *The Bee Gees: Live in Australia*. I watched that band strut their stuff on stage dozens and dozens of times, 'Tragedy' blasting out of the speakers, its sugary lyrics lodging forever in my brain. The second was a highlights reel from the 2005 Tour de France, and even before it became a goal I found myself talking to the TV screen: 'I'm coming to see you, Lance Armstrong. I'm coming to see you.' Sometimes John McCabe would stick his head in with a comment. 'Griffin. Thought you were a hurler, not a cyclist! Come on, man, pick it up!'

I had asked Dr Stephen Cheung, a lecturer in exercise physiology at Dalhousie and an expert cyclist, to become my personal trainer. I called into his office one day out of the blue and told him I wanted to cycle across Canada. He sat back, listened without saying a word for ten minutes, then said, 'Hey, I know you. You're the guy who goes around campus with that big stick.'

He asked me to explain about hurling and my training schedule to play at the top level. He then told me it was the antithesis of what was required to become a long-distance cyclist and said that even though we had five months to prepare, we would still be against the clock. But I was confident Dr Cheung would back me. If his students showed enthusiasm, he was known to go through a wall to assist them.

'Okay,' he said, 'I'll help you.'

Stephen had a cyclist's body and a deep and exact voice, and from the start he was totally professional. We set up base camp in a tiny little room tucked away in the basement of the gym. He fitted me out with an advanced stationary bike and pinned electrodes to my body to monitor every little detail.

For the initial session he had me take two different tests. The first, he asked me to pedal as hard as I could for five minutes, and from this he measured my short-term energy abilities. The second was simply a variation on the theme: flat out for twenty minutes to gauge my stamina. By the time I finished he wasn't overly impressed by the power I could generate.

I'm wider and taller than he is but our outputs were generally similar. My output should have been much higher, but he said I had a good aerobic capacity, that it wasn't like we were building an engine from scratch. The main challenge would be to convert my power and fitness to the lower half of my body.

There were other challenges, like the weather. We were starting training in the middle of winter and would have to wait for the snow to clear to get out on the road. This would take months and it confined our training to indoors, away from the icy roads.

As the weeks went by he continued to monitor my training closely to ensure I was making progress, and he also instilled a sense of discipline. If I were a minute late for a session, he'd berate me. 'I won't continue to train you, Tony, if you keep dis- respecting me.'

He was steely and determined and quite confident. Before he moved to Canada, Stephen's father had had a prominent job in a welding factory in China but also had the foresight to pre- dict that communism could threaten his livelihood. As this threat gradually became a reality, Stephen's dad took some practical action. When he finished his work in the factory office he would go down to the floor and learn to weld from the craftsmen. He wanted a trade to take with him if the need to emigrate ever arose. When it did, he arrived in Canada as a fully trained welder. He put his sons through university and because of his hard work and vision Stephen's father shaped a life for himself and his family.

So Stephen was absorbed in the specifics of the world that can lead to success, and that was exactly what I was looking for.

We had deep conversations on things like religion and faith. He couldn't comprehend that I believed so fully in an after-life and I couldn't understand how he didn't have confidence heaven existed.

But we built a solid friendship and it didn't take long to figure out that like many cyclists, numbers obsessed him. Power outage, wattage, cadence. These were foreign words to me but they were part of Stephen's daily vocabulary.

By now, my life was once again shaped by routine. I'd race from class to this underground cycling clinic, he'd hook me to the computer and I'd pedal for hours.

In this tiny white room, just big enough to hold two people, a bike and a computer, there was no place to hide. In there, under a yellow light and wedged between bare walls, it was difficult to tell if it was night or day. There was something otherworldly about it and that room became my own war zone, the place where I tried, again, to answer questions about my character. I'd look down on the floor, a pool of sweat shining back at me, and wonder why I was putting myself through this. It was grunt work. Pedal, pedal, grunt. Pedal, pedal, grunt.

I was hurting, but I was laying foundations.

When you're not used to cycling a racing bike there's an

adjustment period that nobody tells you about. The saddle is whip thin, no thicker than the width of three fingers. In the evenings I would sometimes put my three middle fingers in front of me and fixate on what happens to the body after an hour sitting on something that narrow, keeping your head as still as possible and remaining in the same arched posture. There are pains you never accounted for. Your back creaks, your shoulders seize, your neck aches, your thighs burn, your hamstrings tighten and your groin numbs. The latter is particularly worrying, and it takes a while for the pins and needles to subside.

Stephen loved to see me in agony. After leaving me for a few hours on the bike he would return to this laboratory of pain, sit down beside me and eat his lunch in my face. My stomach would rumble.

His wife Debbie made these delicious cinnamon rolls. I say delicious but I never got to taste them; it was the smell that bewitched me. Stephen would finish his lunch before tucking into the pastries and the scent would come floating into my nostrils.

'You hungry, Tony?'

I'd curse him but I knew he was testing me.

The mind games continued. Most of the time he wouldn't let me in on what session we were going to do until I was literally sitting on the saddle. It could be a short high-intensity workout or a long, slow slog. I liked to mentally prepare for the session beforehand but this wasn't a luxury Stephen would give me. His thinking was solid. Crossing Canada, I would be in an uncontrolled environment. I would have to deal with punctures, heat, strong winds. He was programming my brain to cope with whatever the next hour threw at me.

In time, he asked me to cut out all other sports, including running, and put me on a programme of pushing the pedals at a high resistance to stress my leg muscles and adapt them to cycling. The previous year I had worked continually on developing my explosive power and my upper body. Now I had to strip this away.

'What we want,' he told me, 'is to make it look like gravity has taken over and moved the strength from above your belt-buckle to below it.'

All of the work I had done with Travis, everything I had focused on physically for the previous six years, was being eroded day by day. My weight dropped, but I accepted that. I had to gain strength in my legs, and after a month I began to notice my jeans were tighter around my thighs. It became agonizing simply to walk up stairs, but I found a way to cheat: I went up backwards. It was less painful that way.

I was forced to change everything. I had to go from an athlete who ran in bursts and recovered in bursts to one who maintained a steady output of energy but didn't get time to recover. Stephen gave me targets to hit. My tendency was to work harder than required, but this approach was useless. He drilled me that I wasn't racing, that I had to ensure that physiologically my body would not break down on the road. It became a regular mantra. 'Tony, if I want you to ride at 300 watts, I do not want to see the printout at 350 or 310. You keep it at 300 for every single push of the pedal.'

Stephen went above and beyond what was required of him. Once we had assembled a road crew to take the trip with me he spoke to them about bike maintenance and told them to think ahead before we reached the bigger towns to book me some time with a physiotherapist. His planning was exact.

I was itching to cycle outdoors with Stephen. When the snow thawed in late March we rode out of Halifax together for the first time. It was an above-zero blue spring morning. We travelled through the beautiful countryside of Nova Scotia, between wheat fields and fishing villages and up over the rolling bumps of this beautiful province of deep green and gold meadows towards the little town of Sambro.

On the hills, Stephen would make a point of eating me alive. His shape was slender but strong, he carried minimal body fat and his thighs looked like the base of a thick oak tree. He was so much faster than me and I'd see his frame getting smaller and smaller in the distance, melting into the landscape, pushing the pedals with ease while I ground down through the gears, the familiar sense of sweat and lactic acid rising in my legs.

'How the hell am I going to get over the Rockies?' I would say to myself. 'How am I going to sit on a bike for eight weeks solid and push myself through changing altitudes?'

Because of our class schedule and the lack of daylight, we never got the opportunity to replicate the type of work I would have to do in the summer. Eight hours after eight hours after eight hours wasn't possible, but Stephen kept the training varied and vigorous.

His interval sessions were tough, intense, more demanding than the vast majority of hurling training I had done. Essentially, an interval session is made up of two components. During the first you work at an extremely high intensity, and during the second you recover before going again.

I always enjoyed these sessions during Clare training but it

119

was a different story on the bike. Inevitably it was a hard, cold, blustery day for our initial session. Stephen had me ride right beside him, not a foot in front or behind but shoulder to shoulder for the entire afternoon. Five minutes of pushing at close to my maximum followed by two minutes' recovery, and this went on for over an hour.

He was really asking big questions of me. I told myself it couldn't last for ever, this pain, that if I quit now, how could I possibly deal with the bigger tests that were to come, not only on the bike in the summer but in my own life.

Sleep became precious. Between training and class and logistics I wasn't getting much rest. My friend and neighbour, Alison, came up with a nice scheme. She was taking a law degree, and in the Law Library students could book a private booth to study for an hour at a time. Whenever I needed a rest during the day, she would book a booth in her name, give me the key to the room and I would curl up in a ball on the floor and fall asleep.

I tried to focus and not waver, but one time Stephen really pushed me past breaking point. I was six weeks into training and for the first time I was slowly allowing myself to believe I was making progress. I was between classes talking to this beautiful girl, Danielle, and we just happened to be outside Stephen's office.

He must have heard my voice. Out he stormed.

'Tony.'

'Yeah?'

'You really messed up the session today. It's just not good enough. If you refuse to do it properly, I'm quitting. You can find somebody else to train you.'

'What?'

'You're not hitting your targets. Your reps are terrible. Your cadence sucks. You're not sticking to the plan.'

'But we're getting so close.'

'Not good enough.'

'You said I was making real progress.'

'Not good enough!'

He was bellowing all of this down the corridor and everybody was looking on. It was embarrassing. After he finished his tirade he slammed the door behind him, leaving me wondering what the hell was going on.

I skulked off home that evening. I was cracking. 'I'm not going to be able to do this cycle. I'm making no progress.' I couldn't sleep, wondering how to back out of the cycle, how to let people down easy. All night I twisted in my bed.

The next morning I found some courage and decided to have it out with him. I walked into his office like a bull but wasn't given the opportunity to talk.

'Tony, by the way, I was only yanking your chain yesterday.'

'What?'

'Yeah. I wanted to see how you'd react.'

'Cheung! You bastard!' I said it with relief.

'Excuse me?'

I didn't exactly break the news officially to my family that I was taking a year out of hurling. I told my brother Sean in early winter and asked him to spread the word. When it finally filtered out that I was taking a year out of hurling I didn't get the response I had hoped for.

There were various reasons why I remained in Halifax that Christmas. With the cycle coming I wished to strengthen my resolve, and maybe spending Christmas away from my family would help build a stronger mentality. It was also the first full Christmas without my father and part of me didn't want to face up to that.

There was an underlying purpose too. I suspected that by coming back to Ireland and laying my plans for the summer on the table I would meet some opposition. People would pass the idea off as a fool's errand, as some mad concoction of my mind, and at that early stage the cycle, as a concept, wasn't strong enough to cope with outside negativity. That's why meeting Bruce on St Stephen's Day had a sense of fate about it, one which reinforced my growing belief in the laws of positive attraction.

When I got the chance to tell my family there was a degree of scepticism. One of my sisters asked could I not just run a marathon in my father's memory, and I was told to think hard about giving up a season of hurling at the pinnacle of my career. It was candid, genuine advice that I appreciated and understood but my determination didn't waver and my plans remained the same.

Tony Considine had taken over as manager of Clare and I needed to explain my plans to him, so on a trip home that winter I arranged to meet him at the Old Ground Hotel in Ennis.

We sat at the corner of the bar, drinking tea. Our location wasn't exactly private and from time to time people approached us looking for an insight into how Clare were shaping up for the summer.

When I broke the news to him, Tony was dismissive. 'Look,'

he said, 'you can do that kind of thing when you're retired. I'll sort a few thousand euro for charity and that's that. Okay?' He thought business had been taken care of and rose from his chair, ready to leave.

'Tony,' I said, 'no, it's not okay. Hold on a second.'

This was one of the first times I had put my foot down and stood up to a person in authority. For a number of months I had been working as a mental skills coach with the Dalhousie men's basketball team, and the experience of communicating with players from all walks of life provided me with confidence. It had begun as a one-off talk to the group but developed into something significant; after a while I began to work one-on-one with guys who were struggling with confidence or nerves. That in itself helped me deal with people.

At the Old Ground I told Tony Considine that I wasn't going to change my plans, but he had a rapid reply: 'How could you do this to Frank Lohan, to Gerry Quinn? How could you do this to them? Your friends. You can't do this. You can't let your county down.'

It was a response I had already met with. Back in Halifax I got a phone call from a friend of mine in Ballyea. In my head I was still worried how people in Clare would translate my decision.

'What do they think at home?' I asked.

'Look, Tony, don't expect everyone to come out and support what you're doing,' he said. 'People have told me that you don't care about Clare, that you got your All Star and you just want to do your own thing now.'

It was the only time a doubt took hold.

I wrote a note to myself and placed it in my wallet to

retrieve whenever uncertainty surfaced. I had to believe that fortune was waiting to be kind.

'You're doing the right thing,' the note said. 'Keep going.'

At the end of February, the Tony Griffin Foundation 7,000-Kilometre Ride for the Cure was officially launched at the Westbury Hotel in Dublin. It took place in a plush, grand room in a plush, grand hotel, but by then we were already in prudent mode to ensure every cent possible went to the foundation's bottom line. The night before, Travis, Bruce and I shared a room in a little hotel close to the Westbury. In what was a long and restless night, we waited up until 6.00 a.m. for footage of Lance Armstrong's endorsement of the Ride for the Cure to drop into my email inbox.

Over twenty-five journalists showed up that morning. On the surface, the story was straightforward: a hurling All Star was giving up his season to cycle across Canada in memory of his father. Nobody knew the complexities behind the mission.

I outlined what I planned to do and was asked how much I wished to raise for cancer research. We had settled on a target of €150,000.

'One million euros,' I replied to the question.

Travis was beside me at the table. He looked over, first with a slack jaw, then with a smile. The stakes were getting higher but the figure felt achievable. In three months we had gone from a little slip of an idea to a strong seed that had the potential to develop into something massive.

Newspapers and radio stations took the story on board. I explained I would cycle over 7,000 kilometres from Vancouver, on the west coast of Canada, to Halifax on the east. I would begin cycling on 2 May and arrive in Halifax on 24 June – a fifty-four-day ride. I would then fly to Dublin where a group of cyclists and I would bike over two days to Ennis.

At that stage, I had yet to break the century milestone of logging 100 kilometres in a single spin and had yet to complete three consecutive spins, but my idea was now on the record. Nobody could turn back.

Afterwards, we drove to Clare and stopped off in Tipperary to grab some food. The six o'clock news had footage of the conference and showed Armstrong's message from Stockton, where he was taking part in the Tour of California. 'Thanks for taking time out of your life to ride your bike across Canada and Ireland,' he said. 'It means the world to us and to the people we are trying to help.'

Back in Halifax, the weeks filled with promise but day-to-day plans needed executing. We needed to secure a title sponsor, we needed food and energy drink supplies, bikes, clothing, fuel, phones, maps, police details, insurance, medical equipment. Every time I looked the list had slinked on and on, and to compound things, I was now in the midst of studying for end-of-term exams. It seemed that at any given time I was juggling a dozen glass balls.

We had amassed a team of over sixty volunteers in Ireland and Canada and everything, I believed, would click into place.

One afternoon I picked up the phone and called the offices of Fraserway, an RV company, and told the owner my story, that this student from Ireland was preparing to cycle across Canada. It must have sounded crazy, but by the time the conversation ended I had secured the use of a brand-new RV with 7,000 complimentary kilometres.

Janice Landry, a renowned and respected public relations and media expert who has worked with politicians and celebrities across Canada, became part of the team and she would get the foundation on every TV station from British Columbia to Newfoundland. Her own father had just passed away from cancer and she wanted to help out.

Through Travis we established a little network of Irish societies and groups on the route across the country and we would tap into that energy and hospitality as we made progress raising funds for the charity.

As the seconds ticked down to lift-off, Bruce would save the day and locate a phone company that offered us unlimited national and international calls, and a Canadian grocery store that provided us with food.

Little things, collective things, kept us going, kept the momentum flowing, kept the spirits high until 2 May, the day I would sit on a bike in Vancouver to pedal back to Halifax, and on to Ennis.

The idea was becoming a reality. A storm was now brewing for the foundation, like in a movie when the wind is picking up and the clouds are gathering and something big is going to happen.

After the video from Lance Armstrong for the press conference, communication with his foundation and his bike sponsor Trek had gone cold. The emails dried up and we hadn't heard from them in weeks. To reach our potential and to keep the news stories stirring in Ireland and in Canada, I knew I needed to meet Lance.

Todd toiled away to arrange the meeting but it looked like we were getting nowhere.

I walked around campus with a picture in my head. I was in Texas, putting out my right hand and saying, 'Nice to meet you, Lance.' I visualized it. *We are going to meet him.* I wrote it down. *We will meet Lance.* I believed it would happen, but still nothing.

One night in April, two weeks before the cycle was to begin, I left the library late. I always enjoyed the walk home, a chance to clear my head strolling down Vernon Street, and again, though time was running out, I pictured the meeting.

When I got home, the phone rang.

'Griffy, it's Todd. What you doing on Tuesday?'

'Another exam.'

'Cancel it. We're going to Austin.'

Before he even said it, I knew why he was ringing, and though I had been waiting for a phone call like that with Christmas-like anticipation, I didn't get excited. Now I knew we could push on and really aim for that million-euro target.

In bed that night I asked myself why I was so caught up with meeting Lance. Was it ego? Was it to rub shoulders with the most successful cyclist in the world? Two years earlier I had left Clare to see his Postal Service team climb one of the toughest ascents in the world, and Armstrong had flashed by me in a luminous whizz. Yes, there was an element of ego involved in my meeting him, but it was far down the list. We really did need as much backing from Armstrong as we could get. The more he associated with us, the greater impact the Tony Griffin Foundation would have and with his support we would raise more money, help more people. I knew the meeting would energize the volunteers who had given themselves over to the cause. I was also seeking confirmation from him that I was doing the right thing by taking a year out of my hurling career. There were in fact a jumble of reasons for meeting Armstrong, and it was a mutually beneficial relationship: we had pledged to give $250,000 of what we raised to the Lance Armstrong Foundation in their fight against cancer.

That April, $250,000 seemed like a mountain. Donations had been trickling in; one for $1,600 had blown me away. But little did I know the generosity we were about to encounter throughout the remainder of the year, or the magic that was about to happen.

Austin is a wonderful city. Locals drive around in beat-up cars with bumper stickers asking visitors to 'Keep Austin Weird'. It's a place that doesn't compromise. In a deeply conservative state, Austin is progressive and open-minded; it's an island of blue, the residents like to say, in an ocean of red. It's also home to Lance Armstrong, and when the plane touched down that Tuesday morning I felt a bolt of excitement push through my veins.

Bruce, Todd and I were met by Chris Brewer, one of Lance's friends and right-hand men. Chris is a cancer survivor and an ex-military man and he talked us through the itinerary for the day before stopping off at a bike shop to rent three bikes. Chris wondered what kind of bike I was using on the ride and I told him I had hoped to secure one from Trek, the company that supplies Armstrong, but I hadn't heard back from them. I wondered if Lance could help.

'Hmm,' mused Brewer. Then he put his index finger in the air and told us to rent three bikes from Trek's main rival company.

At the gates of his home we met Armstrong in his black Audi A5, about to tackle the morning school run. He rolled his window down, shot us a smile, we shook hands and he welcomed us to Austin. In the backseat were his twin daughters, one of whom was teary.

'She's upset to have to leave her piglet behind,' he explained. 'See you all in five.'

We had arranged for a film crew to shoot some footage of Lance and me to post on the website and, perhaps, use in a documentary we had tentatively planned. Initially Armstrong seemed indifferent to my presence, like he was sizing me up. It was clear he had other things going on and he would regularly break from our small talk to remind his manager, Bart Knaggs, of little bits and pieces.

'Hey, Lance,' I said. 'Thanks so much for seeing us today.'

'Don't worry,' he said. 'We did a good background check on you. By the way, how come you hurlers don't get paid?'

Slowly, he began to open up.

I asked him when he was coming to Ireland. He said he didn't know.

'Look,' I said. 'When you do, I'll arrange for you to take a bike ride with Paul Kimmage and David Walsh.' Both are Irish sportswriters and among the most outspoken of Armstrong's critics, implying he has taken performance-enhancing drugs.

By the time I saw the Tour in 2005 I had researched cycling to a certain degree and was aware of the doping tradition that had existed in the peloton since the first days of the Tour. So that day on the mountaintop climb to Courchevel I wasn't oblivious to the fact that souped-up bodies littered the road, but I didn't pin Armstrong as one.

Part of what fascinated me about Armstrong was his training schedule. He seemed to go above and beyond what was physically necessary, and to me, that ability to train at maximum output and that attention to detail were compelling. Months before the Tour, when other riders were still indoors, Armstrong would take out a map, identify a number of crucial stages in the upcoming Tour and go on a reconnaissance mission to France. He would climb the hills of the stage in snow and rain, then turn round, descend and start again. He would do whatever it took to get a strategic advantage, and that way, in his own mind, he would know he had left nothing to chance.

Anyway, I mentioned Kimmage and Walsh to him and as soon as I did I got a reaction. He dissolved into laughter and his demeanour changed. He relaxed.

It was now time to go for a ride. He glanced at our bikes.

'Where d'you get those pieces of crap?'

'This is all we have,' I said. 'Trek won't return our calls.'

He turned again to Bart Knaggs. 'Remind me to talk to Trek.'

Bruce looked at me and flashed a smile. The wheels were moving, and later that week two new Treks were on their way to Halifax, one for the ride and one to act as a backup should I crash. Their combined cost was $15,000.

We went and biked one of his regular loops round the city and chatted for an hour or so. I was captivated by his calves – big, hulking, pulsing chunks of muscle, as big as my thighs. During the ride, seemingly at the last second, Lance called the shots on what direction we went. Left, right, straight on. At times it was difficult to keep up, and once we had warmed up we clipped along at a steady pace.

At one point Bruce and Todd fell behind and it was just me and Lance whizzing through suburban Austin, talking about cycling and hurling.

When we arrived back at his home we expected to leave almost straight away, but Armstrong invited us inside with a 'Come on in.'

On the pathway to his door is a 150-year-old oak tree. One of its branches loops in such a way that you have to walk beneath it to get to the door.

'Cool tree,' I said.

He told me he had moved into this house recently from just up the street and brought the tree with him, had it dug up from his old home and replanted here. 'I love that tree,' he said.

'Really?' I said incredulously. 'Looks like it's been here for ever.' And that's exactly how it looked.

We walked through his carpeted garage into his house, which was a flurry of activity. It seemed like when Lance wanted a drink, somebody would immediately press a Coke into his hand. It felt like he was the nucleus of a world he had created.

He spoke with a lady who was doing an inventory of his wine cellar and then brought me into his office. Behind his desk was a huge fresco of the Madonna. It looked exactly like the one Dan Coyle described in his book as having been in Armstrong's training base in Europe.

'Did you bring that back from Italy?'

'Yup,' he said. 'Love that fresco too.'

I walked upstairs and was struck by the duality of his life, the everyday father and the international athlete. In a room next to his daughter's pink playroom was a wall that housed his framed winning yellow jerseys from the Tour de France, seven in all, and I realized then I was in the home of one of the greatest achievers in sport.

Meeting with Lance had served its purpose. It gave the whole group confidence. Made us hanker to get out on the road.

Most of all, it confirmed that faith in the impossible, the unseen, can move mountains. And if not mountains, then certainly 150-year-old trees.

Matt Bethune and Ben Whidden had signed up for the journey from the very beginning, in the dark, with only the promise of hard work and long days. They would be my crew on the road, driving the RV, handing me energy drinks, ensuring we were moving in the right direction. They gave up on the opportunity of making some cash for the summer to pay back their student loans and instead immersed themselves in the project. They took bike mechanics lessons and developed dietary plans. They mapped out the route in fine detail.

Their loyalty and belief pushed me on.

Ben is now living in northern Quebec, working with the Inuit Canadian people in savagely harsh countryside where the cold bites hard. But then Ben is used to life lived hard. A tough start in life made him the person he is – a born fighter.

He arrived into the world one month premature, with a hole in his heart and a dysfunctional oesophagus. The prospects for this tiny baby were poor. The doctors spoke to his parents and told them to brace themselves for the worst. When he survived the early days of his infancy the medics were astounded but once more called his parents aside.

'Well, it's great news,' the doctors said, 'but you'll be taking care of him much of his life. And for one thing, he will not play sports like other kids.'

They hadn't figured Ben's character into the equation. He sailed through childhood independently, but when he was seven years old he came face to face with his family's 180lb dog, which was in an angry mood that day. The small boy and the angry dog came to blows over a woollen quilt. The dog was of the opinion it was his. Ben didn't agree.

The dog mauled him, ripping his head to shreds. Ben needed over a thousand stitches in his forehead and scalp.

Ben, being Ben, bounced back.

In school they told him once more that he couldn't play sports because of his size, but he took no heed. He played basketball, baseball and ran track, and when I took out my hurleys in Halifax, he began to train with me.

Matt became a driving force as well. He's open, always laughing, and on the road that would be crucial in keeping things light and carefree.

Rob Book, a classmate who at first I didn't really know, signed on as the third member of the crew and we now had a well-prepared and motivated team.

Aside from the day-to-day management of the cycle out there on the road, the guys would help promote the ride and spread the foundation's message: celebrate life and dream big.

After meeting Lance, we searched for ways to bring the cycle to as wide an audience as possible. At the Canadian press launch, the national TV station CTV backed the cycle in a big way. They loved the story and used it as their main night-time feature, bringing the Ride for the Cure to a potential audience of 2.5 million people.

We then heard that the renowned Irish showjumper Eddie Macken was based outside Vancouver and I decided to find out if he would lend his support to the cycle. During the 1980s, Macken was one of our most successful sportspeople on the international scene. His prestige was still strong but he was notoriously slow to get involved in the Irish community in British Columbia. He mainly kept to himself. The Irish in BC knew he was based in Langley and he received regular invitations to social occasions and functions but he rarely, if ever, showed up. Getting him to a Tony Griffin Foundation event the evening before we set sail for Halifax would ensure a big turn-out and well-fed charity coffers.

I had a vision of Eddie and a Canadian Mountie leading me out of the streets of the city on horseback while I pedalled behind them, ready to face whatever the road would throw at me. Eddie and the Mountie. It would be perfect because it would blend the Irish and Canadian elements.

We reached Vancouver on 27 April, and a couple of days before the cycle we drove to Eddie's ranch at Langley, about 25 miles outside the city. I had communicated with him through his wife and had yet to receive a guarantee that he would come on board.

We were brought down to his sprawling stables where he was jumping a strong black stallion. He invited us to his porch so I could explain some more about the cycle. His wife dropped down some tea and biscuits. We were looking out on his vast ranch on an overcast April day with warmth in the air. Eddie was sitting back in his chair, his jodhpurs on and a pair of shiny riding boots up to his knees. He looked out at the vista like the king of the castle and I tried to muster the nerve to ask him to the function.

'Look, Eddie, it would be really great if you could come tomorrow night, just even show your face. It would really help. How about we get a limo to come and collect you and your wife and whoever else you'd like to bring?' The limo idea just sprang into my head. Whether or not we could organize one I didn't know.

'I'll see,' he said. 'I'll see.'

There was a silence before Matt filled the void: 'Jeez, Ed, you've got a fine-looking wife there.'

Eddie was taken aback, like it was the last thing he expected one of us to come out with. 'You think so,' he said.

'Sure do, Ed. Atta boy!'

The ice was broken and we began to endear ourselves to him.

A few hours after we left his home his wife called. 'Eddie says he'll be there tomorrow night,' she said. 'Have the limo pick us up at seven.'

We scrambled about to find a deal on a limo, and the following evening, true to his word, Eddie arrived at the function. He really got involved in the event and people were shocked to see him there. After a while he got up to speak and gave a stirring talk.

'I don't think you all realize what this guy is doing,' he said. 'A lot of us say we will do things and we don't follow through. We have great ideas and we let them slip by. But this is different. This guy has not turned back on what he said he would do. He has followed the idea all the way to Vancouver.'

The start – 2 May 2007. There were no crowds, no cameras flashing. There were no hollers or cheers. Just a small knot of people, drawn from unlikely sources, pulled together by some force to be there at six o'clock in the morning on the Pacific coast of Canada. A Royal Canadian Mounted Police officer, a Mormon from British Columbia, a middle-aged woman with a bell, an emigrant from Dublin, a bagpiper.

A scrim of mist rolled in across the ocean and settled over Stanley Park as Ben's uncle gathered us and called to us to hold hands. It all seemed so surreal. He said a short prayer. 'We just ask that everyone who is suffering from cancer, wherever they are, that they somehow get to hear about what this young man is doing and what we're all here for this morning.'

There was a sense of delicious anticipation to the day.

As we were about to leave, Ben pulled at my arm and muttered some words, but he was overcome by the emotion and power of the moment and I never got to hear what he said. Later, he told me: 'Now go out there and show the world what Jerome Griffin's son can do.'

I dipped the front wheel of my blue Trek bicycle in the Pacific but I didn't take time to savour the moment, to frame it in my mind, this exact morning we had been working towards for the past six months. I was in work mode, anxious to get on the road, anxious to push pedals and complete the first 125 kilometres.

A man suffering with cancer turned up to wave us off. We

spoke for a little while, he showed me his morphine pump. My father had had one just like it, and the value of this cycle was brought home to me once more.

Then the rain began to come down and the time to move arrived. The bagpiper slowly led us out of Stanley Park, the stranger rang her bell. The road crew drove in front of the bicycle and, as if this was the way it was always going to be, I was on the road, the sound of raindrops hitting the ground, wind breaking across my ears, the morning traffic oblivious to where we were going and how we were getting there.

We were off. Into the absolute unknown.

An hour passed. We had sneaked through the suburbs of Vancouver, rain still falling. On a little incline with spray from passing cars rising all around me, I heard a voice from the side of the road.

'Tony. Tony.'

I wasn't sure if she was calling me or somebody else. I stopped. She said she'd heard about the cycle and had stood in the downpour all morning waiting for me to pass by, that it was a wonderful thing I was doing. The connection and the outpouring of kindness knocked me out and I continued with adrenalin in my blood.

After a while we decided that the RV could no longer drive in front of me. Traffic behind us was being held up, drivers were frustrated and complaining. We changed strategy: the RV would now drive ahead 40 or 50 kilometres at a time then wait for me to catch up. When I did, the crew would have a small meal prepared, and I would saddle up once more. But without the protection of the RV I would be exposed to traffic for the following seven weeks.

Once, it was dicey. On a long straight stretch in the middle of God Knows Where a guy in a green sports car overtook a vehicle and decided to play chicken with me. He remained on the wrong side of the road, lining up to ram straight into me. He came so close I had to wheel off the road and into a field. He zoomed by, laughing, and it showed me how vulnerable I was.

The destination for the first night was a little town called Hope, nestled in the mountains just off that boundless road, the Trans Canadian Highway. With 90 kilometres down I hit mountains and decided I would remain positive, that I could live with climbs for the next 35 kilometres, but when I reached the RV the guys had some troubling news. We had underestimated the distance from Vancouver to Hope, hadn't taken into account that we were starting from the most westerly point of the city. On top of that, I had cycled an unnecessary 30-kilometre loop beyond Vancouver, so instead of our planned 125 kilometres on day one, I was now faced with a bike ride of 194 kilometres. We had read the map incorrectly.

It was a simple first-day mistake brought on by nerves and excitement but I was devastated. I had been cycling for six hours now. I was soaking wet and my body was filled with a pain I had never encountered. Daggers in my lungs. Thighs seizing up. Everything ached and I had emptied my tank of energy. A little over 100 kilometres had been logged, but instead of another 20 or so to go I was left with 90 kilometres of torture to navigate. It would take hours. I was tired and I had an endless range of hills still to climb.

The RV pulled away. I was alone again. I felt my spirits drop from my stomach and melt on to the ground. Pain spread across my face.

At that moment I thought I would never reach Hope and I wanted to quit, to simply dump my bike on this mountain, hitch a ride to Vancouver, check into some fancy hotel, eat a plate of hot food then sleep in a warm bed.

Up ahead, the road curved into the mountain and I could hear the screeching of brakes from the logging trucks as they made their way down. Thick beads of rain dripped from my clothes. It was getting dark and the headlights of the traffic shone on the wet road. I didn't even have a light on my bike, didn't think I would need one, and I felt as though a truck could wipe me out at any minute.

I was hanging on to the bicycle with tears streaming down my cheeks. I cried for many reasons. At my father's funeral I'd felt too embarrassed to cry. My teammates were there, people who expected me to be strong and courageous, and I couldn't open up. So I probably cried for my father that day. I cried because of the pain and I cried because I feared the trip was coming to an end before it had even begun. I cried because I would have to go back to Halifax and to Clare in shame.

I was frustrated, angry, dejected, lost. For the first time I felt a desolate loneliness. All I asked was that the passing vehicles wouldn't see my face and my pathetic tears.

Right then I received a text message from my sister: 'Thank you for doing this for our father.' I was hit by the thought that she didn't know I was about to climb off my bike and quit. If I was struggling through day one, how was I supposed to get up the following morning and do it all over again, do it for the next fifty days? All the work of the past six months flashed into my head. Bruce, Todd, Travis, Stephen Cheung. Everybody in Ireland. My family. How could I look these people in the face again?

I thought about the consequences of not finishing, and in my black-and-white winner-or-loser mindset I knew something like that could haunt me for life. I would come home one day and this cycle, this reason I had given up hurling, would be my personal phantom. I would have to live the life of a failure. That thought was darker than the road ahead.

I lifted my eyes into the rain and the wind, looked up at the heavy sky and screamed and screamed, a guttural, angry noise escaping from my mouth. There was nothing to do but keep going.

The final two hours were a blur, like I had fallen into a fog. I became a long-distance cyclist. I just kept going, kept going. I didn't question where I was or how far I had to push. I decided to make progress one pedal at a time.

I hadn't seen a person on the road since late morning but an hour outside Hope I spotted a native Canadian with his little girl. They were coming out of a swollen river and had just washed their clothes in it. The man had flowing black hair and his daughter had a striking face. I stopped and tried to talk to them, took out my energy sweets and offered them to the little girl. She hid behind her father's leg and he looked at me suspiciously. Their clothes were wet and filthy and the father continued to stare at me without saying much. Then they walked across the road into their home, a shack made from pieces of wood and tin.

I hadn't expected to see a scene like this in a country such as Canada and I got back on the road wondering what kind of life the little girl had mapped out for her.

A little after seven o'clock I reached Hope. With the mountains on all sides it was a beautiful town, but there was a strange feel to it, like a setting in that series *Twin Peaks*. It seemed there was no spirit there.

We were met at the edge of town by some local cops. One of them, Chris, was in the Special Drugs Force. His mother was Irish and he had met us in Vancouver the night before. He explained that Hope was the crystal meth capital of Canada and that with the woods and mountaintops surrounding the place it was difficult to track down everybody who produced the drug. Looking up at the hills and knowing we were miles from the next town, it was easy to feel we were in a detached part of the world.

Chris introduced us to Mary, the woman we would stay with for the night. She had moved to Hope from County Meath over three decades back and still had her Irish accent. She'd married a man from Russia who was working in the Tara mines, and together they had travelled to Hope so he could work the mines here and make better money. Her husband had passed away only a month before we arrived. He'd developed cancer from his years working in those mines of Hope, the same cancer that had taken my own father.

She told me that the previous day she'd dropped her son at rehab for the second time, that he was addicted to crystal meth and that Chris, the cop, had had to take care of her husband's funeral arrangements because her son was unable to do so. 'People are made useless from these drugs,' she told me.

This was the first time I had experienced this kind of travel, where other people opened their lives up to you. It seemed as though we were walking the same stretch of road for a single mile before we would have to say goodbye.

Mary brought us to the local Legion Club where those who served in the war for Canada can meet and share a drink. I walked in and was underwhelmed by the moment. It didn't feel right. The great charge of fulfilment I had been expecting was lost in the post. This is the end of the first day? A little bar in Hope telling war veterans that I'm cycling across Canada?

I tried to sleep that night but woke several times to go to the bathroom. My stomach was cut to pieces from eating protein bars and sucking down sugary energy drinks.

In the morning, I walked with Mary and her dog along the river. Her company was soothing and I used the time to stretch and loosen my muscles. She looked at the river as we ambled on and said that in a few weeks the water would rise even more when the snows from the mountain began to melt. She talked about her husband and her family some more, and I mainly listened. She told me she would lead us out of town in her car, just in case we took a wrong turn, and at the foothills of the great, barrelling Rockies we said goodbye.

We had already been warned about the Coquihalla mountain pass in the Canadian Cascades, to treat it with care and patience. It was a 60-kilometre climb up a winding, corkscrew drag of a road and then 70 kilometres down into a lush green valley to our second stop, Merritt.

The climb was tough. Logging trucks dragged their loads up the hill in first gear. My body began to spasm and cramp during the ascent. My left knee was beginning to develop a piercing throb, which was worrying, and I began complaining.

Halfway to the top of the climb I got off the bike and spoke to myself. There would be no more grumbling, and I promised myself that when I got back on the saddle, I would be glad I could do so. I had to choose my attitude, and eventually we made it to the summit, to the sign that told us we were 4,081 feet above sea level. Then the descent started, a hit-a-pebble-and-you're-gone downhiller that at times clipped the 70-kilometre-per-hour mark. The world flashed by with a wind roaring through my ears.

The surroundings were awesome, their sweep a reminder of how small I was in the greater scheme of things, and for the first time on the journey I could see God's hand in the different greens of the fields I passed, in the lakes, and in the rocks.

On the third morning my left knee was so sore I couldn't manage the three steps from the RV to the ground without sitting down on each step. I began to have crazy thoughts. I believed my cruciate had been ruptured. But I was now in a place where I would not go back. I didn't care if the cycle took seven months to complete. If I needed a knee replacement on the road, then so be it. If it meant the end of my hurling career, I was prepared to deal with that.

Before we'd set sail, Rob had received some training in massage. He sat me down on the bed of the RV and began to work on my knee. It was as if he was trying to cut me open with blades it was so painful, but slowly he stripped out all the little knots that had clogged my blood flow. The muscle and ligament had become so inflamed from the repetition of sixteen hours of cycling in two days that my kneecap had been pulled out of its natural alignment.

The most I had cycled prior to this ride was 100 kilometres and I had completed only two of those cycles consecutively. Stephen Cheung had correctly predicted that I would train myself into the hard slog of long-distance cycling, and on the fourth day my knee was ready for more road.

The road can do strange things to a man, plunge him into dreamlike states, and I learned this early on.

Cycling by yourself day after day, it doesn't take long for your mind to wander and the urges to kick in. Some days I longed for any kind of pleasure to break the monotony. Any kind. And once, I could do nothing but succumb.

The night before we reached Merritt there was a big hockey game on TV, which the guys wanted to watch. So we stopped off in a local bar. Afterwards, the karaoke machine started up and a good-looking blonde got up to sing. We became enraptured and charmed. It was like she was drawing us in. We hadn't seen a woman in days and this lent some fire to our collective drooling. To our starved minds, it was like Marilyn Monroe was at the top of the bar giving us the look.

The blonde singer filled our conversation on the way back to the RV and we went to sleep and thought no more of her.

Out on the bike the next day, there was no mobile phone reception and I lost contact with the crew. After the previous night's entertainment I was particularly tired so I stopped for a coffee in a roadside café, and unknown to me, the RV sped by.

Above: 'I am warning you!'
A four-year-old with attitude.

Right: After scoring a point v.
Kilkenny, 2006. Telling Niall
Gilligan it was his score. Now a
grown man, pointing the finger.

Team photo: What hurling is all about: family.
After winning the Senior B Clare championship
with Ballyea. My father, my brother Sean with
his son Oisín and my other brother Frankie. My
father loved to see Ballyea play and was
a happy man that day.

Above (left): The long walk to the dressing room after the Cork game in the Munster championship, 2006. I had just come back home to play full time, and this was a crushing defeat. (**Right**): Striking long v. Kilkenny, 2006.

Above: Running at the Wexford defence, 2006.

Right: Walking off the field with our inspirational manager, Anthony Daly, having beaten Wexford in Croke Park, 2006.

Left: Side-step v. Kilkenny, 2006. I practised this move for months, convinced that if it led to even one score it would be time well spent.

Below: 'Trying' to get away from Kilkenny's J. J. Delaney. I loved playing Kilkenny, even if they broke our hearts on so many occasions. My boyhood hero D. J. Carey hailed from there and, during my career with Clare, Kilkenny were the standard bearers.

Right: A long time coming: All Star night, 2006. With Sean McMahon (*left*) and Frank Lohan (*right*) – two special people.

Above: Getting to know Lance Armstrong in his back garden on our first trip to Austin, Texas, to promote the 7,000-kilometre Ride for the Cure.

Above: A future Clare hurler in the making! Lance tries his hand at the ancient game of hurling.

Below and right: From smiles on the first day at the foot of the Rockies to pain as we pass another time zone.

TIME ZONE CHANGE
SET YOUR WATCH
ONE HOUR AHEAD

Above: The end of the road in Halifax, Nova Scotia, with the road crew. Next stop, Ireland.

Below (left): The finish line in Ennis, County Clare, Ireland. The welcome home was incredible. So many people. It was all worth it. **(Right)**: He ain't heavy, he's my brotha! Matt literally carries Ben to the finish line through O'Connell Street after Ben's knee gave out half way across Ireland. Two of the greatest friends a man could have.

Left: Ball boy and hurley carrier. The results of the cycle are plain to see. I had lost over 20lbs in weight, but was blind to the after-effects of the cycle and decided to return to hurling weeks after coming off the bike.

Below: High fielding v. Waterford in 2008. A good start to what was a tough year.

Above: Evading John Gardiner and Sean Óg Ó hAilpín, one of the modern game's real athletes and a good friend, v. Cork, summer 2008.

Right: I got used to my ice pack in 2008. I have just come off injured v. Limerick. Not a happy man.

Below: Not happy because this is my second hamstring injury of the season and it happens in the opening stages of the game.

Left: Back on the road. Keira and I on the last day of the Ride for Life 2008 Halifax to Texas cycle.

Below: Iten, Kenya, 2009. Beautiful people and a great experience high in the Rift Valley.

I got back on my bike and cycled with no communication for a long time. Suddenly my body needed more rest and I just had to obey the voices that demanded sleep. I clipped out of my pedals and parked the bike against a tree. I wandered into a field, curled up in a ball and drifted off, images of the blonde once again filling my mind.

Up ahead, on the road, I was nowhere to be seen and the three guys began to worry about my location. Wisely, and according to our protocol in such situations, they called the authorities.

As it happened, the police had a helicopter in the air and it combed the area for my whereabouts. A couple of minutes later they spotted me in the field sleeping the sleep of the contented, my yellow windbreaker balled up beneath my head for comfort, dreaming pleasurable dreams.

The helicopter communicated my whereabouts to the guys and they backtracked along the road, curious to know why I had fallen asleep in a field. It took a while to confess, but when I told them the truth, that I had completely lost my focus as a result of that blonde swimming around in my head, they laughed. From then on, any boundaries that had existed between us evaporated.

The Rockies began to recede into the background and we made our way through the state of Alberta. Sometimes, on the tough days, just to keep myself focused, I would peer over my shoulder at the snowcaps and shout, 'I beat you, Rockies! I fuckin' beat you!' But really, it was the mountains that had exacted their toll on me. They had brought me to tears, and sometimes, on the road, I would thank them for what they had taught me – patience, belief, greater appreciation for the natural beauty of the world.

The loneliness of the road forced me to new places. I spoke to the cows I passed, I spoke to the bison in the meadows. I said hello whenever I saw a deer. Anything for interaction. Anything to keep from going crazy. I spoke to my father and I spoke to God. I ran through old games in my head and fixated on how I could have played better.

There were days when I noticed myself nodding off on the bike and I would jerk awake to straighten myself. It got to the point where I had to acknowledge my tiredness and purposely chose long straights if I was to allow myself a few seconds' naptime. I wouldn't be pedalling down a hill or going round a bend, so the chances of a serious accident would be less.

At one particular point in the first week I was struggling, half awake, half asleep. It was late in the evening and a difficult day was almost behind me. Earlier on I had asked my father to help me through the tough times, and that evening, as though in another dream, I sensed a cyclist was tailing me. It felt like I had company, which would have been unusual because once more I had found myself in an isolated, unpopulated part of Canada. Seeing a cyclist out here would have been unexpected. I waited for the best part of a minute and really sensed somebody was on my left shoulder about to pass me. I looked round, ready to greet the cyclist, but nobody was there. Just an empty road. I wondered if it was my father guiding me, pushing me on in some spiritual way, but I can't be sure. It could have been some form of hallucination brought on by tiredness and hunger and cycling alone.

When I spoke to God, I looked for His help in getting me across Canada. I laid my requests on the table, asked Him to guide the crew and the volunteers, asked Him to give faith to those suffering with cancer, asked Him if there was a girl out there for me, somewhere, anywhere, and to help me find her when the time was right.

The unlimited use of the mobile phone that Bruce had secured became a saviour. Not only did it provide a link with the crew, it also allowed me to keep in touch with the world outside. I called my family regularly, and John McCabe. I also stayed in touch with the volunteers in Canada and Ireland, and word got through to me that the foundation had made huge strides since I had been on the road. Donations were pouring in; we were approaching the $250,000 point.

The more we progressed, the less time there was to fully take in the splendour of the scenery. I found myself wishing I could stop off and soak up the panorama but there was always a fundraiser down the line, a couple of days ahead, organized, more often than not, by the Irish community spread across this huge slab of land. It struck me that as a race, as a group of people, the Irish are the greatest in the world to get behind a cause.

The Halifax return on 24 June was the big date that loomed but that was still weeks away, and as we approached the prairies I looked at the map and saw we had barely made headway.

We had great plans and schedules but these began to break down with the weariness of the road. We'd planned to clean the bike every day, to check the tyres for air; we'd promised that we would all stretch together before breakfast and energize ourselves for the day ahead. After two weeks all this became too much of an effort. We were being broken down and there was no light in the tunnel. I was sleeping for longer in the mornings, until nine o'clock, which meant I had to cycle until darkness each night.

We had planned to arrive at a stop-off point every evening, at some little town or village with a campsite, but sometimes we simply pulled the RV on to the side of the road and slept for the night. It became a freedom I enjoyed, but Rob wasn't pleased with the arrangement. He had to hear some background noise in order to sleep and the silence of the road was killing him. Rob needed to go to a campsite or trailer park where we could plug in the RV and turn on the fan heater, and he would drift off to its monotonous whirr.

Spending so long in one another's company in such a tight living space, somebody's little foibles can drive you nuts. It began to frustrate me and I found myself being hard on him. Sometimes we had to drive 30 kilometres in another direction just to find a campsite, which meant the following morning we had to drive back to the exact point I had come off the bike the previous night. I didn't want to break the continuous line from Vancouver to Halifax, and sometimes it took two hours out of the day making that round trip.

For Matt and Ben, the summer was a mission. Both were there the day my father passed away.

I have a clear memory from that morning. Ben was in tears. He put his arm round me and it was the first time I'd had contact with a friend in that way. It was a loyal and deep gesture. A physical act of kindness like this wasn't typical at home in Ireland.

Matt and Ben were also there when the idea of this cycle first came to me, and they were well acquainted with its importance.

It took a while for Rob to put himself in the same story.

In Hope we had bought a bike, figuring that there would be times when the guys might like to get out on the road too and cycle with me for an hour or so. Some days we had a rota where each of them would cycle for 30 kilometres alongside me. That bike became a punchline to a bad joke. It was a heap of junk, designed not for the open roads of Canada but for the streets of a city, but it served to keep the crew occupied when the boredom set in. If they couldn't keep pace with me, it wasn't a problem. They either cycled on their own or jumped into the RV.

On these cycles I found that Rob was testing me. Rob is a fit guy. He's a strong runner and a well-built athlete. Because he was sitting in the RV all day he would come out in the afternoon with pent-up energy and eat the road up. I might average 26 kilometres an hour but Rob would push it to 33. I would ask him to slow down but it was no good, and I knew if I increased my pace I would be in trouble the following day. Cheung had drilled me that I had to keep a steady pace and under no circumstances should I push things. 'You've only got so much in your bank account,' he said, 'so don't take out more than you can afford.'

I became paranoid. I thought Rob was trying to break me, and my competitive streak took over. The next time he came out and pulled the trick on me, I'd show him.

So it happened. Rob came out in the afternoon and charged it to something like 35 kilometres an hour. I didn't care if I couldn't walk the following day, I had to react. I drove on. At one stage I looked at the clock on my bike and I was doing 43 kilometres per hour on the flat, pounding down on the pedals and pulling them up with my cleats. I'd slow, drift back to him, talk to him a little and push forward again. It was childish, but in my paranoia this was all I could counter with. We did this for 40 kilometres, but the thing was, I had already cycled 130 kilometres that day and I had 180 kilometres to tackle in the morning.

When we reached our stop-off point for the night, our legs were mush. It was a senseless act by me, and the next day, as I was paying for that stupidity, I concluded I had been taking Rob too seriously.

Gradually, I came to like and understand Rob and appreciate how vital he was to the journey, and in the end I learned as much about interaction from him as I did from anybody else over those weeks.

My thinking was blinkered on the cycle, and if we were going to reach Halifax as a team, it was important that I bend to other outlooks. Living in tight confines, you have no choice but to adapt, and there were times when I had to wrestle with my ego. Days when the guys came out to bike alongside me I felt aggrieved. I wanted it to be me, on my own, at all times. Me answering my own questions in my own head and me taking all of the pain and the punishment that came with the road.

There's an old saying that you can watch your dog run away for days on the Canadian plains. It's true. Out there you're completely open. There is no protection from the elements, no hill or ridge to shield you from the weather. It's pancake country, and when we reached the flatlands of Manitoba I was unprepared for the sheer force of the wind. It came at me in great slabs. Storms bore over the wheat fields bringing angry gusts and furious gales that made my ears ring.

Worse, the wind direction changed. It became my enemy. I was now cycling into a direct headwind and it was like negotiating my way through thick honey. I went from an average speed of 29 kilometres per hour to 11 kilometres per hour. On those days when the wind was strong and against me, I put the speedometer into the pocket of my cycling top and in the back of my mind I knew we were slipping behind schedule.

The landscape was so vast and even. It was a sea of grain elevators and yellow fields. Barns full of last year's harvest. I passed water towers and endless driveways to farmhouses in the distance.

Trains with dozens of carriages would travel straight through these farms collecting grain before making their way along the railway that hugged the road. A train was like an oasis. It provided a buffer from the wind and it shot out hot air from its engines. I came to love those prairie trains and tried to keep pace with them for as long as possible, indulging myself in the warmth they provided.

Out there on the prairies it lashed down on me. Clouds dumped small wells of water on my body and I was soaked for nine hours each day, but I learned more on those roads than I did in the Rockies. For three days I was pounded by the weather and once more the cycle got on top of me. I was wearier than I had ever been in my life, and I cried with frustration.

Drivers would pull up and ask if I was okay, if I knew where I was going. It was difficult to fathom what a lone cyclist was doing miles and miles from any town. 'You're cycling to Halifax? In Nova Scotia? You're crazy!' Dozens offered a lift, and I wished I could take them up on their offer.

But out there I was being cleansed. I was beginning to come to terms with things, like my father's death and my own demented obsession with having to prove myself. I don't know for sure why the change was coming about. Maybe it was all this time I was spending on my own – time to reflect, to look deep inside – or maybe I knew that, yes, I was going to complete this challenge, I would solve this simple equation of whether or not I really had the right stuff.

There's a scene in the movie *Walk the Line* that becomes the tipping point of the country singer Johnny Cash's story. Johnny and June Carter and both their families are having Thanksgiving dinner at Johnny's new house in the Tennessee woods when Johnny's estranged father, Ray, finds something to taunt his son with. Johnny's life has bottomed out by now and he's hooked on pills. So Ray provokes him.

He calls Johnny a Mister Big Shot. He tells him he's nothing but a pill-popping rock star and says he's got nothing in the world but a big empty house and children he never sees. Ray doesn't stop there. He points out that his son is also the owner of an expensive tractor that's just stuck in the ground, gathering dust.

True enough, outside, by a lake, lies Johnny's tractor, wedged in the mud for a few weeks. Old man Cash says to the whole table that Johnny is such a good-for-nothing soul that this tractor of his is going to remain in the mud for ever.

The comments torment Johnny and he storms from the room to free the tractor, jamming on the gas and rocking the machine from side to side. Both families are leaving by the time he gets it clear of the mud, but the thing is, he loses control and both he and the tractor end up in the lake.

June rushes to him, drags his head out of the water, saves him. It's poignant. It's like a baptismal ceremony, like he's being brought back to life. From here, Johnny begins to clean up his act.

Out on the prairies with the wind howling and the rain teeming down, it felt, in a way, like I was being reborn, that I was changing my attitude towards myself and giving myself a break from my private anguish.

Sky the colour of a pink rose. June bugs in the air. Flat, smooth roads and a brisk tailwind. The evening had been kind as we made our way across the golden prairie headed for Saskatoon. Thankfully, somewhere after Oyen the wind had changed in our favour and we began to make real progress.

Matt rode at my side as the sun was beginning to set and we spoke about the past two weeks. 'The hardest thing,' he said, 'will be going back to normal life and not losing this feeling and this sense of freedom.'

We pushed on to our stop in the little town of McGee, but 30 kilometres out we hit dry gravel.

The crash happened in a millisecond, Matt losing control of his bike, falling, then me piling over his bike and body and landing head-first on the road. I looked up from the roadside and saw that Matt was concussed. My helmet was cracked and I had injured my left hip and shoulder, but the pain subsided when I saw the state of Matt's bike. He hadn't been cycling the touring bike from Hope but our backup Trek racing bike. It was mangled. The back wheel was shaped like the letter S, the handlebars were warped. We were both fine, but lucky. Had we fallen on to the road we could have been eaten up by a line of passing cars. But as I picked myself up, that thought didn't bother me. I was preoccupied with the wreckage of the backup bike and flung down my helmet in disgust. It occurred to me that the cycle was only one mistake away from ending in disaster.

We called the RV back. Matt suggested I finish the remaining 30 kilometres the following day but I wouldn't hear of it. I was angry and full of boiling determination. I wanted to tear the road up. I pushed on for McGee, but when we arrived we found there was no spot to park the RV. I cycled another 15 kilometres to Rosedale and the rage subsided. Under that sky washed in pink I had the surreal experience of watching my shadow pass through the fields in a yellow glow. My anger had disappeared and I was feeling upbeat once more.

At times, my spirits seemed to shift with the wind – pure elation to deep despondency back to elation again. There was no emotional measure to tap into on the bike, only days of pedalling dictated by the progress we made, the scenery in front of us and the state of the weather. Nature and miles became my barometer.

The second crash was a thing purely of my own making. It happened a few weeks after the first as we rounded the great Lake Superior. The heat had been rising all day, peaking in the low thirties, and in the late afternoon, just 5 kilometres from our day's end, I decided to take off my jersey. I held it in my hands and the wind caught it, winding the sleeve on to my wheel and wrapping it in the spokes. It was a rookie mistake. The brakes seized, the bike flipped and I tumbled right out over the handle-bars, this time landing on my shoulder.

I had been so careful since the first crash but one irresponsible decision had put everything on the line.

Immediately a pain shot through me. I was convinced I had broken a bone and I would be forced off the road. We drove to a hospital in Wawa, on the banks of Michipicoten Bay. There, I was told I hadn't broken a bone but I had dislocated the AC joint at the top of my shoulder. We slept in the hospital car park and that whole night I tried to prepare myself for the pain that would accompany tomorrow.

Dan Coyle's *Tour de Force* came to mind again. He had written of Tyler Hamilton, the American cyclist who completed the Tour de France in 2004 with a similar injury. Hamilton had been in such pain climbing in the mountains that he'd gritted his teeth to little stubs and had to have them capped when the race was over.

I let myself remember the torment I went through with Stephen Cheung in the lab and on the road.

The following morning I looked at my bike. 'I cannot get up on you today,' I said.

But I had to. To silence my doubts, to keep my promise, I had to.

On one of the nights we stayed by the roadside, we woke to find a man walking past the RV. We were miles and miles from the nearest community and it was intriguing where this guy was walking to, where he had come from. When we finished eating breakfast I suggested to the three guys they should offer him a lift.

Rob didn't want to do it. 'I don't stop for people.'

'What?' I said. 'What if you see a woman on the side of the road and it's lashing rain on her and she has shopping bags?'

'I just don't stop for people. Somebody could be right there, hiding in the bushes, ready for a carjacking.'

I left the guys, clipped my bike shoes into my pedals and cycled down to this figure, walking slowly to nowhere.

He said his name was Stephen Francis, that he had lived in Toronto but had dropped everything to walk the country and preach. He said he had owned apartment blocks in the city and his wealth had been measured in millions but he'd had vices like drugs and prostitutes. His sister sat him down one day and told him he was going to die before he was forty because of the way he lived and she told him he was going to hell.

Stephen had an awakening. He sold his property and gave his wealth to charity, kept just enough to see him through a few months on the Canadian roads. He had been walking for half a year, he said. 'I've been up past the tree line in Ontario, I walked into towns in the middle of winter snow up to my waist. I've been beaten, I've been run out of towns, but I'm going to keep walking and spreading the word of Christ.'

He was a true man of the road. When he wasn't directly answering a question of mine an avalanche of biblical passages erupted out of his mouth.

We began to meet all sorts on the roads and it became clear I wasn't the only one who had a cross-country challenge to contend with. We met the Pozzolo family who had taken four months out to cycle west to east. A mother and her three kids. They said they wanted to see and experience their own country up close and they pulled and dragged their tents and belongings behind them. It was backbreaking stuff and they made progress at a rate of 30 kilometres each day.

As for me, I was now ripping through the calories, burning about 8,000 per day, over three times the average. I wolfed down protein shakes, weight gain supplements, troughs of pasta, endless sugary cereal bars. When I was on the bike and passed an eating house that looked good, I would park up, wander up to the counter, examine the dessert tray and place my order.

Pie was my addiction. Blueberry pie. Pumpkin pie. Cherry pie. Apple pie. Cranberry pie. Pecan pie. I loved them all.

'What would you like, sir?'

'Pie.'

'One slice?'

'The whole lot, please.'

'Sure thing. Friends waiting on you outside?'

'Nope.'

I would sit at the counter and demolish the pie in a matter of minutes, wiping my lips as I left the waitress with a look of wonder on her face.

One afternoon, eating pancakes at a diner, I met two French Canadians, François and Olivier. They, too, were cycling east. We made a pact to stay in contact and I met them along the road from time to time. Whenever we met, we worked as a team and made rapid progress.

Later, we bumped into two teenagers, blond Canadians, who were on a similar cycling expedition across Canada. These guys had zero money but it didn't stop them. They slept on haystacks, slept under trees. They walked into camping stores and Walmarts, snuck into tents on display and waited for the store to close before they caught some shut-eye.

It seemed anything was possible. All you needed were two ingredients: an idea and some spirit.

On top of this, the pure goodness of those we encountered was staggering. It really did astound me. Even the simple things made you feel that there is warmth and decency within every human being. A waitress heard of our expedition and brought us four desserts when we passed by her diner; a chain of people across the country offered to put us up for a night. We stopped to refuel one day and the owner of the gas station peered out his window at the signage on the RV, which briefly explained the cycle. The guys went in to pay for the gas but by the time they reached the counter the owner had told them the bill was on the house.

Turned out he was going through chemo for cancer of the kidney and while we were filling up he had looked up our website on his laptop.

'Gas is taken care of, guys. And take whatever food supplies you need.'

There was something about the cycle that resonated wherever we went. Cancer patients who heard we were passing through their town came out to greet us. People with chemo bags left their hospital beds to have a quick word, tell us that what we had embarked on was making a huge difference to their lives and brought them hope and energy to continue their fight against the disease. I had never imagined the cycle could have such a positive impact. The Irish community had helped spread the word, as did the media and the LiveStrong organization.

I met people recovering from the disease. Ordinary people with extraordinary courage and optimism. The warmth and decency of these men and women kept the pedals turning, turning when the hill seemed too high and the rest stop seemed forever in the distance.

A few days later we met Greg McGee, whose father was battling cancer. Greg fixed the bike that was disfigured during the first crash, tuned up my own and loaded our RV with energy drinks and recovery shakes. He refused to accept a penny in return. Scenes such as this were replayed on a daily basis.

People opened up to us, too. Outside Saskatoon, a local man in his early seventies with a Clare jersey on his back was waiting for us on his bike. He told us that a month ago his daughter had passed away. He had just landed in Miami for a short vacation when he heard the news.

As it happened, a rest day was scheduled for Saskatoon and we developed a strong bond with him. The night we arrived, he and Ben took a walk – an old man telling a twenty-four-year-old the troubles he was going through, crying openly and allowing Ben into his life.

People sensed we were on a mission. They knew we had a positive goal and they realized we wouldn't be waiting around for ever, that there were no real consequences for what they said, so it was easier for them to be forthright and communicative. It was an aspect of the summer we could never have foreseen.

On the last Sunday of May I could not have been more removed from Thurles, the cathedral of Munster hurling. While Clare played Cork in the opening round of the championship, I found myself in Upsala, a logging outpost in the deep forests of northern Ontario. It's a small grey town founded by Swedish emigrants. The place has few modern services and it felt like I had stepped into a town that hadn't changed in thirty years.

The wind picked up and the rain came at me in slanted waves but I didn't care. My mind and my heart were in Thurles.

I looked at it logically, told myself I was the one who had made the decision to take a year out, reminded my brain that nobody had put a gun to it to cycle Canada. It didn't make a difference. I wished to be at home.

I looked at the clock all day, and when throw-in time came I stepped into the RV and tried to pick up the game on satellite radio, but the reception was down. I stayed in touch with the game via Travis, who began sending through updates with a torrent of text messages.

I pictured each score as the texts came through until the final whistle, when Travis confirmed that Clare had lost by seven points. For a quick moment I was back in the dressing room, sitting, as usual, between Frank Lohan and Diarmuid McMahon. I could feel the cold bank of silence that surrounded the lads.

I stepped out into the wet morning of northern Ontario, the smell of pine drifting in the air, the sound of trains in the distance.

For the rest of the day the fragments of defeat remained with me, but there was good news. It turned out that Travis had been sending his match reports from a maternity ward. Margaret had given birth to their third child, a boy. 'We're going to name him Griffin,' Travis texted. Secretly, privately, I beamed with pride. Upsala or Cork could not take that away.

Back home in Clare, the season had turned into a peculiar beast of a thing, and not for the first time the county's hurling world was in a squabbling state. Tony Considine, the manager, and Davy Fitzgerald, the high-profile goalkeeper, had locked horns early in the year. They'd argued one cold night before training, and after the exchange Davy drove away from training before it even started. He never returned, and a stand-off developed. Neither would give an inch. Tony wouldn't invite Davy back, Davy wouldn't seek reinstatement. Their dispute was the main talking point for a number of weeks and the season had begun without one of the game's greatest goalkeepers. A murky air hung over the team and I was told, regularly, that if I was going to miss a season then maybe 2007 mightn't be such a bad one to sit out. It sounded like people were either in Considine's corner or Davy's corner, a dispute I had no desire to become involved in.

The deeper we travelled into Canada the more the country fascinated me. Sometimes, it seemed like we were the only people in the world. After leaving the prairies we crossed the Canadian Shield on a road that had been blasted through the surrounding rock. I reprimanded myself for complaining about having to cycle when these roads were here, already built for me.

Later, at a point high above Lake Ontario, I stopped at a little place called Kicking Horse Pass. It was a significant point, and in front of me was the only stretch of rail line in North America that doubled back on itself in a figure of eight.

Close to here was the site where the Trans-Canadian rail line had joined. I was gripped by the idea. On the east coast and on the west coast a group of men began building the line separately. They crossed the country and met right here. One piece of rail sleeper completed the mammoth task. I also found out that thousands and thousands of Chinese emigrants had worked on building the line and that, on average, for every mile of line laid one Chinese labourer had died. It was dangerous and difficult work blasting through mountains and crossing rivers and the captains of industry had just used these men as commercial commodities, something that could be replaced.

There were stories tucked away everywhere. Across Manitoba and northern Ontario we passed the reservations of the native people. Cycling along the banks of the mist-covered Lake Superior I could picture them centuries back, gliding through the water in their birch canoes or appearing at the peak of a mountaintop.

Most of the reservations we passed consisted of roughly built huts and run-down cabins, small settlements dotted with burned-out cars and upturned trucks, a scatter of horses and wet metal. Some of the towns looked like the people had just run out of them, they were so empty. It was as if the plague was coming. With no large town in either direction for hundreds of miles, the sense of segregation was clear.

I must have appeared peculiar and alien to these people, a lone cyclist in the middle of nowhere.

We stayed at the edge of the Pays Plats reservation one night and spoke to a group of young native Canadians at the local grocery store. We looked out on a big green area that was overgrown with weeds and long grass. There was a small, creaky amphitheatre in the middle. The guys explained that they used to run big festivals out there but these didn't take place any more. Many of the younger people on the reservation had left for cities like Thunder Bay and Toronto and the place had lost its vibrancy. Many of the elders still hunted and fished and kept up the traditions but the culture was dying out; alcohol and drug abuse had become a problem. Stories like this filled me with a great sadness – to think that this proud, beautiful race had had government dependency forced upon them.

We passed Thunder Bay and stopped at the Terry Fox memorial. His story motivated me further. When he was just eighteen, Terry, from British Columbia, had been diagnosed with bone cancer in his right knee and his leg had had to be amputated. He had also passed through here, in 1980, as part of an epic solo run. After his diagnosis he received an artificial leg and trained for fourteen months before telling his family he would run across Canada to raise awareness for the fight against cancer.

His mother asked him, 'Why don't you just run across British Columbia?'

He said, 'Because it's not only BC people who get cancer.'

Terry started on the east coast of Canada, dipped his leg in the ocean at St John's, Newfoundland, and planned to keep running until he hit the Pacific, covering 26 miles – a marathon – every day. By the time he reached Thunder Bay he had clocked 3,339 miles. This wasn't simply an athletic feat, it was a triumph of the human spirit.

A couple of miles after leaving Thunder Bay, on a lonesome stretch of highway, he asked to be taken off the road. He was brought to hospital where he was told he had two large tumours in his lungs. His cancer had intensified to the point where he couldn't continue his journey, but by then he had become a hero of humanity. A simple white marker recalls the point at which Terry's journey ended.

For three days after Thunder Bay the landscape undulated in great swells of hilly road. I was tiring. It seemed like I had been cycling for years as I inched my way up the climbs. My thighs and calves were stiff. My neck was locked into position and I struggled to push. But I drew hope from Terry Fox, from the thought that he had travelled these exact roads, running in the opposite direction to which I was now cycling.

I crossed the road and cycled on the same side he'd run on.

After leaving his memorial, the wilderness of northern Ontario became more vivid. Bear, moose and coyote roamed the dense forests that hugged the road. Days of solitude rolled by, but Toronto was in the distance and a hot summer gust was at my back. The biggest fundraiser of the trip was taking place in the city, planned by the Irish community, and it became a beacon in the distance.

Terrace Bay, White River, Blind River, Espanola, Copper Cliff, Key Harbour, Parry Sound – all passed by. By 9 June we had covered a little over 5,000 kilometres, with 2,000 kilometres logged in the previous sixteen days.

After the boondocks and backwoods of northern Ontario we approached Toronto in the midst of a freak summer storm. The city loomed and sparkled in the distance like a shelter from the elements. We drove along the streets looking at the brilliance of the place through our innocent road eyes and knew Toronto would devour our senses.

We were met by a flood of well-wishers. Newspapers and radio stations lined up to hear our story. CTV scheduled another interview, which took place at Ireland Park, the Toronto location that commemorates the Irish who fled the famine in 1847. Michael Donnellan and Priscilla Hall, champion Irish dancers from home, had travelled from Ireland to perform at that evening's fundraiser. The popular leader of the National Democratic Party, Jack Layton, arrived, and his political and parliamentary colleague Alexa McDonough, Travis's mother, flew in from Halifax.

Alexa's arrival was gratifying, a familiar face from my second home. Like John McCabe, she'd played a familial role when I was in Nova Scotia, providing me with furniture for my apartment and food for my belly. It was difficult to grasp the scale of Alexa's distinction in Canadian society. She made headlines for her policies and her parliamentary addresses, she even made headlines if she moved house, but to me, this was the lady who left fresh home-baked cookies outside my apartment door at six in the morning. Her father, Lloyd Shaw, had also been a key political figure, and his daughter had clearly helped push Canada forward. When she was elected, the parliamentary buildings didn't even have ladies' washrooms. At eleven a.m., the men's washroom would become the ladies' washroom for thirty minutes, and again two hours later.

Thanks to Alexa, celebrations at the Board of Trade in the heart of Toronto took on a life of their own. I was overcome by the reception and it struck me that I had grown unaccustomed to large crowds and cameras. Usually I enjoy the hum of company, but that night was in sharp contrast to the open road. It finished in a burger joint, Donnellan tap-dancing his way to the counter through a hail of applause from beery and bedazzled Canadians.

The next morning I rode on, bound for Halifax. My mother and three of my four sisters would meet with us later in the week for the final leg of the journey. Milestones such as that kept me moving.

After Toronto the sun grew warmer, the mosquitoes bit and the tar bubbled. We made Ottawa a few days later and were received by the Irish ambassador. A reception at Parliament Hill had been arranged where we met civic lobbyists and elected members, and I spoke to them of the need to support the fight to eradicate cancer, both financially and in spirit.

It was remarkable. A little idea one November evening had weaved itself three-quarters of the way across Canada, seeped into the media, negotiated its way into the political world and, most importantly, reached those who were suffering. An idea, belief and support had carried us this far. Several times I had questioned whether or not we were making a difference on the trip. Speaking at Parliament Hill, it struck me that the past month had provided a concrete reply.

I met my mother and sisters in the searing heat near the town of Nicolet, just outside Quebec City, and they travelled with us for the final leg. They saw up close what the previous few weeks had been like.

I would rise in the morning and set sail on the desert of concrete, then meet up with my family in the evening. We'd stop at roadside picnic tables, gather wood, cook a meal. The presence of my family was something I really treasured and I knew my father was looking down, smiling at the happy times we were sharing.

We still were not out of the woods. Ben joined me one evening a few days out from Halifax and on the road his knee began to act up. He slowed to a crawl and we ran the risk of being out on the road in the black of night. I urged him to get in the RV and allow me to finish the day on my own, and on time. He wouldn't take no for an answer.

His strong will frustrated me. I cursed him, pushed on alone, and my sister came out on the spare bike to keep him company to the finish. He came in one slow pedal push at a time, his knee creaking beneath his body weight.

When he arrived at our destination I was still annoyed and told him he had put our safety at risk.

'Griff,' he said, 'I had to finish, man. Don't you see? All my life people have told me I can't do this and I can't do that. I had to finish.'

Stephen Cheung's theory had proved true. After two weeks I trained into the long distances of the cycle, and for a fortnight in the middle I'd felt as though I could tackle any distance, but with 1,000 kilometres to go my body was beginning to give. My legs felt sluggish and my engine was breaking down, though this was offset by the image and anticipation of the finish line. I still worried, though. Worried that we might crash on the final day, that the weather might turn and slow us down.

The evening before we reached Halifax, my family left Ben, Matt, Rob and me by ourselves and drove towards the city. Our final night as a crew. On the road we had been the nucleus of the team, but around us literally hundreds of people had kept the wheels of the foundation moving.

We spoke about the preparation for the cycle, the time on the bike. It had all developed into something magnificent.

With 120 kilometres to go to the Atlantic Ocean we were met on the roadside by eight or ten riders. The sun was rising when we gathered in a deserted parking lot to take off as a small group, the rain of the previous three days having vanished. As we moved closer to Halifax we picked up more and more cyclists, and by the time we hit the city limits there was a little peloton of over forty bikes.

Stephen Cheung was among the little army, and as we cycled alongside each other he looked at my body. It had become skeletal and my facial features were noticeably sharper. In total, I had dropped over 20lb, almost a stone and a half, and whatever excess weight I was carrying had been transferred to my lower body.

'Yup,' he said, nodding his head, 'gravity's been working hard.'

We wheeled past Citadel Hill behind a cavalcade of police cars, sirens blazing. As we approached the waterfront, two bagpipers led us to our destination, the ocean. The hairs on my neck bolted upright and the day became blurry.

Up ahead the crowd could hear the pipers in the distance signalling our return. A stage had been erected for our arrival, and people seemed to pour across the streets. Here I was, a stranger to the city a mere two years earlier, yet now I was being accepted into their hearts, our stories intertwined.

On the stage a little girl of no more than ten read a speech into the microphone. That day she was a one-year cancer survivor, and she came to tell the crowd that the fight would never stop until the disease became a thing of the past. Sadly since then she has passed away.

I felt many emotions, but most of all I felt small. I was met by prostate cancer survivors, ovarian cancer survivors, brain tumour survivors. I was met by those suffering the effects of treatment and those waiting for results. A woman with no hair approached and kissed me on the cheek. I felt small beside this woman, such was the aura of courage that surrounded her.

Later on, a stranger with a husky voice who was suffering from throat cancer asked if we were the guys he had seen on television. When I confirmed that we were, he raised his finger and told us we had done a great thing. Then he turned and walked away.

I felt small all day beside every survivor and sufferer. I felt small in the face of what every volunteer had achieved and I felt small because of the goodness shown to us by every stranger who had crossed our paths over the previous weeks.

I had grown to learn that the concept of loving one another is real, not just a sentimental, syrupy saying, and that this is how life should be.

That was the essence of what I took away from that day, 24 June 2007. Everything else, everything, paled into insignificance.

Saffron and Blue. Black and Amber. The colours of Clare and Ballyea dressed the town of Ennis when we cycled in to complete our mission that Saturday afternoon. It took two days to cross from Dublin, and on the road from Galway to Ennis, when we passed the sign that welcomes visitors to Clare, I allowed myself to relax for the first time in two months.

For 20 miles outside Ennis the roads were filled with banners to greet us and people to shout us on, and at the final stopping point before the cycle ended I met a girl who had cycled the last 30 kilometres with us. Her name was Keira-Eva and she transfixed me. Hooked me in. Amid the hoopla of Ennis there was barely time to get to know her, but coming when our meeting did, on the last leg of the last day, I wondered if somebody significant had been placed in my life.

She was a friend of my sister and had been in Clare to take part in a triathlon the day before. Even though we only spoke briefly, I felt a connection, and two weeks later we went out for the first time, a walk along Dublin's Howth Head. I was returning to Canada, but after a short time we both knew we wanted a relationship to work.

When we arrived in Ennis the streets were closed off, the town was at a standstill. I couldn't believe the reception. We rolled down the main thoroughfare, all 120 of us who had made the trip from Dublin, and it was only then that it hit me. I had done it. Through mountain and prairie and wilderness and hot road, I had done it, and I thanked my father for guiding me through it all. Every ounce of energy that had gone into the project over the previous months led us to this moment. One simple concept, an idea, had brought a town to a halt. Those pains and doubts while I was on the bike vanished in this one moment.

The response to the cycle and its concept humbled me and

embarrassed me. Thousands of people had packed on to O'Connell Street. Hurlers I had played against, strangers, people from miles and miles away, men and women in tears. The effect of the cycle was astonishing.

Just outside Ennis, Ben's knee injury had flared up again and he was forced to go to hospital. It didn't halt him, though. Against doctor's orders he discharged himself early, arranged a drive into Ennis and met the group as we made our way down O'Connell Street towards a stage that had been erected in the middle of town, Matt carrying him and his busted knee on his back.

When I reached the stage I was asked to say some words, but I had no idea what to say. I thought I had been guided this far, so the speech would come to me. I still cannot recall what I said, but I can remember the energy that was within me, as well as the first sentence: 'I would like to thank all the people listening all over the world.' During the cycle I had received emails from all corners of the globe – Australia, Mauritius, the United States – and many had said that on the final day they would tune into the local radio station in Clare, which was broadcasting my return to Ennis.

When I got off the stage I spoke to the media and said that the human spirit is very powerful. I said that when we realize what we really have inside us, every day becomes a journey into the unknown but also a journey to discover what we are really capable of. I couldn't believe I was verbalizing these thoughts. 'This journey left me in no doubt about the existence of a divine power. I would have never said this publicly last year, but if we are willing to place our trust in this power, our path will become clear.'

I uttered some more words to the crowd, but once I'd climbed down off the stage I'd forgotten what I'd said. The sea of faces in front of me was all I could focus on.

I didn't want the feeling, the day, to end. Everything seemed vivid and clear.

When it came time to leave, my family and friends offered a drive. 'No,' I said. 'I'll cycle.'

Those 7 kilometres from Ennis to Ballyea were the most rewarding of the previous 7,000.

I turned right on the main road that links Ennis to the ferry further west and pushed into that little climb on the grassy lane that leads to Ballyea. I rolled up and down those gentle hills until I could see my father's fields. My body was no longer in pain. My shoulders relaxed, my neck loosened. In my happiness I screamed once more.

Home.

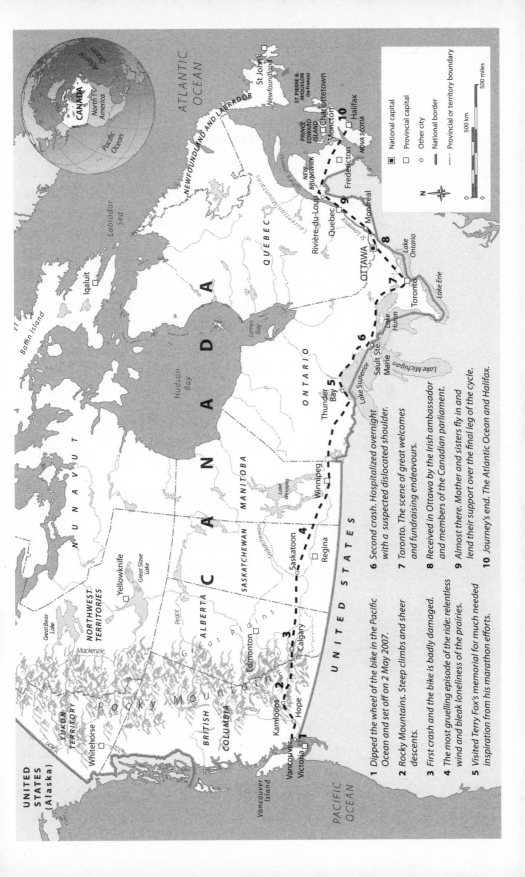

UNITED STATES (Alaska)

ATLANTIC OCEAN

CANADA

North America

Pacific Ocean

Atlantic Ocean

NEWFOUNDLAND AND LABRADOR

St John's
Newfoundland

ST PIERRE & MIQUELON (to France)

PRINCE EDWARD ISLAND

Charlottetown

Moncton

Halifax

10

NOVA SCOTIA

NEW BRUNSWICK

Fredericton

9

Rivière-du-Loup

Québec

Montréal

Laurentian Mountains

St Lawrence

QUEBEC

OTTAWA

8

Lake Ontario

7

Toronto

Lake Erie

Labrador Sea

Iqaluit

Baffin Island

Hudson Bay

James Bay

ONTARIO

6

Sault Ste. Marie

Lake Huron

Lake Michigan

Lake Superior

5

Thunder Bay

NUNAVUT

Great Bear Lake

Yellowknife

NORTHWEST TERRITORIES

Great Slave Lake

Mackenzie

MANITOBA

Lake Winnipeg

Winnipeg

Saskatchewan

SASKATCHEWAN

Saskatoon

Regina

4

ALBERTA

Peace

Edmonton

Calgary

3

UNITED STATES

YUKON TERRITORY

Whitehorse

Rocky Mountains

BRITISH COLUMBIA

Fraser

Kamloops

Hope

2

Vancouver

Vancouver Island

Victoria

1

PACIFIC OCEAN

■ National capital
□ Provincial capital
○ Other city
━━ National border
- - - Provincial or territory boundary

N

500 km

500 miles

1 Dipped the wheel of the bike in the Pacific Ocean and set off on 2 May 2007.

2 Rocky Mountains. Steep climbs and sheer descents.

3 First crash and the bike is badly damaged.

4 The most gruelling episode of the ride: relentless wind and bleak loneliness of the prairies.

5 Visited Terry Fox's memorial for much needed inspiration from his marathon efforts.

6 Second crash. Hospitalized overnight with a suspected dislocated shoulder.

7 Toronto. The scene of great welcomes and fundraising endeavours.

8 Received in Ottawa by the Irish ambassador and members of the Canadian parliament.

9 Almost there. Mother and sisters fly in and lend their support over the final leg of the cycle.

10 Journey's end. The Atlantic Ocean and Halifax.

2008

I should have seen it coming but it took me by surprise, hit me from behind like a bullet to the back. For five months after I climbed off my bike outside my home in Ballyea that early July evening, pressure from all angles rolled over me in waves. It was pressure I had never experienced before, and because of that I was too short-sighted to see where it could lead and to realize that I was burned out and flat and running on empty.

Those mounting pressures culminated one cold night in January after I had returned to Halifax to complete my final year at university. It was as if I had stepped out on an icy lake and at any minute I might fall through the crack that was emerging. I cannot say for sure if I experienced some form of breakdown that evening because I have never examined what happened for fear of what it may tell me. I can simply recall the intense feeling of anxiety and being in a state of mind I was unfamiliar with.

For sure and for definite it was one of those bitter nights when the Atlantic dumps ferocious rain and wind on the Canadian coast. I sat by myself in my apartment on Pepperell Street and so many pressures came crashing into my head. I was still probing to make sense of the cycle but failing to find complete answers, the reasons behind why I had chosen to do it and what I had tried to achieve. I had final exams to prepare for but I could not face opening a book. I thought about my father. I beat myself up for ignoring hurling throughout the winter. With Keira in Ireland, I wondered how we would make it work. There were outside pressures because of the cycle, too. The previous months had been a whirlwind of appointments and speeches about the Ride for the Cure. It was a full timetable of presentations and social engagements. Combined, these were forces I couldn't deal with. I wanted to detach myself from everyday life. I craved a quiet place to go and remain invisible.

Sitting in my apartment, it was clear I hadn't been myself that day and hadn't been myself most of the week. I was jittery and shaky. In class, I couldn't focus. I didn't want to be in a lecture room full of people any more. I longed for the feeling of space and openness I had experienced on the road. I would sit there, look across at the rows of students and try and plan an escape route. This wasn't normal behaviour for me and I was unable to make sense of what was going on.

I was obsessing over the future and what it would bring. Where would I find a job? What career should I pursue? I couldn't work things out, and it felt as though dark blood was running through my body.

So, that night I had no appetite for study; instead I had a vague idea that I needed to get money. I zipped a jacket over my hoodie and walked into the weather, dipping my head against the gale. A blizzard was hanging low above the city, stalking it, testing my resolve.

But I didn't make my way to the ATM on Pepperell Street. My senses were switching off. I found myself on Oxford Street and turned on to the city's main drag, Quinpool Road. It was deserted. Sleet fell against the streetlights, the trees were bare again. I felt the chill of the wintry air rub against my back. It seemed like I was the only person on the planet.

Some nights, when the weather comes from a certain direction, Quinpool Road is transformed into a wind tunnel with careening walls of gusts channelling through the street, stabbing their way between the canyons of buildings on either side. My clothes were soaked by the time I reached Quinpool Road, then I was hit by those walls of wind.

I didn't even think about turning back, just kept on walking. This night had menace. It had the power to take me down. My body felt strange, like only half of it existed, like there was some invisible ball trapped in my stomach.

I crossed the road and stepped off the kerb. My head was swirling. I wished a car or bus would come and chop me down, break my legs so I could find some peace and maybe rest up in hospital for a few months.

I was seeing things from an unlit room in my mind, and there seemed to be no escape.

I looked up ahead along Quinpool Road towards a small incline. I realized this was the same patch of road we had cycled those Saturday mornings as a group. That little incline was the final sting in the tail, the sign that we were coming back into the city with a tough morning of work completed and the reward of a breakfast to follow.

I remembered so many beautiful spring days cycling that little rise, days that were filled with promise and satisfaction. I remembered conversations with Bruce, wondering if sponsorship would come, wondering if Lance Armstrong would agree to meet us. It felt like we were in the middle of something honourable back then, but now here I was, on the same road, drenched, cold, feeling trapped. I had no perspective or purpose.

The cycle was over. Months of preparation and weeks on the road had passed in an instant. Was that it?

On the cycle I'd been able to make sense of what I was doing and where I was going, but when I got off the bike I lost my way. Matt's words on the road came back to me: 'The challenge will be to hold on to this feeling.'

When I got home to Ballyea I had promised myself to keep pushing forward, to get out into nature every day, to celebrate life, but those plans had fallen by the wayside.

It was like a pilgrimage. When you're in the midst of your mission you have clarity and a sense of who you are, but when it's finished it's difficult to carry those things with you. My promises were eaten up by the routine of everyday life.

That night in Halifax I longed for the road again, the smell of the forest after it rains, days when the only worry was getting to the next rest stop. Weeks of simplicity.

I needed something big again. There was no substance to what I was doing now, no challenge on the horizon to excite me. I was lacking inspiration. It felt like I was standing on wet sand, sinking, about to burst at the seams.

It's the previous July, the day the cycle finished in Ennis. I've just deposited my bike in the shed at home and already it is becoming clear that to others, cycling has overtaken hurling in defining my identity. For the remainder of the summer of 2007 an array of people call in at Ballyea to catch up and see how the cycle went. They have genuine curiosity about the trans-Canada trip. Did you think a lot about your father? How much did you raise? What effect will the cycle have on cancer research? What's Lance Armstrong like? On the street, when I meet people, it is the obvious topic of conversation. I am no longer the guy with the yellow and black helmet who plays hurling for Clare. Instead I am the guy who cycled across Canada in memory of his father.

This wasn't something I was uncomfortable with because at least some people were beginning to notice that a hurler did exist beyond the cage of his helmet. But as time wore on the attention began to overwhelm me. After fifty-six days on the road, the majority spent only with the crew, I was still, despite Toronto, Halifax and Ennis, unaccustomed to society. Being in a room full of people was an assault on the senses.

It got to the point where if somebody called by I would make myself unavailable because I couldn't face talking about the cycle again. All the questions people had for me – honest, well-meaning questions – simply presented more and more problems in my head. It was like I had to really come to a conclusion about what the cycle had been about. So I decided to avoid people as much as I could, and after a fortnight I began to dread the doorbell ringing. A social aspect of my personality shut down during those fifty-six days on the road and it had yet to return.

Meanwhile I was being pulled in directions I didn't want to go. Clare had a crucial game with Galway four weeks after I arrived home and Tony Considine invited me on to the squad.

I initially refused, but Frank Lohan, captain for the year, asked me to reconsider and I changed my mind.

The first night at training, I was held back afterwards for extra running with a couple of others and I lagged behind by a long way. It felt like I was carrying bags of lead from the waist down, and even when I swung a hurley it caused a sharp pain due to the dislocation of my shoulder on the ride.

From my background in sports science I knew that my body was now unequipped for the mix of sprinting and long-distance running that hurling demands, but when you're in a group of thirty players and confronted by a manager who is trying to assert his authority, the easiest thing to do is get on with it.

So I now found myself in the unfamiliar position of coming last in each run.

I was sprinting alongside players who had worked all season to enable them to play a high-tempo game in the middle of summer and I had underestimated the changes the cycle had made to my body.

For a long time I had wondered why each player on the team carries out the same type of training. A midfielder can cover over 16 kilometres during the course of a game, consisting of a mix of mid-tempo runs and full-on sprints to reach a breaking ball. A good midfielder is always on the move, trying to read where the ball will land. On the other hand, a corner-forward will cover less ground but will explosively sprint from a standing position much more than a midfielder. He's built for short intervals of high speed. In running terms, it's a bit like comparing Haile Gebrselassie to Usain Bolt. Yet both players will be given the same training programme and both will take part in the same drills. There is little appreciation for the specific needs of the individual.

Coaches tend to use the same methods they were exposed to as players, because it's the only way they know how, but the game has evolved dramatically over the past decade and many of those methods are now being questioned.

In Clare, what worked in the 1990s during the county's most successful days is still prevalent, meaning there is a tendency to overtrain and push the limits. If we lose, we're not putting in the effort, so we train harder. If we win, we must be doing something right, so we train harder.

Lining up for those post-training sprints, I knew those runs could end in injury. I drove on but found my capacity for running after seven months on a bicycle was lower than I could have ever imagined. Tony Considine didn't seem to mind. I got the sense he liked me being around because in a turbulent hurling year I was a feel-good story for the media.

He offered to send me for cryogenic therapy in Wexford to speed up the healing in the shoulder. During those weeks I had kept in contact with Keira, I did the maths in my head. Wexford was close to Kildare, where she was living, so I told Tony yes, I would go to Wexford for therapy. I did not say yes to improve my shoulder and I did not say yes to get to a stage where I could play for Clare later that summer. Wexford merely meant I could hop to Kildare afterwards and see Keira.

That was the level of my interest in hurling. It wasn't even secondary in my mind. It was peripheral to almost everything else, but I remained involved through a sense of obligation.

When we took on Galway two weeks after the cryogenics

I was still not fit enough to play or even to be considered as one of the substitutes, so I carried the hurleys and water bottles in Cusack Park that evening. The reception I received from the crowd was warm and heartening.

Clare won by a couple of points, and when I watched the game's highlights that evening and saw the camera focus on me, I was struck by how gaunt I looked. My shoulders had shrunk and my features had hollowed out into an image that wasn't familiar to me.

Next we played Limerick in the All Ireland quarter-final in Croke Park and I knew that physically I wasn't prepared or ready to play in the game. I was named as a substitute and the game looked so fast and quick I wondered if I would settle in if I was introduced. After a few minutes, the natural urge of any player to get on to the field kicked in and I began to twitch. I never got on, though. As Limerick began to pull away out on the field, I remained on the bench.

Afterwards, the lads went to drown their sorrows. I had one drink then slipped away.

Keira had cycled to the game from the other side of the city and I decided to spend some time with her. In essence, that's all I wanted to do, but those opportunities were limited. I cycled her bike through the streets, Keira on the bar, me with my hurley on the handlebars and my gear bag on my back. Clare people driving home from the game rolled down their windows and shouted some support.

'Are you cycling all the way to Clare again?'

That spin through Dublin was the highlight of the day, and it once again struck me that there were other things in life than hurling.

*

If I had been looking for a mission that November day cross-ing the bridge in Killaloe, then for good or for ill that's what I got. I was now bogged down in every aspect of the Tony Griffin Foundation and thought I had to continue to provide it with oxygen if it was not going to fade away and become something I just did one summer, a yarn to spin at the dinner table.

Travis had been looking after the foundation's day-to-day matters in Ireland from the outset, but he was now in the process of moving back to Canada, spending most of his time in Halifax. I wasn't due back at university until September and that gave me the best part of three months to concentrate on the foundation.

I had barely stepped off the bike, and there I was, locked away in Travis's old office, sending hundreds of thank you cards and making endless phone calls to express my gratitude for the hard work people had done on the foundation's behalf.

At the time I didn't have a car so even getting to the office required planning. It seemed like nothing was straightforward any more. Everything was loaded with effort.

I was asked to speak at schools and talk to GAA clubs and businesses about the bike ride. I enjoyed those projects and said yes to every single one for those three months at home, but unknown to myself, my own battery was slowly dying and my enthusiasm was draining away.

On one trip to a school near Limerick, my mother picked me up from the office. I loaded myself into the back of the car and slept for the forty-five-minute drive. She later told me that she looked in the rearview mirror that day and thought that if I didn't take my foot off the pedal, I would soon crash. I was constantly going from place to place, trying hard to keep the spirit of the foundation alive. But only I could decide to take a step back. Had anybody advised me to apply the brakes I wouldn't have listened.

When I did get time to myself at home, I became anxious and unsettled. Instead of using the solitude to energize my body and mind, I would go to Lahinch and walk the strand where people would approach me with donations and press €50 and €100 notes into my hand, telling me they hadn't had the opportunity to support the foundation during the summer. Then we would break into a conversation about the challenge and all the questions would flow, but I had no answers. After the cycle, because I'd refused to take a break, I hadn't processed the experiences or given my body or mind the chance to recover. I couldn't escape. I was peering at the rocks but refused to walk away from the cliff edge.

Sponsorship had gone extremely well. By now we had raised $225,000 for LiveStrong, €200,000 for the Irish Cancer Society, €50,000 for Cahercalla Hospice, where my father spent his final days, and $50,000 for Ovarian Cancer Canada. We were halfway to our target of €1 million, and the final fundraising initiative of 2007 was a black-tie ball in Galway that August. The problem was ticket sales had been slow, so I began making phone calls for the event to potential sponsors. But by now the thought of asking for more support filled me with dread. Seven full months of calls and bartering for bikes and supplies and transport had weakened my passion for seeking funds.

With the Galway event approaching, I had to go on. Early

one morning, the week before the ball, I dropped a friend at the train station in Limerick, a half-hour drive from my home. Driving back on my own, out of the blue, tears began to fall down my face. Without realizing what I was doing, I was crying.

For some reason I had to figure out the cycle, and this was proving impossible. I began to think I was like one of those guys who ran behind Forrest Gump in the film, waiting for Forrest to turn round and reveal some secret message that was never there in the first place.

I had to secure money to continue my studies, and now I had to drive to an office and make calls about a fundraising event.

That moment in the car should have been a signal. Fault lines were appearing, but I kept moving through them.

When I went back to Halifax in September my mother said the break from Ireland would be a huge relief, that I could finally take a step back from the foundation and find some perspective. I looked forward to the space in Nova Scotia, thought I would finally be able to begin framing things in my mind, but when I arrived it was Ireland all over again. I had only briefly seen friends when I finished the cycle in Halifax and the Irish reception was replayed when I returned to university. More questions and requests. Professors wanted me to speak in front of their class. I was asked to address sports teams in Dalhousie and talk about motivation and remaining true to a dream. In my own head, I came to think that this dream I had was slowly eating away at me now, and at times, speaking about inspiration seemed like I was selling something I didn't believe in.

Taken on its own, dealing with the aftermath of the cycle

would have been manageable, but the overriding responsibilities began to take control and weigh me down.

I just couldn't deal with everything.

I was flown to Toronto to give a presentation to a room of 250 people. I had been invited to talk about motivation, and this was something that should have filled me with spirit and fire. I used to enjoy the company of strangers and grew comfortable addressing crowds. On the cycle I had looked forward to occasions such as this, pictured them in my mind, but I stood at the top of the conference room in Toronto and drew a blank. People were reaching out for me but I was drowning too. I looked out at the room of faces and nothing came to me. I felt a lump in my throat and I was speechless.

There I was, given the task to motivate others, and I had been unable to motivate myself for the previous three months. Was I becoming a fake, a fraud? I felt like turning round and walking out of the room.

Moments passed, and in a nearby function room, where a separate party was meeting, an Abba song blasted out of the speakers. It saved me. Our room was submerged in a swamp of Euro-pop. Somebody went to ask if the music could be turned down and I had a few minutes to gather myself and find my autopilot button.

In the midst of these challenges, I found some respite in Austin. We flew down to present the Lance Armstrong Foundation with their cheque for $225,000 as part of the annual Ride for the Roses weekend, organized by Armstrong's foundation. It's a huge event. The city is speckled with cyclists and cancer patients and survivors of all ages and shapes, most of them dressed in yellow.

I got back on the bike for the ride that Sunday morning, rising early to get a bus to the start line. I had planned on cycling easy, taking in some of the sweeping Texan landscape that surrounds Austin and enjoying my time on the bike, something I couldn't afford to do on the Canadian ride. But 10 miles in I found myself at the back of a group of Mexican riders, a team of a dozen or so. They were moving fast, and again, something clicked in my head. These guys were aiming to win the team medal and they were taking it seriously.

Another 10 miles on and I was still with them and decided to push for the remaining 80 miles, drafting along in their slipstream, unconcerned if the Irish guy wasn't adhering to peloton etiquette.

I figured that with my Canada experience I was as good as a professional cyclist now and that nothing would or could stop me. But as we moved through the course, we passed food stations with tables wedged with all kinds of food. Big Texan portions, sandwiches the size of birthday cakes, chocolate cookies that could refuel a small country. We zipped by these with lightning-fast speed. My stomach rumbled. My new 'team' were feasting on high-carb gels and all I had was one bottle of blue Gatorade.

Halfway through, the Mexicans stopped to refill their water bottles. I managed to have a few words with them and we whizzed on. Thirty miles later we stopped again, but this time I visited the buffet. I wolfed down two peanut butter sandwiches and they tasted like gold. When I got back to my bike the Mexicans had vanished. I thought about trying to catch them but the buffet won out – I stayed on and filled my belly. I was beginning to realize that I didn't need to prove myself to anybody any more. Most of all I didn't have to prove anything to myself.

I struggled home with a full stomach and heavy legs.

In the communal area beyond the finish line, I saw the Mexicans. They had showered and changed. They were sipping coffee and eating. They nodded at me. I nodded back, broken and tired, laughing at myself, but a lesson learned.

I went back to Ballyea for Christmas and served as best man at my brother Frankie's wedding. I celebrated that night, but the following morning we had our first game of the new season with Clare, the pre-season Waterford Crystal tournament.

Tony Considine had departed as manager, Mike McNamara had taken his place. There was talk and reports that political forces within the county board were at play when it came to the make-up of Clare's management for 2008, and if that was the case then I wasn't concerned. I had worries of my own, like paying off a €12,000 college debt and regaining my fitness. But the most immediate was shaking off the wedding hangover.

I woke that morning and didn't want to get out of bed. Two years earlier I had ticked off the days to the start of the season; now I had no desire to play for Clare on a cold, damp morning in late December in front of a handful of supporters for a warm-up tournament. It was a similar time of year and a similar setting to the pre-season opener two years back but those days had felt different because of the state of my mind and my own expectations.

With little training under my belt, I walked on to the field the least prepared I had been for any game. It showed. I tore my hamstring early on and limped on to the plane to Halifax a few days later.

It was shortly after this that I laboured through that awful, crooked, stormy Halifax night on the edge of breakdown.

Spring was usually a time to get back into the air of Nova Scotia, but by March I hadn't risen from my funk. I had no desire to go back to training and playing for Clare was no longer the most important thing in my life.

Every few weeks I would receive a phone call from the new management and they would wonder how my fitness was coming along. I would tell them I was making progress, that I was looking forward to the championship season and looking forward to moving back to Ireland at the start of summer. In reality, Bruce would come round early in the morning and try to rouse me from my bed to go for a run. I normally pulled the sheets back over my head. It was my first encounter with zero motivation.

After a few days of this, Bruce tried to shake me back to reality. He said to start from the very beginning of the day, to get up when my alarm went off and immediately make my bed. He said to use this as a starting point.

One morning I woke and decided to fly to South Africa later in the week. Keira was there to take part in a training programme with her triathlon coach and I wanted to see her again. It would mean putting the cost of the flights on my credit card and increasing debt, but I didn't care. It would mean missing crucial classes and falling behind for my final exams, but I knew that if I didn't get out of Canada I would spiral further. I might have been running away from responsibilities but it was the only door I could go through.

The flight to Cape Town had a transfer in London and I used the time to spend a few days with my sister Angela, who was living in the south of England in a town called Lyndhurst, situated in the beautiful region of the New Forest. When I arrived at their home, Angela and her husband Paul were at work. The house was quiet and peaceful. The fridge and cupboards were stocked with food. Raspberries, yogurt, juices. Luxury food. The kind of food that is not the staple diet of a university student. I allowed myself to relax, and when they arrived home we drank some wine, cooked a meal and spoke about my father.

I went to bed at nine and slept the following day until two in the afternoon. The house was empty again. I sucked in the silence, then went outside. The New Forest had been William the Conqueror's private hunting ground, and it's easy to see why. The area is known for its wild horses and there are miles and miles of dense woodland and trails and moory bogs.

I got lost on one of the trails, just wandered deeper and deeper into the woods. I approached a small river, a canopy of trees overhead, the leaves just beginning to bud. On the bank was a white stone, a funny-looking shape. It seemed like it shouldn't be there. It was smooth and light and the stones around it were dark and jagged. I put it into my pocket.

The next day I explored some more and found my way back to the same river. I felt the stone in my pocket, rubbed it between my fingers.

Just then, a conversation from a few weeks earlier returned to me. I had bumped into a friend of my thesis adviser

192

in downtown Halifax, a bereavement councillor who worked on campus.

'I believe your father passed away a while back,' she said. 'It must have been tough. How did you cope with it?'

I thought this to be a strange question.

'I don't know really. I suppose I did the cycle.'

'Subconsciously that may have been your way of coping. To take on something new. To take on a challenge. But have you said goodbye to him?'

I told her we had the funeral after he passed away.

'No, no, no,' she said. 'Have you said goodbye to him in a personal way?'

I hadn't.

'Okay. Something I tell people to do when they've lost a loved one is to make a statement. Say you plant a tree, or make a scrapbook, or write a poem. A final mark to say, "I'm leaving it here now. I'm leaving the bereavement stage and I'm going on to the acceptance stage."'

I thought it sounded corny but I listened anyway. 'Interesting,' I said.

We talked a little longer. She told me that a real high like the cycle can lead to depression in the same way as the loss of a parent can. 'You've had a huge bereavement followed by an immense high. That can result in times of feeling down.'

What she was saying made sense. We said goodbye, and she told me to make sure I took care of myself.

The white stone brought that chat back into my head. She had been so understanding and insightful. She had, in fact, hit the nail on the head.

I stood on the bank of the river, thinking, 'What can I do to come to terms with all of this?' I needed to put some finality to my father's death.

Every time my father came into my head, I was met with an image of suffering. I was feeling sorry for him, dwelling on the pain he'd had to go through. I remembered how weak he had been the last time I saw him but how dignified he'd remained, and I thought he deserved better than to die the way he did. When I thought about him, I felt anger and despair. This wasn't healthy.

I didn't care how corny it was, I took off my shoes and socks and waded into the middle of the river. I took the stone from my pocket and burrowed it into the bed of the river. I got back out and sat for a while. It was a beautiful crisp April day.

'Right, Dad,' I said. 'This is it. This is my goodbye. I'm not going to feel sorry any more. When I think about you from now on, I will think about you with joy. I won't feel bad for myself and I won't feel bad for everybody at home who misses you. I'm drawing a line in the sand.'

It worked. Almost immediately it gave me the sense of peace I required. It wasn't the cycle, it wasn't the funeral or the months of grieving. The acceptance of my father's death arrived at a time when I was ready, when I needed it most.

Since that moment I haven't felt sad for my father, and when I think about him now it's the good times I recall – the evenings he drove me to hurling training, the work we did together on the farm, the look on his face after I made my championship debut for Clare in 2002.

After the New Forest, I spent eight days with Keira in South Africa and some worries began to fall from my shoulders.

We returned to the New Forest a year later and I walked back to the river and waded in once more. The stone was still there, wedged in the riverbed. It had become faded and discoloured against the gushing water, but it was there.

I completed my final exams and moved back to Ireland. With a certain sense of inevitability, I'd decided to get straight back into training with the Clare squad, but I still didn't know what the future would hold. Even though I didn't dwell on this lack of focus and control, it was always there, always steaming along in the background.

I moved into my sister Rosaleen's house in Ennis and thought this would present me with an opportunity I had thought about for a while. In Halifax I'd slept on an old mattress I had found on the side of the street, probably a donation from some prosperous Nova Scotian with one too many beds in his redbrick mansion. Anyway, I never did like sleeping on that mattress, particularly in the mornings, when I would simply roll on to the ground and slowly straighten my body. Now that I had finished university I figured I needed something with a little more dignity.

Before I left Halifax I had eventually got round to visiting Cape Split, a peninsula in Nova Scotia John McCabe had said was beautiful. It turned out the professor was right. It was an inspiring place. There's a 7-kilometre trail through the woods from the car park to a lookout point and this trek takes you through a dense covering of trees. At the end of the trail, after you pass beyond the dark and muffled overhead canopy, you reach the lookout and the light and the sound of the water crashing on the rocks below the ridge immediately strike you. You gaze across the Bay of Fundy, which has some of the highest tides in the world, and it's a powerful sight. Just like Spanish Point, it's a place to think big.

On a subsequent trip with Keira we found a place to stay in Grand-Pré, about 40 kilometres away, cycled to Cape Split then ran the 7 kilometres to the lookout. We arrived back at our lodgings in complete darkness, sunk with fatigue. Luckily, we had a bed appropriate to our needs. This was definitely no mattress on the ground, it was a magnificent piece of crafts-manship, standing a full 4 feet off the ground with steps to help you climb in. When I woke in the morning, I had to jump off the bed just to land on the ground.

This was something different. I reckoned it was a great way to greet a new day. Attack it, leap into it, ready for what-ever it has to offer.

When I moved into my sister's house that summer I wanted to build a bed just like the one in Grand-Pré. Problem was, I didn't have DIY fingers. But I knew some friends who did.

One night at training, I told the lads about my plans for the big bed. Our midfielder Brian O'Connell, an engineer, said he would come up with a design. When he had this completed, Diarmuid McMahon, our centre-forward, travelled with us to choose the wood. We settled on 5-foot-high staircase banisters for the legs of the bed and 8-foot planks for the two long sides.

While we were assembling this freak of furniture on my sister's lawn, our centre-back, Gerry Quinn – a businessman – called by in his suit and tie. He felt obliged to oversee the project. But we only made real progress when Alan Markham, a wing-back on the hurling field and a carpenter off it, showed up in the evening. He stitched the whole thing together, and shortly before midnight the bed was completed and placed in my bedroom.

We called it the BFG – the Big Friendly Giant.

The bed became a source of amusement for the team for a few weeks. Niall Gilligan repeated the words of Fr Harry Bohan. 'You know,' he said, 'there's no point in being mad unless you can prove it!'

For me, though, I had achieved something. In a small way, I was taking control of where I was at a time when I still felt directionless in other areas of my life.

As hurling was cranking into gear again, I knew I was lacking in preparation. I was out of shape. The only time I'd worked on my fitness and hurling between the close of the 2007 season and the beginning of 2008 was a four-week spell before I travelled to New York to play in the annual hurling All Stars game. I was still based in Halifax then and knew that the best players in the game were travelling from Ireland to New York to play the exhibition. I wanted to ensure I could compete in a game I had longed to play in for years. So for a month I went back to the soccer field at Dalhousie with another Irish student. We met each morning at 6.30, ran a couple of laps and created our own drills.

This was early November and the mornings were cold. Each morning you looked up at the clouds overhead and wondered if this was the day when the winter snows would come.

Like clockwork, John McCabe would pass by at eight on his way to class and peer in through the wire. He always brought a joke with him. 'Hey, Griffin!' he'd yell. 'You're useless, man! Where's the coach? Take him off, coach!'

He was closer to the truth than either of us suspected.

After I pulled my hamstring, I hadn't cared enough to organize treatment, so even if I'd wanted to train it would have been difficult. I carried the injury for two months and the tear simply lingered. This meant that for the first time in my career I had not worked on my game, my fitness or my strength during the pre-season months, and this would have a knock-on effect.

I had always generated confidence in my hurling simply from putting in hours in the gym and on the field, on top of team training. I've heard athletes and sportspeople say that confidence is a disposition you're born with, that it's either in your DNA or it's not. For me, this was never the case. If I worked hard and put time into my game, I was ready and prepared, therefore I was confident. The whole season of 2008 made me think there were certain boxes that could be ticked in order to build confidence.

In 2006, during the days of the week and minutes of a game when I began to question my ability, I would return to the work of the winter and the spring and draw strength from it. If the game was tight and the doubts crept in, I would quiet my mind by telling myself I had done more work than anybody on the field.

With Travis now in Canada, the physical therapist Ger Hartmann began treating my leg once I moved back to Ireland.

'You know,' he told me once, 'some guys can play a game if they're only eighty per cent right. Take Ollie Baker. He could play with a busted knee. But you're different. You need to know that your body is functioning to its potential.'

Hartmann was right.

In May, not long after I moved back to Ireland, we had our first championship game of the year, against Waterford. The league had gone reasonably with two wins, two losses and one draw, and even though I hadn't been involved I sensed there was a degree of enthusiasm about the new management.

A new manager brings some vibrancy, and it seemed like the slate was being wiped clean by Mike McNamara. The previous year had brought that public fallout between Tony Considine and Davy Fitzgerald, and the season had ended with a whimper. So for Clare, the 2008 season began with a degree of optimism.

I tried to rouse myself and find some pleasure in hurling but it was proving difficult. When I stood on the grass of the Gaelic Grounds on that May day, I had nothing to call on. No reservoir of belief. No positive background to quiet the gremlins. Just a tight strap wound around my right thigh and a river of doubts about to flood forth.

It was one of the hottest days of the summer, and as I stood there in the baking heat, waiting for the game to start, I wondered if I would even see out the first half. I questioned the strength of my hamstring, I questioned whether or not it would collapse if I pushed it too hard, I questioned my engine and energy levels.

But early in the contest I got lost in the familiar flow of the game. I clipped over the first score of the day and discovered some temporary conviction. In all I scored five good points from play that afternoon, and we eased past Waterford by nine points. Space on the field simply seemed to open up and I ran until the end.

The following evening I drove to County Mayo and climbed Croagh Patrick mountain, my hamstring pushed to the back of my mind once more.

It was an encouraging beginning to the summer but, unknown to us, Waterford were in disarray. In the fallout of that defeat, the Waterford players gathered together to communicate a lack of confidence in their management, and within a week Justin McCarthy, the manager, had resigned.

In Clare, we took little notice. We had Limerick in the next round. But on the Sunday morning a week before the game I was struck by another blow.

The previous day we had put down a particularly heavy session. When I arrived home I was tired, but my young nephew Oisín was on a sleepover and giant bed or no giant bed, I didn't get a good night's sleep. The following morning we assembled for another session and played a practice game. I knew my hamstring wasn't strong enough to take two sessions within the space of twenty-four hours and I should have listened to my body and sat out that second session. I didn't, and I ruptured the injury again.

Seven days to rehab for Limerick wasn't giving me much time. Had I been removed from the situation and reading it from afar, I would have told myself to pack away my hurley for the year. Because of my lack of preparation and low confidence levels, I still wasn't enjoying the game; like many things in my life that year, it had become a struggle.

But again, I lacked the perspective to make the wise choice. For the rest of the week I drove from my sister's house to the nearest pub a mile away and loaded the boot with bags of ice to carry home to my bath. I would mix the ice with cold water in the hope that I could bring down the swelling and heal the muscle in time for the game. I would sit in that freezing tub every evening and shake my head at how far I had slipped from two seasons earlier, dwelling on my apathy for the game.

Neither the injury nor my mindset improved. Less than three minutes into the Limerick game, as I won my first ball of the day and struck over my head, the hamstring on my other leg tore. It felt like a knife had punctured my thigh. I remained on the field for a little under twenty minutes before hobbling off, my season in serious doubt, Clare people throughout the stadium surmising that I had lost my appetite for the battle. When you live in the community that supports and follows your team, word from the terrace filters back quickly. Clare supporters had expected me to reproduce my 2006 form, as I had myself, but physically and mentally the building blocks were not there.

When that game was over we had beaten Limerick and made a Munster final for only the second time since I began playing for Clare. I tried to lift my enthusiasm during the three-week lead-in to the game but by now the two hamstring injuries were playing all kinds of games in my head.

If I quit hurling now, or if injury forced me out, what was

I if I wasn't Griffin the Hurler? Somewhere along the line I had become attached to that label and had accepted it as a source of comfort. It was a spooky concept.

Ever since I could walk I had played the game and had wanted to play for Clare. If I no longer existed within the world of hurling, then where did I exist? I had no job, I had no career. Whether I was still in love with the game or not suddenly didn't matter because at least I could still pick up a hurley and hit a ball, but now those two hamstrings were going to take that away from me.

With three weeks to go to the Munster final the management were patient with me at first, but after a week the mood was swaying. They were anxious to have every player fit and ready. At training they began to question things, and after a challenge game against Offaly before the Munster final some of the management expressed their doubts about the authenticity of the injury.

I began to explain that I had a tear in my semi-membranosus on the left hamstring and my biceps femoris on the right, but I was cut off. I was told to look at Gerry O'Grady, that he had broken his hand two weeks before and was back training. I tried to make light of it and said you don't need your hands to run but the legs were pretty important. The management weren't interested.

I then began to wonder if the injury was just a creation of my imagination, so I booked an appointment at a sports surgery clinic in Dublin and asked the specialist to give me a scan and then point out on the image exactly where the tears in the hamstrings had occurred. He pointed to two clear micro-tears and a large build-up of scar tissue at the site of each tear. Once again, I learned the value of trusting my gut instinct.

On one of his trips back from Canada, I got Travis to examine me. He produced a three-point medical report on the injury, which was presented to the management, and I continued to push myself in training.

Travis also gave me an insight into why exactly these injuries had occurred. My legs were quadricept-dominant, which essentially meant that because of the cycle the front of my thighs were considerably over-developed. I had not worked sufficiently on building up the normal ratio of quadricept to hamstring strength. As a result of being quad-dominant, my hamstrings were overly stretched and weakened. They were an injury waiting to happen. And when I damaged the left hamstring, this put even more stress on the right one. My pelvis had shifted slightly, too, and because I was putting more pressure on my healthy right leg every time I sprinted, inevitably it gave way.

Because the work I had done with Stephen Cheung in preparing my body for the cycle hadn't been redressed, in 2008 I was playing hurling with a cyclist's body. A physiotherapist once described it perfectly. He said moving from endurance cycling to playing hurling was like asking an arm that had regularly lifted a 1kg bag of sugar two hundred times in a row to now lift a 200kg bag of sugar once. The muscles in the arm would tear, which is exactly what happened with my hamstring.

I had spent half a year creating the engine and the anatomy to allow me to cycle across Canada but hadn't spent one day to try to correct this to enable me to hurl at the top level again. In the aftermath of the cycle it hadn't even occurred to me that I needed to tackle this. In any case, I'd had neither the time nor the motivation to do so.

The least I needed was six months to train on my own and build back my upper-body strength. Training with Clare at the end of 2007 was the wrong decision. I went through the same drills and running sequences as players who had been preparing for the entire season. What I'd needed was physical rehab and four months in the gym to rebuild my body.

I didn't do this, and I continued to pay for it throughout 2008.

During the summer I spoke with a writer for a Sunday newspaper for an interview piece he was putting together and briefly explained to him that the cycle had altered my view on how I approached hurling.

In most dressing rooms, a player is told that he must hate the player he will mark in the game and disrespect the team he is up against. As I became more acquainted with the new management team for 2008, I realized this approach was being used with more frequency than I had experienced before. I told the writer I was having difficulty hating anybody these days because the two months on the bike had enhanced my outlook on life. I felt connected to humanity in a way I had never expected. I told him about the courage and strength I had witnessed in people I met on the roads of Canada who were going through their battles with cancer. I told him I was welcomed into strangers' homes and I still thought and cared deeply about all the people who affected me and encouraged me on the trip. I was now trying to live my life with the aim of seeing only the good in people, and I asked the writer how anybody could expect me to change this attitude for a seventy-minute sports game, to hate a player I had probably never met in my life, a player I had no grievance with.

When our interview was finished, the writer ambled away to his car wondering if I had gone crazy, ready to commit me to some oddball hurlers' asylum. The following Sunday I read his piece, and he speculated that I couldn't continue to live in the world of hurling with this frame of mind.

I hadn't fully figured it out at that stage, but moving from such an uplifting experience as the cycle into a generally negative dressing room where a mantra of hatred was regularly preached didn't motivate me.

It would take another year for that penny to drop.

The Munster final against Tipperary represented a possible new dawn for Clare. Our first Munster final in five years, and again, the chance to bypass the difficult backroad to Croke Park.

Because of my injury I had to sit out more than three-quarters of our training sessions in the three weeks leading up to the Tipperary game. It was a big occasion, one of the most prestigious games on the year's hurling calendar – a crowd of 48,000 was at the Gaelic Grounds to watch the encounter – and I told myself that I played best when I was under pressure on important days, but I was struggling to win over my mind.

Like the Waterford game, I made a promising start, turning my marker, racing through the Tipperary defence and winning a free. But I knew my sprint lacked power, and ten minutes into the game I allowed my hamstrings to dictate my day.

I was marking their corner-back, and even though I was grappling with my confidence and my hurling, he still did a fine job in ensuring I didn't influence the game. Like many corner-backs in hurling, he was a typically tigerish defender, the sort who will try to shake you up. I had dealt with this for years and had grown accustomed to ignoring these tactics, but on this day my resolve was weak. I played into his hands and became sidetracked in a physical duel rather than focus on the game.

Afterwards, it sounded like people felt sorry for me. 'He was in your face, you didn't get the protection you needed from the referee.' The truth was, he did nothing out of order. He tried to ruffle my feathers, chop his hurley on my hands, get in my face. Big deal. He did what any decent corner-back should do. The difference was I allowed him to dictate the terms. I knew I wasn't playing well. I felt frustrated.

Between wondering if my legs would hold the pace and my struggle with my marker, the game passed me by.

Had I had a stronger mindset on the day, I would have concluded that if one of my hamstrings snapped again, then to hell with it, let it go. Either way, I should have said, 'I'm going to put in the effort a Munster final deserves, and if that means a torn hamstring in the process, so be it.' Instead I played it safe and allowed fear to control me, and in that sense I didn't play at all.

Tipperary forged ahead. They cut through us with penetrating runs and had built up a twelve-point lead early in the second half. We panicked and deviated from our game plan, and in doing so allowed them to get further ahead than their momentum deserved.

Later in the game, when we went on a roll and took the game to them, they didn't waver. They retained their game plan and held their shape. That was the difference. That was why they became Munster champions that afternoon.

During the closing stages of the game I began to hope the ball wouldn't travel to my side of the field. From talking to colleagues I know this is something players go through from time to time but rarely verbalize, because it's a tough admission. It can shake you to your very core.

For me, slowly, and because of everything that had gone before, my passion for the game was evaporating. I had emptied the well two years before, and now that I hadn't given my mind or body time to rest, I was lacking motivation. Hurling didn't occupy the same pedestal it once had.

Late in the game against Tipperary, my confidence was rock bottom. I felt I had nothing to contribute. This was the second Munster final of my career, who knew if I would even reach another in the future, yet there I was, ambivalent about whether or not I would be involved in a match every kid who picks up a hurley wants to play in.

Something was seriously askew.

On a warm day in Thurles our season ended against Cork, but even before the year came to a halt I sensed that the good work of 2006 had been undone. Self-doubts that had been put to bed had resurfaced. I was returning to the same scars and scratching at them once more. Questions needed answering again.

If anything, I had regressed even further. I wasn't simply uncertain of my ability as a hurler any more, I was now out of love with the game and unsure how I could rekindle my appetite.

It reminded me of a harsh day I spent on the Canadian prairies, one of those days when wind and rain were whipping at my face and the rain was coming down in buckets. Inevitably I was cycling at a crawl, and a kind old lady slowed down her car and drove alongside me.

'Where you going, son?'

'Ennis.'

'I think you're lost, son. Jump in and I'll give you a ride to the next town.'

'Can't,' I said. 'Can't do that.'

She drove off into the distance, and I remember my hands shaking with the cold and the wet. I looked down at my two water bottles which I'd picked up in Austin and took a sip from one. The LiveStrong logo was blazoned across them. I was ready to quit, I was hacked up from the road and the weather, and these bottles were telling me to live strong? I grabbed the two bottles and fired them into the distance.

'Fuckin' LiveStrong!'

About half an hour later I wasn't just cold and wet and tired, I was thirsty too. I called the crew and asked them to turn back. I loaded up on water again and Matt put my feet into two pots of hot water to warm them up. In the RV, I managed to dominate my attitude and got back out on the bike until sundown.

That's what I needed in Ireland, that's what I needed throughout the entire hurling season – a tiny flame to light a bonfire. But when I sat back and thought about it, there was a series of events that led to my lack of passion for the game.

The cycle was immediately followed by the wrong kind of training, which was followed by no training at all, which was followed by the injuries, which was followed by a creeping sense of distance from the management, which was followed by two poor championship performances. If I had broken the chain somewhere along the line maybe I wouldn't have found myself playing against Cork and praying for the season to end. Maybe if I had spoken with the management and told them I wasn't buying into their approach . . . but I hadn't the strength of belief to do this.

My year was played out in a bubble. It felt like nobody could understand what I was experiencing.

So Cork beat us and I watched from the sideline, substituted midway through the second half. To the hurling world it had been a satisfactory season for Clare, reaching the Munster final and being knocked out of the championship by a talented Cork team. But for me, it was the most difficult season of my life.

Later that evening I travelled home with Keira. We walked a couple of miles to her car, which was parked on the edge of town. I told her I didn't care if I never played again.

The drive home was slow and comforting. It was a familiar routine as we drove the same roads I had driven with my father a few years before. We stopped at the side of the road to look at a beautiful horse farm in Tipperary.

Three young geldings out in the field came over to the gate.

'You know,' I said, 'the thought of having time to do something like this on a Sunday evening in summer appeals to me far more than hurling.'

With Clare's season over, we went back to play for our clubs. I had simple, basic aims: perform well, help Ballyea in the club championship and regain my sparkle for hurling.

At the beginning of the club championship we met Tulla, a parish from the other side of Ennis and the county champions the previous year. It was their hard-hitting, never-say-die attitude that saw them win the championship in 2007, and they retained that edge in 2008, sharpened it a little to cope with the special attention champions will always receive.

As a Clare player, you expect a little more attention from the opposition when you play for your club, and throughout the game one of their players constantly sniped at me. 'Useless Griffin. Useless boy. You can't do it for Clare any more. Stick to the cycling. It's all you're good for.' The usual. He served this up with a couple of digs in the ribs and the odd stray pull of the hurley.

Normally I wouldn't have paid attention, but this day was different. I was struggling to cope with my own voices let alone those from somebody else. My form was poor, my hamstring was heavily strapped, the day was cold and bleak. I was irritated. I wanted a release. I wanted to fight. I'd had enough.

For the last five minutes of the game, I had no interest in

the ball. The only thing on my mind was nailing my man from Tulla. I never did get the chance, so I finished the game like a wound-up coil, ready to snap.

As I was walking off the pitch and into the dressing room, a couple of their supporters got in my face. 'Ah Griffin. Get back on your bike. Go back to Canada.' Innocent enough comments that supporters of one club might let slip when they're in the flush of victory, but as I got closer to the dressing room a man approached me and let loose with a particularly nasty tirade.

I kept going, but one second later I thought, 'No, I'm not taking this.'

In the short length of time it took me to wheel round, grab him and pin him against a wall, I had found my fight. I began to roar. 'Say it now! Say it now!' I could feel the pulse throb on my neck. 'Say it fuckin' now!'

Supporters from both clubs came rushing in and a brawl broke out. No punches, just pulling and dragging, but I had definitely lost control of my emotions, something that rarely happens.

When things died down, I finally made it back to the dressing room and sat inside with my head in my hands, wondering what had driven me to react so strongly. I had never reacted to a comment like that before, but then again I had never been so disappointed with a season or disillusioned with where I was going.

I jumped into my car and drove to Dublin, pounding the steering wheel with my fist all the way through the backroads of Clare.

'Fuck 'em!' I bellowed. 'Fuck 'em all!'

The spark had yet to arrive and I began to think of life away from hurling. Deep down I had never closed the door to retiring from the game. Even when 2006 had ended I had considered retiring from the game, but now the idea seemed more tangible.

My thinking was simple. Hurling had always occupied a central strand of my life, but the world was a big place and I could survive without the tag of a Clare hurler on my back. Even though I relished playing and had defined my own character in terms of the game, I had often thought about walking away to embrace some new aspect of life.

It was all about perspective. Some days I wanted to continue, others I had no desire to, but I didn't want to move on with the sense of unfinished business. Maybe I would never win an All Ireland with Clare, maybe that was a dream too far, but my performance in 2008 wasn't me.

I couldn't go out on that note.

Away from hurling, I began to process my mental state that year and figured I couldn't be the only hurler to experience the lows I had gone through.

At one of those dark winter training sessions when the season seems like years away, one of the lads turned to me as we were warming up.

'You know what,' he said, 'I don't understand how you can remain so positive all the time.'

We were probably shivering at the time with only the thought of torturous laps to look forward to, but his comment surprised me because I hadn't pinned myself as having the image of a terminally positive person. 'You'd be amazed at what goes on in my head at times,' was all I managed to say, but I felt like I had let him down with that response.

A season is a long, drawn-out series of good days and bad. Wins and losses. Injury and fitness. It's impossible to remain upbeat throughout it all, and at that moment, maybe my team-mate was reaching out, feeling disconsolate, looking for some support.

But he couldn't ask for it and I couldn't give it.

It's a complete paradox. We share serious peaks and troughs out on the field, we share a bond that's as strong as a brotherhood, we share sessions and stories and spend as much time together as we do with our families, but a team environment is not a place where you can be emotionally expressive.

In fact, it's the exact opposite. As a race, us Irish are typically closed when it comes to speaking about our feelings, and the world of hurling and Gaelic football is seen as the true essence of Irishness. And so within this frame the expression of emotion is seen as a sign of weakness. We camouflage misery with bad jokes and fake laughs. I know of players who have locked themselves into a room for days and days not wanting to face the world because their hurling form is bad, and there are players who fail to separate the player from the man. Yet there is no official support system for those going through a rough patch.

Some players can shake it off like water. They can hit the beer for two days and drink their way out of a slump. I was never one of those guys. Alcohol made the problem worse, pushed me into darker places.

With the season over, I made a call to the Gaelic Players Association, the official group that looks after the needs of current and former players. I spoke with the chief executive, the former Dublin footballer Dessie Farrell, who himself had suffered from a bout of depression during his career, and asked was there a role within the organization for a mental health service.

After that Toronto presentation when I drew a blank, I'd begun to realize that I was sinking into the sand and I figured I couldn't be the only person experiencing these feelings. I felt that no matter how deep anybody's resources are, a period sometimes arrives when the world seems like an overwhelming place. After that Toronto experience, I promised myself that when I got stronger, I would speak to others about what I had gone through.

That's what led me to phone Dessie Farrell. I wanted to find out if the players association was doing anything to promote mental health, particularly for young men, who, traditionally in Ireland, are reluctant to speak about their emotions and troubles. I thought that through sport there was an opportunity to de-stigmatize mental health issues.

Dessie agreed, and while the idea was in its early stages, I helped establish a relevant focus within the players organization.

The next phase of the foundation had been mapped out and it was scheduled to kick into place in October. In my absence, the Canadian troop had planned a relay cycle from Halifax to Austin. We were nearing our goal of raising €1 million and the foundation in Canada was in the process of changing its name to Give to Live. With most foundation activity now taking place on Canadian soil, it seemed wise to step back considering I was living in Ireland.

Todd McDonald had arranged for fifty Canadians to take on the 6,000-kilometre charity cycle and six of us travelled across the Atlantic to form an Irish team. For Todd to convince this number of riders to take on such a difficult task and raise $5,000 each into the bargain was a magnificent feat. This was how far the foundation had come. People joined up because they had heard about the Ride for the Cure and wanted a similar experience; people jumped on board because they had been touched by cancer and wanted to get active; people came because they believed they could make a difference and wished to fight on their feet. Many hadn't cycled before they began training for the trip, but combined, we formed a motivated peloton filled with spirit.

So we glided down Citadel Hill one chilly autumn morning for another escapade, a phalanx of fifty-six riders snaking through the city streets of Halifax and out once more into the beautiful, lush countryside of Nova Scotia.

The starting point wasn't like Vancouver the previous year. This time there were cameras and news crews and crowds of people to see us freewheel from the top of the hill as we began the slow crawl for the baking roads of Texas.

When we reached Maine in the north-east of the United States a couple of days later, I left the group for a short spell to fly back home. Ballyea were involved in a crucial relegation playoff, and if we didn't win the game we would lose our senior status, something that a little club like ours had worked for years to achieve. I felt a duty to return home for the encounter. This was the parish whose people had formed a guard of honour for me as I pedalled into Ennis that July day in 2007. These were the men and women who had put money into church gate collections for the foundation, great people who understood why I had to cycle across Canada.

The relegation playoff was no different in that sense, and bringing me home was a serious financial outlay for the club. Because the schedule was so tight and because I was flying out of Maine and returning to meet the cycle three days later in Ohio, the flights home would cost in excess of €2,000. Again, one last time, the people of the parish made my return for the game happen.

We played the Éire Óg club from Ennis in the relegation decider and were given only a fighting chance. I was still trying to find my own game, but on the flight home I promised myself that I would not leave Ireland with regrets.

Before throw-in, I spoke to our players and told them that at some point we were going to find ourselves in a corner, find ourselves trailing in the game, and things might look bleak, but that was when we had to forge forward, together. This was something I had failed to comprehend myself all year.

That afternoon we did stare into the void, but we ignored it. When it looked like we would lose, we fought back.

Some moments take their time and pass slowly. They give you an opportunity to be understood.

The game was finished, into its last attack, and we were level on the scoreboard. Frankie, my brother, had broken down an attack at his end of the field and the ball made its way to my hands. I stood at the side of the field, 50 or 60 yards out.

A difficult shot. Then time slowed down, and that's when the moment slid by my eyelids like pure honey. I remember the sensation of the ball in my hand and thinking that my whole year could be put to rest with this one point.

A defender was tight by my side. I looked at the posts and struck. The feeling of ash on leather. I liked the connection I made. The ball fizzed its way through the air and between the posts and we had won the game by that single point.

Word reached the Irish cycle team that we had won, and somewhere in the Adirondack Mountains in upstate New York, a roar went out for Ballyea.

In the big scheme of things, in the world of sports, that simple club game didn't even register, but for the people of my parish it was the defining point of a season.

In my interpretation the game had provided me with that important test of character. Could I produce it when it mattered? It wasn't Croke Park and it wasn't Thurles, but it was a game watched by friends, neighbours. The people I move through life beside.

I didn't decide to continue playing for Clare because of that one score, but it began to represent the reasons why I decided to continue. On the return flight to America and in the skies above Ohio I reckoned there were only four months to spring. Four months to prepare for a season during which I had to put ghosts to rest. Ironically, with hurling for the entire year just concluded, I felt my first sense of hope.

Ten days later we finished the cycle trip in a green park on the edge of Austin with an emotional celebration. People laughed, people cried. People jumped up and down and drank beer. Some were tired, some were ready to party. Most had just completed something that didn't seem possible a few weeks earlier. Everybody had a smile on their face.

In the midst of a sea of cyclists embracing one another, Bruce sidled up to me. 'Hey Griffy. Look around, man. Just think of the difference the foundation has made to the lives of others. Not just these people here, but the people they will tell this story to. It's never-ending.'

2009

This is an account of a season gone wrong, of buried hopes, of wrong decisions, of mistrust and breakdown. It is an account of two cultures meeting head on and the consequences this brings.

But there's more to it than that. Off the field, this is the story of a year when fear was dismantled piece by piece, when the athlete was finally separated from the man, when a poor performance didn't represent a weak character. This was the year I realized I could push boundaries with balance and awareness, that I could walk right up to the line but refuse to cross beyond it.

I would do things differently. I would still train feverishly but I would do so with more objectivity and less obsession and therefore I would find perspective.

There were definite repercussions.

In 2009, to the outside world, my performance on the hurling field did not compare to 2006, but to me, I found stability. I found complete faith in myself as a hurler. I found a future and I found life.

The story starts at the end of the championship season, in Cusack Park, Ennis. July. A soaking summer's day. Clare versus Galway. Last-chance saloon for both teams.

Three hundred and eighty-three days have passed since

we won a competitive game of any kind. Frustration hangs in the air.

This afternoon we will lose again, and six minutes into the second half I will be withdrawn from play. No injury. No explanation. Just withdrawn. I will feel aggrieved, but that emotion will subside and for the first time I will not allow the negative thoughts to fester or colour my outlook.

If you look inside the cage of my helmet, you will see that my face is hard. You will see that I'm shocked and I'm angry. The hurley is gripped tight in my hand. My eyebrows are furrowed. You can see light wrinkles on my forehead and beads of sweat on my nose. But you cannot see that my head is clear.

I'm thinking that this decision to wrench me from the game is harsh, but I'm also thinking that I cannot pity myself. I decide not to jog quickly off the field in the usual manner of a player who is substituted prematurely. I will not depart with my shoulders hunched and my eyes bent to the ground. Instead, I will walk slowly and keep my head high.

Young John Conlon takes my place. I pass him, shake his hand and wish him luck, a younger version of me making his way forward in the game.

As I'm walking now, irritation begins to rise. I think my substitution was a rash decision because John Lee has caught one puckout. One bloody puckout!

In fact, when I heard the ball make that hard smacking noise against Lee's hand as his arm surged into the air, I could already picture the scene on the sideline: our management turning in unison and saying, 'Griffin, off. Somebody take him off.'

Three years ago, four years ago, something like that would have brought me to my knees. I could have crumbled in front of the stand at Cusack Park. But not now.

I look into the crowd, and perhaps I'm being judged by some of the faces up there. Maybe they believe I have lost my edge, that I've only had a couple of decent games in the past three years, but I'm not worried. I know I'm a good player. I know I gave the season and this game everything I had, and I take strength from this thought.

Tonight, I will look in the mirror and I will feel comfortable with the person I see.

So I'm going to walk off at my own pace. I'm not going to jog. I'm going to sit in that empty dugout over there and stay quiet. For certain, anger now bubbles somewhere in my body, but at this moment, walking off, I somehow feel defiant and free. Even though this season and the potential it once had has been taken from my hands, I am taking charge of the only thing I can – my reaction.

I wasn't sure of it then, but that was my last championship game for my county, and my final act in front of my home crowd was a slow march to the sideline.

When I finally reach the sideline, one of the county board officials comes over.

'You're going to have to go up to the stand and sit with the rest of the substitutes,' he says.

'What?'

'We'll get a fine from the GAA if you don't.'

'No, I'm good here.'

'You have to move,' he continued bullishly.

'Fuck off.'

As I mutter those words, they surprise even me. Fury and dismay exist within them.

'What?' he repeats.

'Go away and leave me alone.'

'No. You listen to me now. You've got to go up to the stand.'

I am losing my temper now. I feel my opportunity to put 2008 to bed has been snatched away from me. Six minutes into the second half! Was our management trying to make a statement?

In the opening half I felt I played well. Not great, but well. I ran at Galway, I covered ground; my marker hit a lot of ball, but so did I. I scored and set up scores and was gaining momentum. I genuinely felt I could put some ghosts to rest, but no. Our sideline saw John Lee catch a ball and then they said, 'Griffin, off.'

The official is still standing over me, barking at me.

'You see this hurley?' I say. 'I'm only looking for someone to hit with it, so if you want that person to be you, then tell me to go up to the stand again.'

My anger and reaction are startling and offensive. The official eventually shuffles away, up along the sideline in front of the crowd.

When I regain some composure I feel horrible for what I said. He was, after all, just following rules and doing his job. I was carried away by a whole range of emotions.

Shortly after that, a senior official walks over and shows some understanding. 'Tony, please, just go up. Just to save trouble.'

'Don't,' I say. 'I want to stay here.'

'Tony, we'll just get a fine if you do.'

'That's no problem. Tell me how much it is. I'll pay it.'

I am being abrupt and snappy and smart, and once more I will regret this reaction, but I just want to be by myself.

'You know it's not about the money,' he says, 'and I know you're disappointed, but please, Tony, just go to the stand.'

He manages to calm me down, and a short time later Tony Carmody is also taken off. I leave the dugout to greet him, and both of us join the remaining substitutes in the stand to watch from a respectable distance as Galway take us out of the championship. Yet another year is over and I realize my opportunity of redemption on the hurling field has vanished.

At that point I thought the clouds of 2008 would live on and the wounds would fester, but I hadn't grasped how far I had come. Hurling was over, but the future was not dead. Only in the days following the game did I come to know this.

In those difficult moments immediately after the defeat I knew I shouldn't brood. I wanted to support the lads who'd finished the game, especially the younger guys who I felt could give hope to the county in the future. But in the dressing room I was thinking they deserved more from our management. For many it was their first year on the senior squad and they deserved honest, truthful, respectful leadership. But we didn't get that.

Inside this defeated dressing room at Cusack Park it's as silent as ever. Dark. Damp. Banks of steam rise from the shower area. I slap a few lads on the back. I tell Diarmuid to keep the head up. I tog in, and Gazzy, our kitman, comes over to shake my hand.

'I can't stand this, Gaz. I have to go. Can you do me a huge favour and look after my gear bag?'

I know I have to get out of there, and carrying my bag through the crowds still leaving the stadium doesn't seem wise. It will merely draw unwanted attention to me.

So I walk out of the dressing room because I can't sit and listen to our manager any more, because I feel he could erupt and I've had enough of that all year.

I walk out into the wet town and Floyd Patterson comes into my head – the boxer who brought fake glasses and a fake beard to his fights so he could flee anonymously through the crowd should he lose. I don't need a mask to escape. A few years ago perhaps, but not now. I don't care who sees me leave early. I am blind to how anybody may perceive me.

I was too involved with the moment and couldn't have known it then, but the three previous years had shaped me in a fundamental way. I was no longer concerned with external matters. I had found some confidence and grown to be my own man.

I had not just overcome the early doubts of the Canada cycle but had grown the idea into something significant. I had climbed out of that bleak night in Halifax. I had eventually come to terms with the death of my father, and if anything, the events and the smaller challenges of those years provided me with real faith and prepared me to deal with whatever came my way.

When I arrive at where I thought my car would be, I remember I left it in a different car park closer to the ground – a slip of the mind that means I'll have to walk back against the crowd. I am still confused and out of sync with my surroundings. I'm not thinking straight. My head is still processing the game and I am also working to control my reaction.

As I weave my way through the crowd I can hear people muttering, pointing me out, deducing the reason why I'm out on the streets so quickly, among the paying punters, saying look, there's Griffin, the guy who was taken off early. I keep moving and speak to nobody.

When I find my car I jump in and turn the key. I realize this is it. A season finished and dreams vanished after a seventy-minute game of hurling. A shot of fear suddenly zips through me.

I drive home, wondering if I can cope with the night.

I joined some friends for a Josh Ritter concert in Dublin the winter before that Galway game and drove home the following night to make a training session in Crusheen. In the car on the return trip the conversation rolled on to the concept of 'the line', that invisible place everybody has which defines the boundary between healthy and obsessive behaviour. How close can you get to the line – in terms of relationships, work, life in general – without stepping beyond it and spiralling out of control? What are your limits? Too much obsession about a relationship and you will doom it to failure. Similarly, if you obsess over the breakdown of that relationship, it will force you to live in the shadows of your mind. It's the same with obsession over work, because at some point, other elements in your life, important elements, will collapse.

It was an interesting notion. I believed at times I had

crossed the line, breached the boundary. I had obsessed about hurling and maybe even the cycle and had done so for the wrong reasons. Initially, I had looked at hurling as a method of finding out who I was as a person, whether or not I had the mettle to produce the goods, the true grit. Later, I had used both hurling and the cycle to allow me to cope with my father passing away. Both had merely lengthened the time it took to deal with his death. I hadn't faced up to the cold fact that he wasn't here any more and instead shifted my entire energy to another focus. It made the inevitable crash all the more difficult to take.

That stone in the river in the New Forest was a farewell to many things, but it had taken almost three years to get there. That moment, in itself, was one step back from the line.

In the past, I hadn't been fully aware of my boundary, but once I looked at it from a distance and recognized where the line was drawn, I could operate within a healthy limit.

The idea of the line stayed with me throughout the season and I began to see it elsewhere. A few weeks after the concert in Dublin I read a book by the English rugby player Jonny Wilkinson. His story resonated deeply and I saw some unhealthy similarities in his approach to rugby and my approach to hurling. He obsessed over training and dwelled on losses and mistakes as though an examination of them could alter their existence. Most of all, in Wilkinson I saw a man who struggled to know where the line between enjoyment and fixation existed.

Eventually, through experience, he learned to navigate his way back from the line after a heavy loss or an injury setback. He began to see the world through a wider lens, and in a roundabout way this relinquishing of control brought a new freedom. It allowed him to develop his self-expression, and rather than replay a missed tackle he would exist in the moment. This was what I had achieved in 2006, but I needed to apply the principle not only during a game, but to the sport itself.

In 2009, I slowly came to recognize when I was edging towards this line and began to figure out when to step back. So, days after that Galway game, as the anger seeped away like a slow hangover, it was replaced by a sense of perspective that had eluded me throughout my career.

It was simple. Tony Griffin the man is not defined by Tony Griffin the hurler, and when the hurler has a bad day on the field, this does not diminish the man in any way. It was simple, but difficult to fathom, because I knew no other way.

Because of other things that were happening in my life, I began to appreciate that I was doing my best on the field, and rather than scrape at my sense of self, I would take what I could from any experience and shelve it as a lesson learned.

It was like knocking down my very own Berlin Wall, but it could never happen in one big swoop. It would be a brick by brick process. It didn't even happen entirely in 2009, rather in the circumstances that brought me to that point in my life.

I was amazed that I had been unable to see this earlier in my career. If I had, I wondered, would I have achieved some goals like playing for Clare or winning that All Star? Can an athlete be the best he can be without that obsessive streak that means he trains when his opponent does not? Must he thrive on the fact that he is out on the road as his opponent sleeps? It's like those writers who lock themselves away for weeks and months to create the novel, or the tortured artist who must live in a dark place to produce the masterpiece. It's like Bob Dylan splitting from his first wife and writing all those haunting songs of lost love.

But none of those scenarios is entirely healthy. In the bigger scheme, too much is sacrificed. In 2009, I realized I could push my boundaries and still do it with balance. The key was not to allow my self-worth to plummet if my performance waned. Those faces in the crowd might judge me and conclude I wasn't the hurler I had been in the past, but I knew, deep down, that my life was better. Once I realized this to be true, that was all that mattered.

For too long I had been unbalanced. I was now learning that while a healthy obsession is absolutely necessary and the closer I could get to the line the better I would perform, I no longer needed to push beyond it.

Killaloe is an ancient old place. There's history in the silt of the lake, history in the giant trees and mountains around Lough Derg.

I moved to this sleepy postcard village on the lower tip of Clare in the early summer of 2009. It provided space and detachment from the world I had been living in, where a trip for groceries meant a conversation on hurling. In one sense, the move allowed me to exist in my own world and on my own terms. Living alone in my apartment on the edge of the lake, I had the scope to allow ideas to grow, and as the year pushed on, this would be critical.

After the move, I also got back into the fields and

mountains, into nature. There's a rough trail a couple of miles outside the village that travels to the heart of the rolling Ballycugguran Woods. The trail tilts away from the main road to Ennis and winds its way up the side of a hill. From a clearing at the top there is a sweeping view out across the lake, across to the fields of Tipperary. I found myself coming to this spot regularly.

The season had yet to start and I needed to inject some confidence back into my game. I put down a good winter of training and had assembled a background team, a circle of people to help propel me forward. In one way, this was bordering on obsessive, but as yet, I knew no other way to compete. Aside from the pure work this background team put in and the function each one served, their combined effort would allow me to win over my mind and reassure myself in the summer that I had prepared properly.

So that winter I met with Liam Moggan, the performance expert from Anthony Daly's term, and went through some of my personal doubts about my form with him, told him how I wanted to put right the poor season of 2008. His advice was straightforward but valuable. Go back to basics, he said, control the controllable.

I spoke to Johnny Glynn, the trainer under Daly, and he designed a daily pre-season programme to increase my strength and conditioning.

I was treated by Ger Hartmann at his clinic in Limerick, where we would go through a lively aqua session before working on my hamstrings.

The hamstrings were a big thing, not just physically but mentally.

Every Monday I would visit Hayden Landry, a chiropractor from Canada, and he would scan my entire body from head to toe before loosening out any tight spots. He would stretch my hamstrings and help rebuild them so I could have total confidence in my legs for the year ahead. I still wasn't as fit and strong as I had been in 2006, but I was getting there.

For every game I had somebody in the stand taking notes on my performance, just like Travis had done. A second pair of eyes. Every possible detail was recorded, including little things like unseen moments when I failed to make a run to contest a puckout, or occasions when I failed to break a tackle or provide support for a teammate in possession. This way I could see if I was making progress or not. It also gave me cold hard facts and the illusion of some control.

Though I still had the desire to control my game and my mind, it was clear I was no longer the same person I had been during and before 2006. Back then, because I defined myself through my game, my emotions swayed dramatically according to my performances, and while 2008 had been a difficult year personally, hurling was only one piece of a larger jigsaw. The unhealthy, obsessive weight I had attached to the game was lifting. It was becoming less and less rational to interpret my reality through a ball and stick.

My relationship with Keira was strong and I was taking my first steps towards setting up a sports business. Both excited me. Both deserved time that I was more than willing to give. My life, for the first time, had a future away from the game. This was perspective, and it meant that finding a broader frame of reference for the game wasn't just an abstract notion. There were real, tangible reasons why the urgency of hurling was diminishing.

Even though that gave me a certain release and a certain amount of freedom, it was also unnerving. One way or the other the game would still occupy an important part of my life and part of me would still find its identity through the game, so there were times when I became uneasy about my calmer approach. I wondered if I could still produce a high-intensity, effective performance if the stakes were not as high, if I wasn't prepared to visit the darker places after a poor display. Because come game time, the stick and the ball would still be all that mattered.

Early in the season, I delighted in the sense of freedom the new approach to hurling had given me. I was playing with abandon, flicking the ball over the heads of onrushing defenders, shooting from distance. Whenever these plays didn't come off, I lived with it because I was no longer wagering my identity on the outcome.

I chose not to rip myself to pieces with manic weights sessions and late-night runs. I was now finding a balance. The foundation was in place and gradually I chose not to put my self-worth on the line.

So the season unravelled and we lost to Galway, cast out of the championship at the first available opportunity.

There are many reasons why a season ends in deep disappointment and frustration, and even though, in the end, the year developed into a long and public stand-off between the players and the management, it's one-dimensional to come to a straightforward and concrete conclusion. I have learned enough about people to know that a breakdown in communication is a complex element of life. The rope didn't simply split in one neat cut, it splintered along several microscopic fissures, and management, players and administrators must share collective responsibility.

Two days after that Galway game, I sat in my apartment for a couple of hours and once more looked out across the lake at Tipperary. I enjoyed the view from my place, liked looking at the drift of water that leads across to the opposite shore. The trees were still green, it was the full flush of summer, but our season was dead.

Aside from Galway, Tipperary had beaten us earlier in the championship, and before that game I had sat in the same chair and looked at the same view but with totally different thoughts. That week, before we played Tipperary, we were asked to hate our opponents with a great and deep hostility. We were told we had to stand up and be men and represent our county with pride.

The night prior to the game, I looked across Lough Derg as the lights flicked on in the opposite valley in Tipperary. It was windy, and the boats moored at the edge of the lake rattled against one another. I sat there listening to this soothing noise for a long time and tried to fill my body with venom.

Traditionally, because of complex reasons but mainly because of the counties' proximity to each other, Clare and Tipperary have been strong rivals. These days, though, things are moving on. Tipperary are not the antagonists they once were, despite having had the upper hand against Clare in the past. There used to be a gulf in class between the two counties, but the Clare team of the 1990s bridged that gap. Anyway, Kilkenny had dominated the game over the past number of years, so the Clare–Tipperary relationship had evolved. Most Clare players now look upon Tipperary as just another team, another hurdle to prepare for in the great steeplechase that is the All Ireland championship.

Most of our Clare management, though, were drawn from that period of time when the sole function of Tipperary hurling was perceived to be to keep Clare down, and prior to the game our management had yet to acknowledge that things had pushed forward.

So we had to hate Tipperary. They were the enemy for the week, until we played Cork or Waterford or Limerick, and then they would become the great monsters of the world.

For the week before we played Tipperary, I tried to do what we'd been told to do in training. I looked across Lough Derg and ripped myself to pieces. 'Bastards. Nothing but bastards. That's all you are over there across the river is bastards. That's right. You bastards will shit on top of us over here if we give you the chance.'

That was the doctrine in training all week. 'Hate Tipperary. Hate Tipperary. Stand up, lads. Be men. Get the poison going.'

Of course, there is a grain of wisdom in this thinking because we play a hard, physical game where you have to put your body on the line, where you have to be willing to take a man down and be taken down yourself; but when the whistle blows to start the game and the adrenalin begins to course, you naturally slip into that way of thinking. You don't need seven days of incitement. Or at least I don't.

Normally, this sort of preparation would be at the opposite

end of the scale for me, but I was overcome by the steady stream of messages we received at training so I failed to listen to my instincts. I deviated from what I knew worked for me.

I wound myself up for days but merely ensured I focused on the wrong things. I gave all of my energy to the opposition and felt flat in the game. Out on the field, we were so focused on killing Tipperary and hating Tipperary that we forgot our pattern of play, forgot to stick to our tactics.

Sitting in Killaloe after the Galway game, everything came back to me. I went through my season with a microscope. Analysed everything. Questioned everything. Tried to draw some conclusions. Right then the obsession still lived because questions needed to be answered, but I worked to control the depths to which I plunged.

These are the moments nobody sees, the hidden life. When the rest of the county is back at work and the rest of the world is going about its business, you walk around for days after a defeat and become consumed. No subject remains untouched. If I'd trained through that injury, could I have been more prepared? If I'd passed on that radio interview, would my concentration have been sharper? In these private moments you don't want to talk about the game, you don't want to meet supporters. You don't need your back slapped and you don't need to be told that there's next year to think about, always next year.

The Galway anger was waning but I was still mentally restless. What even drove me to go back and play for Clare when other important elements of life were coming my way?

*

Eight months before this, on 12 November 2008, my season had begun. Not with any fanfare but with a phone call from Eoin Kelly, Tipperary's free-scoring forward and one of the greatest players of his generation.

As I was driving home from Dublin, we spoke about the season ahead. He knew I had struggled in 2008 and he knew my hamstring injuries had hampered me. It was an injury he had suffered with as well, and like me, he said it had shaken his confidence. Simply knowing that somebody like Eoin had questioned his ability to return to his high level of performance post-injury was a chink of light for me. It reassured me that I wasn't the only hurler in Ireland who had doubts about his ability when injury struck. Over the phone, he offered a few words of advice, but we mainly spoke about those negative thoughts that can float into your head when you're hampered by a setback.

After the phone call, and in the falling November sun, I reached Ennis, walked on to the hurling field at St Flannan's and began to take some shots at the posts. The place was empty and quiet. This season I wanted to find some pleasure in simply striking a ball between two posts. As the evening wore on, I imagined I was playing in Croke Park once more.

I thought about the season. Throughout 2008 I'd been so carried away with my own problems and difficulties I hadn't had room to process the usual challenges each hurling season brings. Niggling injuries, dips in form. Yet I'd soaked up enough to know that at some point I would be faced with a difficult dilemma.

We would be bombarded by speeches that preached hostility, but this flew in the face of the way I had chosen to live my life. I didn't want to walk through the world with my body as a vessel filled with hatred yet I knew this would be asked of me at certain times of the season.

Because of this, I worried that I would find myself existing in limbo, wavering between what I would be told to think and what I wanted to think. At some point I would have a decision to make.

The Clare manager, Mike McNamara, is a strong figure. His body is housed in a sturdy frame. He has large facial features and a contagious and genuine grin, but he uses it rarely this season.

He likes to fish and speaks about his boat a lot. There are times this season when I will see him sitting alone in his car before training, puffing on a cigar, exhaling in a worried manner, and I will think that Mike would prefer to be out on his boat fishing the little green inlets of Lough Derg rather than pushing a group of twentysomethings to their limits.

When he was part of that legendary management triumvirate that led Clare to glory in the nineties, Mike got the most out of teams. He was the man who shuttled players up the Shannon hill to the point where they could run no more. Mike could see the line and knew how to work it, driving those men until they could feel the fog of their breath rebound from it. Then he would conclude the torture, and players would literally stagger back to their cars, their heads spinning. Experiences like that welded that Clare team together, made them feel as though nothing – not Kilkenny, not Cork, not even Tipperary – could be as hard on them as that hill in Shannon.

His sessions in the nineties were legendary, and those tales were passed down year after year like fables from the Coliseum.

Once, after he saw me held up signing match programmes outside Cusack Park, he told me I was too soft. He owns a bar a few miles up the road from Killaloe, in the village of Scariff, and people would often trundle in looking for one thing or another, a favour here or a dig-out there. He would always supply whatever they wanted, until one day he figured that he, too, was soft. So Mike decided he had had enough. After this, whenever people walked into his bar with a sponsorship card or a fundraising idea, he would shoo them back out on to the street. Then his conscience would click into action and he would follow them out the door, calling them back, wondering how he could help or how much they needed.

When games are finished and people are milling about waiting for players to emerge from the dressing room, Mike has the courtesy to ask the girlfriends and wives of players how they are doing and would they like to join the team in the hotel for a meal. He has an old-world way about him, the characteristics of a real country gentleman.

But this season, as a manager, I would lose my faith in him.

The team started out positively, and even though we were operating more in hope than belief, we felt we were moving in the right direction.

Mike was upbeat early on and we won a competition – the only silverware in my time with Clare. It was nothing to get too excited about, but we beat Tipperary in the Waterford Crystal Cup final on a cold day in east Clare. With the Irish recession biting hard, the sponsor company, which was going out of business, minted only seventeen replica trophies. After the game I wandered back to the warmth of the dressing room, late, and found that all the trophies had been handed out.

It wasn't a problem: I would wait for a Munster medal or, who knew, an All Ireland medal in the autumn.

You take confidence wherever you can find it, and as the crowd ambled back to their cars in overcoats and caps, they must have garnered some hope from the win.

If they did, then so too did the players. That night, over a few drinks in Ennis, Niall Gilligan wheeled away from the group and told me he was impressed by how we'd kept Tipperary at bay late on. I was excited by this interpretation. We had shown composure and leadership when it mattered, and even if it was a pre-season competition, when it came to playing Tipp later on in the championship, we could gain comfort from the thought that we had stood up to their challenge.

Mike had developed a good rapport with Gerry Quinn too. Gerry is our finest defender, one of our most intelligent players, but in the eyes of the public he's seen as the funny man, the prankster. He is one of the guys who can swat away bad defeats and come out the following day with a reservoir full of confidence. He saves his best for the big stage and isn't too concerned about those Off-Broadway performances that are part and parcel of every season. Because of this, people don't always note the crucial role he plays in the team and his early-season performances are sometimes used to diminish the vital contribution he makes. He's a tough, hard player but there's flair and intelligence to his game that most other defenders don't possess. Gerry will take an extra second when he is in possession of the ball and drop a 90-yard pass into your hand instead of merely driving the ball into space.

As an attacking player, you want Gerry Quinn on your team. You also want him firing on all cylinders and some managers have found this to be a challenge, especially in the early part of the season before the curtain comes up.

In all aspects of his life, Gerry is fearless, and at times this can come across as being impetuous or disrespectful. Anthony Daly, struggled to understand the intricacies of his personality, but Mike didn't seem to have the same problem. He would joke around with him and throw some innocent one-liners his way.

For an early Waterford Crystal Cup game, Gerry failed to show. He sent word that he had crashed his car over the weekend, but a few nights later he showed up in the same car. Not a scratch on it. Again, this could be interpreted as not having respect, but the bigger picture dictates that this was merely one blip on the graph.

When word spread that he had arrived driving his unblemished car, players waited to see how Mike would react. And he managed the situation perfectly. Before training, we gathered round for our usual talk and he brought the issue out into the open.

'Lads, before we start, if you're ever stuck for a mechanic to work on your car, just get in touch with Quinn. He has obviously found somebody who can work miracles.'

That was it. Issue over. We got on with training.

*

It's difficult, maybe even impossible, to pinpoint where and when a team loses its way. Several instances join together, and slowly but certainly the team loses faith in its leader before losing faith in itself. When this happens, disappointment and frustration are inevitable. If communication lines are clear then perhaps the ship can be turned before it loses its way. It didn't work like that with us in 2009, and that's not just down to management. The players should have demanded a better relationship.

The league began like the inevitable chime at midnight and a new slate was ours. We played Limerick in the first round, and despite being beaten I was happy with my performance in the first half, in fact, I considered it my best display for Clare in three years.

On the back of Limerick and after the win in the Waterford Crystal Cup, confidence was still high for the next league game, at home to Waterford.

The day before, we arrived for training, like we had done before the league opener against Limerick, but the pre-Waterford training was a severe session. It developed into a two-hour beast. Two hours of training before an important league game is one thing, but the intensity of what we were asked to do was surprising.

During a regular tackling drill, I was put head-to-head with a young player just breaking on to the panel, hungry for a place on the team, not playing the following day. Eager to impress, he gave the drill every ounce of power he had. My own competitive streak kicked in and, game or no game, I tackled with such ferocity that by the time the drill was finished the energy was bleeding out of me. Other players looked weary too. In another corner of the field, Gerry Quinn had broken his nose, and we were still only halfway through the afternoon.

At home that evening, I sat in front of the television watching a rugby game. I felt drained and lifeless. On the way back I had picked up three bottles of Volvic water to help me rehydrate for the following day's encounter, so I sat there, on the couch, sipping water. I was so tired that it soon became difficult to drag myself upstairs to go to the bathroom. It's never wise to go into a game with an empty tank but this was exactly what was going to happen. I wanted to save every ounce of energy I could, and strange as it may sound, those trips to the bathroom were taking their toll. I had cycled across Canada but that evening I couldn't even manage the twelve steps to the top of the stairs. I went to the kitchen, cut the top off the three Volvic bottles and used those to go to the toilet in for the rest of the evening.

When I woke the following morning, jumping from my bed and attacking the day was never going to happen. My legs throbbed with a dull pain when they touched the floor. My body was sore. The last thing I wanted to do was face Waterford.

On the field, I was stuck to the ground. My marker, Shane 'Brick' Walsh, roamed from one wing to the other. I couldn't catch his coat-tails.

During the game, word made its way through the crowd that we had been put through a hard session on the Saturday. Some supporters were baffled by this approach, others thought we should be able to withstand the ferocity. Either way, they had paid in to Cusack Park to see a tired, beaten-down Clare team record a tired, beaten-down performance.

After that Saturday and Sunday, players must have felt physically shattered, but because nobody wished to appear weak, this feeling wasn't expressed.

We lacked voices, guys to come out and call it as they saw it.

At half-time against Limerick there had been a similar situation. We'd had a silent dressing room for ten minutes as we waited for the management to come in and deliver their verdict. We had just conceded some sloppy scores, but nobody addressed it. Nobody said, 'Look, it's only February. We've let in some soft scores, big deal. What are we going to do about it?' I had remained quiet, dwelling, again, on my own game.

In the week after the Waterford game, it became clear that I wasn't the only one who had felt physically shattered that afternoon. One by one, players let it slip that they lacked energy.

It turned out the management had looked upon the Saturday session as a mental test. They wished to know if we could cope under pressure when we were tired. It was a worthwhile exercise in principle, but in my eyes we had played with one hand tied behind our backs against Waterford. We were not physically prepared for the game and we had given ourselves no chance to compete. If anything, it made us ask questions of our ability.

But seasons are fickle. If we had beaten Limerick that first day, maybe we could have surged on against Waterford, heavy training session or not.

One win can bring sunshine into a dark dressing room, but now we had lost to Limerick and Waterford in the league.

When we lost to Tipperary, we were three games in and the dressing room remained gloomy. The Waterford Crystal win had faded into the background.

During the warm-up for that league game against Tipperary, I looked down to the other side of the field. Our opponents were dressed identically. Same shorts, same training tops, same wet gear. There was a military precision about how they looked. We looked like a hastily assembled group of rebels. Simple things like that can put small doubts into your head. *They've got matching gear, they're obviously well prepared. We've got a thrown-together warm-up kit. Hence, we're not prepared.* When it comes to the last five minutes in a game, those doubts will multiply like toxic cells inside your head. With the hard slog of winter at our backs and the need for protection from the weather becoming obsolete, we had yet to even receive our wet gear, despite asking for it on numerous occasions.

There were other things, little details that when added up make a difference. So let's get these seemingly small things out of the way.

For three months at the start of the year we didn't use the correct sliotars. We were using older sliotars with bigger rims, and when they get wet they become heavier. Freetakers and goalkeepers, in particular, thought it was like playing with a different ball, and they were handicapped from the start. It got to the stage where players were buying their own new sliotars and bringing them to training.

I questioned whether or not I was nitpicking after I met a Kenyan athlete at Ger Hartmann's clinic. This athlete told me he had run to school in his bare feet, and when I heard this I thought, 'Who am I to complain about sliotars?' But I was missing the point. Other teams were training with the correct structures and equipment in place. We were not given those basic tools.

As administrators with a role to look at the bottom line, a county board will come at things a little differently to a manager, whose sole function is to produce results for a county at the top level. Because of this, squabbles over facilities and training equipment will always arise. They did in Anthony Daly's time, too, but when Daly felt he and his players were not being treated properly, he tackled the board head on and threatened to resign if standards for his team were not improved. Daly would take this stance over a seemingly small issue like the quality of training sliotars and had always gone the distance for his team.

When you exist in the bubble of a sports season, your daily routine is critical. Your environment exists within the lines of a field. For that season, your manager is one of the most influential people in your life. Hurleys, sliotars, tackle bags – these are your tools. If you commission The David, you don't hand the sculptor a blunt chisel.

After the Tipperary defeat, we spent a weekend in Killarney. It's relatively close to Clare and there are plenty of appropriate facilities. After the Killarney weekend, it seemed like we could bounce back from our string of three defeats. We made progress. On Saturday, we trained for three hours and afterwards had a lengthy team talk. We had a few beers. We bonded. We were ready to take on the world once more.

During one of the meetings, players were broken up into groups and asked to write a list of suggestions they had for the management. One of mine was to bring in Jamesie O'Connor to work with the forwards, but one of the younger players in our group expressed caution. 'What will the management think? They'll say we're telling them they're no good.' We eventually agreed to write it down and we didn't need to worry. Jamesie was asked by the management to take some drills shortly after.

We also suggested we begin giving the Clare jersey the respect it deserved. Up until then the custom had been for players to put jerseys on in their own time, but we had recently heard how the Munster rugby team treated their jersey and the symbolic strength they drew from pulling those red tops over their shoulders. With this in mind, it was suggested we incorporate some of their thinking in our dressing room. We asked for our jerseys to be hung up on the wall before every game, and at an assigned time we would stand up together and put the jerseys on as a team. It's a small thing, but players know that within the confines of a team, small things take on greater weight.

This suggestion was taken on board by the management and delivered upon.

Something Colin Lynch said that weekend stayed with me. He pointed out that he was coming to the end of his career and that every game would have huge significance for him. He said we needed to begin believing we could beat any team.

Even though I was twenty-eight and potentially had six seasons left in my body, I felt I would only continue for two or three more years at most.

We played Cork the following Sunday. Their leading players were returning for their first game after a high-profile strike when they took on their own county board. They were travelling to Ennis with a big crowd and a united attitude. Recording a good performance against Cork, considering my display against the same team the previous season, would be one step towards putting 2008 to rest.

After listening to Lynch, I found myself looking forward to the game with great excitement.

Two days before we played Cork, I checked into a hotel in north Clare and hid away from any talk of hurling. I wanted to rest my body, sleep, eat healthy food and hydrate properly.

That Saturday night in the hotel room, I sat back on my knees and roared at the television as Bernard Dunne rolled with the punches in the fifth round of his world super bantamweight title fight against Ricardo Cordoba. The contest had developed into a huge battle.

Almost two years earlier I had been ringside when the Spaniard Kiko Martinez caught Dunne cold and knocked him out in the first round. I had never appreciated the punishment these boxers took until I was so close to the action, listening to the thud of glove on bone. After the fight, I watched as a supporter broke through the security line to verbally abuse the boxer. Dunne was out on his feet, sitting still in his corner, hawking blood into his slop bucket. The supporter was right beside Dunne, tearing up his ticket in his face, throwing the pieces at him, spitting at him, telling him he was a pathetic boxer.

In the days after that defeat, Dunne's world changed drastically. He had lost his title in deflating circumstances and had done so in front of the boxing world. So in that Doolin hotel I screamed for Dunne, and later thought that if I had needed to lift myself from the mire that winter night in Halifax, then Dunne must have required all the strength in the world to get him to the position he was now in, on the cusp of reclaiming his world title. It was an amazing comeback, and he had emerged from his dark place in the full glare of the public. My emergence, on the other hand, had been private and personal. I had only had to contend with the icy rain of a Nova Scotia winter.

I had respected Dunne ever since I got to know him on the final day of the cycle when he led me through the streets of Ennis, invited by our mutual friend Martin Donnelly. By then, he was already climbing his way to the top of his sport.

The fight rumbled on, and in the eleventh round, with the title in the balance and both boxers tired and worn, Bernard struck for the last time to end an epic contest and become the world super bantamweight champion.

That night made me think that I could bounce back from 2008 and all it had brought, and that this would start against Cork.

In the days before the game, the wheels came off. Before we even got to play Cork, a cloud had formed above our heads and the good work of Killarney was undone.

We were told Gerry Quinn was no longer part of the squad, that he had been late one time too many and therefore he had disrespected the players and management.

Initially we thought it would blow over, that Gerry would be back the following week.

That Saturday morning I phoned Mike McNamara from

north Clare and asked him what needed to be done to get Gerry back into the set-up.

'That man has disrespected me and the players,' I was told. 'I won't allow it.'

It was true that early in 2009 Gerry's timekeeping wasn't always accurate, but without a transparent team code that applied to every player, the crime of sporadic tardiness could never fit the punishment of cutting him from the squad. His exclusion came out of the blue and made other players jittery, as if this could happen to them, too, at any given time. This was reinforced considering the jovial way Mike had treated Gerry's crashed car story.

After we lost to Cork, a group of players met and agreed to approach Mike at training to discuss a way of getting Gerry back into the squad, but he got wind of our plans and cut us off at the pass. Before training began, players were told that he knew we were cooking something up. 'I'm not having that. The matter is closed. It's done and dusted.' You got the feeling that he was looking at you straight in the eye when he spoke, that he was talking directly to you. It was the same after we lost the Munster final in 2008. He said five players had shirked their responsibility. Given the way I had played, I automatically assumed I was one of those five, but his ambiguity meant that every other player also assumed he was implicated. It meant you couldn't relax.

That night, when he told us in his roundabout way to relinquish the Gerry Quinn issue, he was pushing us into a more passive role, laying down the law but building a blockade between players and management at the same time. We simply accepted it. Nobody was prepared to buck the system.

It festered, though. As the season wore on and as trust dis-integrated further, we used gallows humour purely as a release valve. We continued to laugh during sessions, but nobody joked about Gerry Quinn. Players rarely brought that situation up. We hadn't supported a colleague who had been isolated by the management for minor misconduct. He had been wronged, we had let him down, and privately each of us knew that. As people, we were weaker for it.

A few weeks later, Gerry drew a line under the whole thing. In a newspaper interview he said he would not play for Mike again. We moved on but the fallout refused to go away.

Against Cork, I was selected in my 2006 position of corner-forward and was beginning to revel in it when I received a yellow card for a clumsy tackle. I now had two yellow cards in two consecutive games, and according to new rules I was suspended for the next game, against Kilkenny. Considering my preparation that weekend, that yellow card was a real anti-climax.

I sat on the bench and was struck by Kilkenny's ability to increase their intensity at will. A small cameo spoke volumes and shed some light on our shortcomings. Eoin Larkin, the previous season's Player of the Year, missed a tackle, and as soon as he did, one of his teammates took him aside and berated him, telling him this wasn't good enough. This was a team where mediocrity was not acceptable and it was the play-ers who held one another accountable. In our team, we were afraid to hurt one another's feelings by demanding more.

This had to change.

When you sat back and assessed things forensically, you had to conclude we didn't have enough leaders in the team. Colin Lynch retired during the season with a recurring injury, Niall Gilligan missed a few weeks on honeymoon, Alan Markham was out with a back problem. These were the remaining players from Clare's glory years, and without them, a void began to develop.

For a while I had been criticized for not leading, so I began to take on more responsibility and help our younger players find their voice. I had been told that whenever a new player came into the Cork dressing room, Seán Óg Ó hAilpín would be the first player over to him, introducing himself by name despite the fact that he's the most recognizable hurler on the planet. It meant that any intimidation the new guy felt coming into the dressing room was immediately washed away. This impressed me, and this was the role I wanted to fill.

When an established player initially draws you into his personal circle, you're taken aback in a good way. The first time I felt this was one night at training a few months into my second year, when I was still finding my legs on the team. Davy Fitzgerald approached me and said I was the person he always looked for whenever he took a puckout. Whether it was true or not, it filled me with confidence. Then, while he was captain, Sean McMahon would ring up and ask if I thought he was doing a good job. This was a guy I had idolized as a kid. Moments like that, when your old heroes seek out your opinion, can make a younger player feel part of a team.

With less than two months to our first championship game with Tipperary, we needed to put things in perspective. As I drove to training one evening I felt I should say something to the team but wasn't sure. Given the year I had recorded in 2008 I wondered if I had earned the right to address the players and began to weigh things up. By the time I arrived at training I'd decided I cared more about where the team was going than where I was coming from, and I asked the management if I could speak to the lads before training.

We gathered in a corner of the field. 'Let's be brutally honest,' I said. 'Where are we going, lads? Where? Questions will be asked of us, and if they're not answered now, in these two months, then we won't answer them then. We'll wake up the morning after Tipperary and have these same questions, and they'll linger for the next twelve months. Let's answer them now. Let's face the doubt and the fear before they get any bigger.'

I said our management could do only so much for us over the following eight weeks, that we were the ones who wore the jersey, we played the game. I challenged players to speak more and take more responsibility, and told them to demand more from one another.

I didn't know if I was getting my message across, but we went through training with zip and commitment. We hit hard, hurled fast.

I walk around carrying big dreams in my head that nobody knows about. I want to kayak the Colorado River, hike the Andes, climb the mountains of Nepal. I want to build my house of stone and wood, full of sunlight. I want to develop my business. I want a family. I want to break new ground, breed horses, land a water plane on a lake somewhere in the Canadian wilderness.

For now, I must put those dreams on ice. Until then, I want to be the best hurler I can be, play for two more years, continue to strangle my demons on the field and then walk away from the game.

Your thoughts on a season are not easily defined. Despite all the evidence in the world, you never actually give up on the idea that you can win an All Ireland. We drew our last game of the league against Dublin. Normally we would have travelled to Parnell Park and swatted Dublin away, but they had Anthony Daly to lead them now and we were caught in some abstract limbo, shuffling from one week to the next, unsure whether we were coming or going. So we drew.

It meant we were relegated from the top division for the first time in many years, but even after this I could still picture us winning a Munster title.

When he was interviewed at Parnell Park after the Dublin game, Mike told the media Clare would not play against the lesser teams of Division Two in the league of 2010, effectively saying we wouldn't compete in hurling's secondary competition. These were flammable comments, and in the following day's newspapers his quotes deflected from the fact that Clare were actually demoted from Division One.

I eventually came to the conclusion that our failure to win even one game in the league was partly down to a lack of professionalism in our management set-up. Aside from the tangibles like sliotars and training gear, we played the league without a definite game plan or general target. Every team requires regular assessments of how it is doing, where it is falling down and how this can be rectified.

The only time that happened was in Killarney. That weekend brought a lot of issues to the surface and it felt that at last we could throw the shackles off and maybe, just maybe, get that one win that could turn our entire season round, so we could focus, for once, on a job well done. But then the Gerry Quinn situation arose immediately after and the good ship we had built in Killarney began to take on water. Our focus and belief bobbed back and forth. One day you overlook the shortcomings of yourself, your team and your management and figure you are destined for great things. The following day you are bogged down by thoughts of those shortcomings.

A season is a calendar of swings and roundabouts, of shapes and snatched memories. It is not a continuous upward curve on a graph.

Driving home after the Dublin game, I thought of my father again. The last time we played at Parnell Park I had travelled home with him. He had complained of his back feeling itchy, and we later realized this was the tumour.

Years pass by. Life rumbles on. Some things don't change. I find myself back in Ireland, still caring about Clare, still pulled along by some invisible piece of string to some invisible destination, the dream always running up ahead.

To live with it for just one moment, to catch it – that would be happiness.

A professional set-up is well organized. Things work on time. Transport is punctual, meals run to schedule, training camps are enjoyable, physios are available when needed, nutrition is in place, and after the players pushed hard enough, these basics were, in general, implemented by our management.

But next come the people, the faces. Each must have a clearly defined role, each must know what he is doing and communicate his plan in a way that's understood by the team. That way, everybody fights for the same thing. That way, you have some direction. In that sense, it's probably no different to a medium-sized company.

This is where we began to fall down. Most of the time we were kept in the dark. Some coaches like to operate that way, but this strategy didn't work with me. I'm one of those players who likes to know what's going on. If we're at a training camp, I like to know when we have a free hour or two so I can take a walk by myself, catch a nap, use the pool.

My sports management business had got off the ground, and in the summer we began to facilitate training weekends for Gaelic football teams during the season and I got to see what life was like on the other side of the fence. I was impressed by the structures other teams had in place, particularly one team from Ulster. Everything was planned out. Every player had an itinerary for the weekend and it operated like clockwork. The way their backroom staff dealt with our company was impressive. It was clear they had a vision, and their class and will to win were apparent.

As for Clare, on any given evening our plans could change, and this directly led to one of our most influential players walking away. We had arrived at Clareabbey, on the outskirts of Ennis, for our regular Thursday training. In the middle of the session, we noticed that a stream of players from the Under-21 squad had arrived with gear bags on their backs. It seemed curious but we continued to train.

We discovered that Mike had arranged for us to play the Under-21s in a challenge game that evening.

This one player had already arranged to pick up his kid immediately after training. 'Mike,' he explained, 'I'd like to go.' He was told he wasn't starting the game that was going ahead after training but he should stay around because he might be required at some stage. So our man is late to pick up his kid, and he thinks, 'I've had enough of this.' He walks away from the squad and we're down another key player.

At our next meeting, Mike called me aside and asked would I make contact and try to coax our teammate back. I agreed. We're good, close friends. 'Call him tomorrow, talk to him,' Mike said.

When I did, I heard frustration and a guy questioning his involvement in a set-up he had lost faith in. I understood his predicament. We talked things over and he came back.

At the heart of a professional set-up is a basic respect for the people you work with. As a player, you sense this in the way you're spoken to and dealt with, and this becomes more important than expensive gear or the right jerseys. It's more important than running a training session on time or laying out an itinerary for your players.

Sometimes, the voice of the management felt like a lead balloon.

You can take one night of being shouted at. You can actually take three or four. But after weeks and months the air remains septic even though the words have lost their bite.

The negatives were accentuated, and without a win or

anything positive to cling to, those negatives grew out of all proportion.

'How the fuck do ye expect to win playing like that?' This was one of the central themes to the year.

Seasons are built around voices. Who you hear and what you hear becomes your own internal voice, and in the same way that there is only so much you can process, there is, too, only so much you can filter.

Subconsciously, you begin to live in a shifting world where anything can happen. As things go on, you realize you could be taken off in a game or become the butt of a joke for no apparent reason. Players become unstable. They fail to completely express themselves.

Some managers know no other way. It's the legacy that has been handed to them, and perhaps it has worked in the past.

The constant negativity and belligerence wore me down. Clare, as a society and as a hurling force, was a different animal in 1995 compared to what it was in 2009. What motivated players then could not motivate players a decade and a half later because so many things had changed in that space of time.

In 1995, Loughnane recognized what was needed. It was the world against Clare, and those fierce sessions brought players together. That's where the long, hard runs and the verbal abuse to push players up those hills came in. But the game was dramatically slower then; players could cope with heavy training that focused on distance and stamina as opposed to power and explosive energy, which is what is now required.

As a county, even as a country, we're in a different place. Players investigate new training methods on the internet; we tap players from other teams to see what they're doing week by week; we hear that a soccer legend like Roy Keane, for God's sake, practises yoga. So we've moved on.

Or maybe that's just some elaborate sociological excuse. Maybe the cycle had taken the ingredients I needed to compete at this level away from me, ingredients like anger and hatred. Maybe I got from the cycle what I'd been looking for in hurling, or maybe my obsessive nature was waning.

To the management's credit, they did line up some outside voices and provided a great calibre of sportsperson to address us from time to time. The former Irish and Lions rugby international Keith Wood, who is from Killaloe, gave an illuminating talk about what being a winner requires. He told a story about his time playing for Harlequins.

After a training session he took a couple of hurleys out of his car to show his teammates this Irish game he was always talking about. The New Zealand international Zinzan Brooke took a hurley and couldn't hit the ball. Wood could see the Kiwi was annoyed but thought nothing of it. The next day, Brooke came to Wood and asked could they hit some more ball after training. So later on, Wood took out two hurleys, Brooke grabbed one, and with his first attempt he drove the ball 60 yards.

'How the hell did you manage that?' Wood asked. 'You couldn't even hit the ball yesterday.'

'Oh,' Brooke replied, 'I took a stick and ball home yesterday and practised until it got dark.'

Winners, Wood told us, do not accept failure.

A short time later Bernard Dunne stood in front of us. He told us of his crushing loss to Kiko Martinez and how that affected his confidence but he was determined to get back into the ring and regain the world title.

Nearly two years later came that world super bantamweight title fight against Ricardo Cordoba in Dublin, and when Dunne was floored in the fifth round he told us he heard a strong voice in his head telling him to get up, get up, and he did get up, and in an epic fight he knocked Cordoba out in the eleventh round. 'Even if you're down, you've got to believe and keep on striving,' Dunne said. 'You must overcome failure to be the best.'

Those talks helped sharpen our focus, but in the overall environment of 2009 they couldn't push us on to greater things.

In the days after we lost to Galway and our season had ended, I admonished myself for not standing up to the management during the summer. In this respect I had failed.

I knew that belief in our training methods had seeped away. Why didn't I say something? I knew that the greatest chance of damaging my hamstring would arrive at the end of a session. Most of our sessions trundled on for two hours, and at the end, when our muscles were fatigued, we would be put through speed and reaction work. The science of training is no longer a hidden subject found in some dusty manual. These days, every player knows something about the mechanics of exercise. Players know that the end of a session is not the time to take on shuttle sprints, where you run small distances flat out, turning and twisting your body. Yet this was the normal routine, and once more, we complied. Despite a poor training approach and an atmosphere that didn't encourage communication, by failing to stand up and express our worries, we players were also responsible for a receding season.

I remained silent during the season because I chose, regretfully, to remain part of the chorus. I didn't think it was a player's responsibility to speak to our management and inform them I didn't believe in their methods, and by definition I was accepting mediocrity.

As a senior player, I have to hold my hand up and take some of the rap for Clare having a dismal 2009.

There were little fallouts and lapses of communication that built up and festered, and the thing was, nobody – players or management – shouted stop.

In preparation for the championship, we arranged a training weekend in Wexford. I travelled separately and, stupidly, I hadn't checked what time we were due to meet at the ground for our first training session. When I did find out, it turned out I was running behind schedule. I rang Mike and told him I was half an hour away.

'Tony,' he said, 'we're on the field. Kennedy Park. Get directions. Get here now.'

I was on a leafy backroad and flagged down an old timer, asked him did he know where Kennedy Park was.

'Ah,' he said, 'John F. Kennedy Park. Know it well. Follow me.'

He took me down a labyrinthine network of small roads. I was guessing he knew a shortcut and I'd be there before the first half of training was finished. Pressure off.

Twenty minutes passed. Half an hour passed. I was

becoming sceptical. I flashed my headlights at my navigator. He stopped.

'Where exactly are you bringing me?'

'John F. Kennedy Park. The homestead.'

'What?'

'Birthplace of the ancestors of the great JFK?'

Oh Jesus. I'm going to be tortured!

'But I'm looking for the hurling field?'

'Ah,' he said again. 'Hurling field's right beside the homestead. Follow me.'

So I did.

We arrived at the field. Empty. Not a car or bus in sight.

Oh Jesus. I'm going to be killed!

I rang Mike again. Told him I'd been led astray.

'Tony, you're a disgrace. You'd want to take a good look at yourself.' He fired off a few other volleys.

'Mike, I'll get there as fast as I can and do some extra training on my own.'

'Don't bother. See you at the hotel.'

When I arrived at the hotel, I decided to face the music straight away. Nip it in the bud. I walked up to Mike and apologized.

'Mike, I'm sorry. This old fella—'

'Tony,' he said, 'don't worry about it. These things happen. Forget about it.'

I was left bewildered. He had shrugged off his earlier hostility, but we never resolved anything. It was as though he was getting rid of some anger on the phone and once that purpose was served it was like it hadn't even happened.

In any other season, this wouldn't be worth mentioning.

But to me, it encapsulates something. I hadn't checked the schedule. That was my responsibility, and in other years I wouldn't have been as flippant. Now, I was returning from a work meeting and hurling wasn't my only priority.

Mike didn't handle the situation the way he should have and his reaction was indefinite. It veered from anger to acceptance. Not for the first time, he didn't send a clear message.

It should have been obvious that as a group of players and as a management, we were not communicating. We didn't face up to this, so we drifted.

Shortly after this we travelled to Waterford to play a challenge game in preparation for the championship and returned a deflated team with the life sucked out of us.

It was a Tuesday night, and we left Clare in a group of cars. We wouldn't be travelling by bus, which was a relief to some. It meant we could complete the three-hour drive back to Ennis a little quicker and arrive home before midnight. Sitting on a bus for a few hours midweek for a challenge match isn't anybody's idea of entertainment.

We happily agreed to divide the journey between ten or twelve cars, but once more travel directions became a problem. The group gathered in Clonmel, about an hour's drive outside Waterford, for soup and sandwiches.

When it came time to leave, some players who had arrived in Clonmel behind schedule, including me, were still finishing their food. It meant that four cars remained after the main group had departed for Waterford.

Ten minutes later, we followed one of the lads who said he knew the way but before long found ourselves driving the scenic route, adding a further 30 miles to the journey. It meant a dozen players were now running late and game time was approaching.

One of the lads received a phone call from a board official who travels with the team.

'Where are ye?'

'We're still about forty minutes away.'

'What? Wait, Mike wants to say something.'

The official handed the phone to Mike.

'Ye're late? How did that happen? Get here in twenty minutes. We'll delay the start of the game.'

'But Mike, we're—'

The phone went dead.

We had no chance of arriving at the ground in twenty minutes. We broke every speed limit in Waterford to get there as quickly as possible but the game had already started when we arrived. We togged off and took our place on the sideline, but those of us who were late were surplus to requirements.

When the game was over we sat in the dressing room waiting for the inevitable fallout. Twenty minutes passed. No sign of the management. Thirty minutes passed. Players were becoming aware of the time. It was getting late. The atmosphere was getting edgy.

One of the lads broke the silence. 'Fuck it. If he has something to say, let him say it and not have us sitting around and it's all hours by the time we get home.'

When the management showed up, Mike let us have it. He told us we had put Clare hurling back fifteen years; he said we didn't have respect for hurling or for Clare; he said we had embarrassed the management, we had embarrassed the county board.

The dressing rooms at Waterford are small and compact. We were squashed tight on the benches, cramped up, listening to him as he went on, heads bowed, trying to ration the number of times we made eye contact.

He told us we were some shower of arseholes if we couldn't get there on time; he said if we had been driving to a golf game we wouldn't have been late; he told us if we had arranged to meet a journalist back in Clare we wouldn't be late.

Eventually, after almost thirty minutes, he ran dry.

'The lot of ye,' he said, 'get out of here!'

Our tardiness was inexcusable and spoke of an amateur approach on our behalf, but Mike's reaction, again, had been excessive. Taken on its own, the incident might not have merited a second thought, but on the back of the Gerry Quinn fallout and on top of the lack of belief in our training and the increasing amount of negative feedback we were receiving, a tirade like that had the ability to rip us apart.

At the next training session the mood didn't lighten. By then we had already lost to Tipperary in the championship and the crucial game with Galway was approaching. The incident knocked the energy out of us. It's all we were talking about for the following week, wondering, like kids, if we were going to get another tongue lashing at training. And so our focus shifted off Galway.

A few days later Mike came up and told me he needed to get some things off his chest about that night in Waterford, that he needed to let players know he still had it. 'Look,' he said, 'you wouldn't take any notice of that. I was just letting off steam.'

It was more mixed signals. If he wanted to lay down the law, then so be it. There was no need subsequently to trivialize things.

But he probably felt bad about his reaction. Not as a manager but as a human, because Mike, beneath a gruff exterior, has a big heart.

Playing full-time and trying to kickstart a career is a challenge, but between player meetings and training and games you find time, and bit by bit we ploughed on, making inroads, raising a trickle of income.

Sports Academy International was launched earlier in the year and we aimed high and never allowed our dreams to be pulled down. For a long time after coming back from Canada I heard people tell me I should go out and look for a job, to give up on the idea of building a sports management business in these recessionary times. I had learned to listen to my gut by then, to believe in the idea if it was strong enough. I was learning that most ideas will hit a wall, that even if you begin to believe an idea is strong enough to develop into something real there will probably come a time when doubts exist.

Once I pushed past this stage with Sports Academy, I knew we could get the business moving.

The idea of working with international teams got my blood pumping, but because of my hurling commitments, I didn't have time in the summer to push the business forward in the manner I felt was necessary. But I would live with that and I would work around the season.

And then it came to pass that Muhammad Ali was coming to town, to visit the Turnpike area. Ennis, it turned out, is the birthplace of Ali's great-grandfather, a man called Abe Grady.

The boxer has been my greatest sporting hero since I was a kid. When we cycled through Kentucky horse-country on our way to Texas in 2008, I had planned on waiting outside Ali's house for a couple of days until I caught a glimpse of the great man – before I found out he had moved to Michigan.

So the boxer was coming to Ennis. The town had Ali fever. Shop windows welcomed the return of their prodigal son. Streets were decorated in the stars and stripes of the United States.

The local council had arranged a civic reception to greet Ali, but due to space constraints only forty people could attend. What about the great populace of Clare and beyond? The council hadn't yet made provision, so our company came up with an idea.

We needed to transform Ali's visit into a spectacle for the people. At the time, due to his health, there were suggestions that this might be his final overseas trip for some time, and in any case, this would surely be the only time he would set foot on Clare soil.

My business partner Tomás and I walked into the council chambers one morning and told them we planned on developing Ali's visit. We were met with questions about logistics and financing but we vowed to the council we would make this work. This I could not have promised without enthusiasm and faith. I also couldn't have believed without living in the space that Killaloe provided. It was like my decision way back in 2006 to remain in Halifax for Christmas. That space removed me from any negative feedback.

Bruce Mansour – our man who can make things happen – arrived in Clare from Canada to lend his weight to the project. Potentially, if we did not receive sponsorship, our new business would be faced with a debt of €25,000, enough to bring us to our knees, but in less than three weeks we had hit our target.

We'd raised enough to provide the town with a grand ceremony so we organized a large stage in an open space beside the river, a giant screen and some of the country's finest entertainers like Sharon Shannon and Mundy. Over eight thousand people showed up to watch the big screen as Ali was bestowed with the honour of becoming the first Free Man of Ennis.

I had dreamed of meeting Ali at some stage, but it didn't come to pass. Instead, I saw the huge wave of joy and excitement his visit brought to the town. This was clear from the faces that lined the streets and in those who were lucky enough to meet the great boxer. Later, his wife Lonnie told us her husband had enjoyed one of his most memorable days in recent years.

At one point during proceedings it dawned on me that my focus had changed dramatically in three years. I was making calls to clients, answering questions, keeping receipts. Even my clothes were different. In 2006, I went from Monday to Sunday dressed as an athlete. Trainers, tracksuit bottoms, hoodie. Now I was wearing a shirt and pants.

The business was now a serious consideration, but more importantly, I was enjoying it and I had the desire to bring it to the next level. I knew, too, that I couldn't do this the following year and continue to give hurling thirty hours each week.

It's funny, but even though I didn't enjoy training, even though it didn't fit my personality, and even though life as a hurler in 2009 was a strain, I found my love of hurling had returned. In May, during the first half of our championship opener against Tipperary, I looked into the stand and up to the terrace and a huge surge of adrenalin rushed through my body, the kind I hadn't experienced the previous year. At that point, I wished to be nowhere else on the planet than at the Gaelic Grounds, doing battle with Tipperary.

At times that day we looked fit and well prepared, and near the end we pulled Tipp back on the scoreboard, but it simply looked like they had eased off the gas and allowed us into the game. Something was holding us back and we couldn't push on, as if a piece of cord was tied to our waists and we couldn't get free. Tipperary pushed us just far enough to make us ask questions of ourselves, and eventually they steered us away from victory.

What do you take from those games? The defeat, or the sense that you got close and could have won? You focus on the positive, but you cannot discount the reality.

In his analysis of the game Mike told us that one senior player had dropped two balls, and when his calculations were done, this player had contributed minus three to the scoreline. 'Imagine that,' he said. 'Minus three.'

I had dropped two balls, if not more. He could have been talking about me. He could have been talking about any of us.

But instead of taking the player aside or identifying him publicly, we were operating under the threat of innuendo.

At times you just didn't know what you would get with the management. There was a hazy undercurrent.

When I stepped back from it, I reckoned the atmosphere had really hardened after the league. Defeat after defeat became the players' fault. 'Ye're not doing it right.' 'Ye don't have the killer instinct.' 'Have ye any stomach for battle?'

In the past, Clare had thrived under an 'us versus them' mentality; it was Clare taking on the world. Now it was becoming management versus players.

Pat Summitt is one of the greatest coaches in women's basketball. She was ruthless with players on the court and pushed them in every way possible. In that sense she operated with sharpened rods of lightning on her tongue, whipping players verbally, but under that churlish layer her team knew she cared about them, that she would bat for them whenever she was needed.

We no longer had that bond with Mike. It vaporized along the line.

With the season moving on and Galway on the radar, I looked back at my preparation for the Tipperary game and concluded easily that it didn't work for me. Staring at a patch of land across the lake and telling myself that I must be prepared to inflict damage on those who represent that patch of land had simply worn me out.

For Galway, I chose to be more relaxed. In Killaloe, I felt more removed from the hurling scene. The week of a game the chances of meeting somebody who recognized me were slim and whenever the game did come into my mind, I pushed it to one side. I didn't obsess over match-day scenarios like I had done in the past because I wanted to conserve energy; I trusted that when the scenario presented itself I would choose the right option.

Personally, Galway was an important game for me. When I was given the chance of orthodox preparation, I was satisfied with my performance throughout the year. I was being criticized by those in the hurling community who felt my consistency had dropped, but their opinions no longer mattered. I was my own judge now.

Two years earlier we had beaten Galway in Cusack Park against the odds. We needed to do this once more. Though I was putting things in proper perspective and not dwelling on the negatives during a game, those phantoms of 2008 were still floating about, popping into my head from time to time. I had to extinguish them for good, and the Galway game could allow me to do that.

The Thursday before the game we trained for the last time.

Mike told me he reckoned I was having a poor year, but I disagreed. I wanted to take on Galway and felt I was ready, but by now I was demoralized by the training we'd been given and the guidance we'd been shown. Being constantly shouted at hadn't worked for me. 'We need to kill these fuckers because we're from Clare and they're not!' It simply did not push my buttons.

I wanted to explore what playing for Clare actually meant. It couldn't simply be true that because we were from Clare we had some higher invisible moral ground. We needed to sit down, just once, and determine exactly who and what we represented. Then we would know what we stood for; we would have something to believe in rather than outmoded rhetoric.

Ten minutes into the game on a black, wet day, I still hadn't got to the pitch of things. I was tackling well but it began like one of those games where you just don't seem to occupy the same space as the ball.

After six or seven minutes, Brendan Bugler found me with a pass. Immediately, a negative thought consumed me: 'Shit! What if I drop this?' But in those crucial split seconds I managed to override it. I turned, opened my shoulders and launched the ball downfield. After this, I settled in, covered ground, contributed well. We were down six at the break but still in the game.

Before the management came in, it was clear to the players that the Galway defender John Lee had been doing some serious damage. At the break, I was moved from midfield to cover Lee in the second half, instructed to push forward, to move him out of his central defensive position and give him something to think about.

Our situation was obvious. Nobody had to be told. This was it. Crunch time.

Mike began to speak. 'We've signed up to our side of the bargain, everything ye've wanted we've given ye.'

In a way that was true. If I had to see a physio any morning of the week, then a physio was provided, but there was something missing: that basic human interaction, that respect for players. Simply and truthfully, I had lost belief in the leadership we had been given, and the words I was hearing sounded hollow.

'So, lads, ye've got to deliver,' he said.

Before we went back out, we were told emphatically that whoever allowed Lee to catch the next ball in the air was going to be pulled right out of the game.

Seven minutes in, that's exactly what happened. He beat me for one ball in the air. One ball!

In my dream, in my last game with Clare I'm walking off the pitch drenched in September sunlight and applause. Demons are buried and burned, Croke Park is spilling over with saffron and blue colours, the Liam McCarthy Cup is waiting in the Hogan Stand. I'm savouring the moment, embracing my family, pressing through a happy, swaying crowd before stretching to get my hands on that glorious, shining cup. The Holy Grail reached. A flagpole lodged forever on the peak of the mountain. A chapter closed.

Reality is a little different. In real life, I walk off in the Saturday rain of Cusack Park, my tank of energy unnecessary. I walk off drenched, confused, angry, my moment snatched from my grasp.

The thing was, though, I didn't get swallowed. I remained strong, and my faith in myself held firm. Three days after being taken off, my mind was beginning to rest. I would hold no grudge with any of the management, I would not take their decision personally.

There's a certain irony here. The most debasing passage in the story of my career arrived during my last proper championship game, in front of my home crowd and in the most public way possible. Yet I dealt with it.

One mistake in the uncontrollable heat of a game had crippled me in the past but now I was able to deal with this early substitution, and in that alone the fears and the doubts, not only from 2008 but from seasons past, were being overcome.

So I walked from the field against Galway with a furrowed brow and an angry grip on my hurley, but I reached the sideline with my head high.

It's not that simple, though. A shift of any significance never happens in the blink of an eye. It's a process. Once more I began to dwell on the season because, inevitably, most players will.

So it's two days after the game and nothing but hurling is occupying my thoughts. I ask myself if I could have done more, if I could have been fitter, if I have lost my hunger. I put this against the backdrop of setting up a business, of living in a relationship, and conclude that for sure my hunger has changed. I don't define myself purely as a hurler any more, and this is good. A lot of what gave me an edge as a hurler – the obsessive streak, the expression of myself through the game – has vanished. This wasn't healthy for me as a person, but perhaps it was beneficial to my game, to my team. For good or for ill, it has vanished.

Other players have noticed this too, including guys from other teams. Ger Hartmann told me he had treated an opposing player who observed I had lost my passion since the cycle. That might have been true of 2008, but certainly not of this season. In 2009, I still enjoyed playing and had complete motivation to perform.

Eoin Kelly from Tipperary also told me he believed I was playing with no confidence in 2008. 'What struck me about you in '05 and '06 was you played with your chest out. You didn't do that in 2008.' He was right, but that confidence did come back the following year.

At times after that Galway game I found myself approaching the line with my pattern of thinking, telling myself I hadn't been committed enough, that sometimes I had opted out of collective training. But then I looked at our season and saw that I made those decisions because I wasn't feeling fresh, I wasn't enjoying training. Due to the number and nature of our sessions, I began to lose my zip and speed and my body was breaking down. My bones were throbbing, I began to get cold sores – early signs that I was overtraining and pushing my body too far. So I made my excuses and removed myself from a handful of sessions.

I could have been up front, and Mike may have liked me to be up front, but I couldn't be sure he would take my line of thinking on board. Somewhere that season he became a brick wall and I began to wish he would give us something positive to cling to, just one comment or action to give us a lift. That's the environment I thrive in. Good vibes, productive thoughts, a little shot of inspiration. I even wrote my university thesis on the effect a positive attitude can have on pain endurance.

In the void after Galway, I looked further down the line and tried to figure out What's Important Now. I couldn't go through another season like 2009 simply because I couldn't devote thirty hours a week to something I couldn't believe in. I couldn't go through the motions. I was enjoying hurling for Ballyea far more than I was for Clare, learning far more with the club, and I could still cultivate my love of the game there.

In the past, retiring from inter-county hurling was a choice I considered from time to time. Now it was becoming the only option.

I was sitting in a café in Killaloe near my apartment, drinking coffee with a friend. The evening light outside was streaming in. Wet horses were spread across the field over the road. Blackberries about to turn an inky colour lined the ditches. It was the middle of autumn and that Bob Dylan song 'Hurricane' was playing through the speakers.

We got to talking about the musician, and this friend began telling me how Dylan had continued to reinvent himself, how he never stood still and how, when he woke each morning, he knew it was possible to be a new person.

He had torn the rule book to pieces. He pushed folk music to one side, transformed himself into a rock star and at the height of his fame turned his back on the whole music industry to hide away in some little town in upstate New York to raise a family. When he resurfaced, he was into Christianity and continued to push into other corners of music. He confounded the whole world when he signed up to advertising campaigns for major companies like Cadillac and Victoria's Secret. What was his angle?

Nothing seemed impossible to him, no single box could fence him in. I began to think that this guy Dylan had it figured.

Something about the concept of reinvention was mind-blowing. Why typecast yourself with anything?

I wondered if I retired this year but kept my body in top condition, could I return to the game in three or four years' time? Could I come off the bench with fifteen minutes to go, shape the course of a game and become a different type of player? I had never wished to be boxed in purely as a hurler, so why paint myself as a particular type of player?

It's something that isn't really done in hurling, preparing and coaching a player to fill the role of a substitute and then introducing him to the game when the time is right, to operate in the centre of the pitch if the midfielders are tiring, or to sit in the front of the goal if scores are required.

Sitting in that café, I knew I couldn't play for Clare any longer. It wasn't just because of the way the season had turned out. My life was pulling me in other directions and I couldn't fight those desires any longer.

I was still reluctant to leave playing with Clare in the past, though. I had four good seasons in my body if I got the right environment, but this year I had followed the regime and it hadn't worked. I couldn't return to it, but down the line, maybe I could return to something, to that bench player who can come on and change the flow of a game.

Hurling wasn't done with yet. All of a sudden we found ourselves staring down the barrel of a cocked gun. We were two defeats away from losing our place in the All Ireland championship the following year.

Because we had been knocked out of the championship so early, we would now play Wexford in a relegation semi-final. The loser would play in a relegation final, and whoever lost that would lose their championship status.

Two defeats from disaster.

This relegation element of the championship is something no team wants to get involved in. It's removed from any glamour or major crowds, and those who compete here are cast aside as the real competition powers on, parallel to it, but in a different universe.

Yet that's where we were, and our predicament was simple: two losses and Clare hurling would be in its lowest position in history.

None of our players wished to play Wexford in that relegation playoff. Without a single win all season, we genuinely felt we could lose this game and then run the real risk of losing the relegation decider. Call it negative momentum.

These were bleak days, but during that time something notable occurred: we slowly found a voice. We became empowered. We took responsibility for the future.

As it happened, Wexford felt the same about the game as we did – they had no intention of playing if they could help it. The relegation concept was a relatively new introduction to the hurling calendar and we both felt we could fight it.

The week before the fixture, Clare players heard Gizzy Lyng, the Wexford captain, inform us of his team's position on a mobile phone loudspeaker. Wexford wanted us to agree to join them in backing out of the fixture. We voted unanimously for the proposal, even though it was clear some players were still unsure what they were voting for and what the implications might be.

After this, the administrative wheels cranked into action.

Phone calls from the GAA and the county board piled up. They felt we were backing them, the authorities, into a corner.

Mike spoke to us. He said he didn't want the game to go ahead either but said we had to play. He told us he couldn't be seen to support any player's decision not to go ahead with the game and told us not to expect any support from Wexford.

By then, his words sounded vacant to us. The Wexford manager had threatened to resign if his players were forced to play the game. We didn't receive or expect the same from our manager.

Along with two or three others, I began to lead the charge to back out of the game. I led because I was now one of the senior players on the panel and I led because I felt strongly about what we were doing.

The challenge in itself gradually grew to empower us. After the season we had just put down, it felt like there was plenty to rise up against, and looking back, the Wexford issue merely served to unite players, which ultimately led to the end-of-season stand-off with our management.

A few nights before the game, I received a call from administration in Croke Park.

'We made a mistake,' I was told, 'but we need this game to go ahead. I guarantee we will have a meeting the night before the game and the outcome will be that no team will be relegated. Playing the game is the lesser of two evils.'

It was like a conversation in a spy movie, and it meant the Wexford game was meaningless.

On top of this, each player was threatened with a forty-eight-week ban from hurling if we didn't play, which had implications for our Under-21 team, who were competing in a

Munster final the following week and looking good to capture an All Ireland title for the first time in the county's history. If we didn't play Wexford, the insinuation was that Clare would be kicked out of the Under-21 competition.

We listened to advice and were told that, given the GAA had agreed to meet us halfway and given they would do something unprecedented and go back on a previous decision, we should comply. That, and the Under-21 factor, led to a change of mind.

Strange as it may sound, the game gave us heart. I found my voice, as did the rest of the players, and this was the overriding positive of the season. In the midst of quicksand, we managed to stay afloat.

After three hours on the bus to Wexford we stopped at a hotel in the midlands, and when we arrived, players were starving. We were given white scones, tea or coffee. I was dumbfounded at the treatment we were getting.

Before the game, Mike was brutally honest. For once, there was no roaring and shouting. He simply said he knew it wasn't easy to play under the circumstances. A paltry crowd had travelled from Clare, a couple of hundred people at best. He said we needed to win for those people because they were the ones who truly supported us.

It was the most honourable speech I had heard all year.

I put in a good first half and at the break he told us we were doing well. 'Well done, Griff,' he said. 'You're defying all your critics.'

I didn't really know what he had meant, but in any case the emotion of the season came at me.

I spoke. I said our loved ones, those who really matter,

were the only people there to see us end a catastrophic year. They were backing us when we needed it most. I told them my mother was out in the stands supporting us. 'She still believes in us even though we're down and we haven't won in a year and there's other people out there today – your own families – that feel the same way.'

At the start of the second half, one of our players hit a short pass that was intercepted by Wexford and they scored directly from this. Our manager ran 15 yards on to the field to bellow into the face of our guy who made the pass.

I'd had enough. I shouted back: 'Get off the fuckin' pitch and leave us to do what we want to do for the first time this year!'

Regretfully, this was the only time all season I had expressed our frustrations with the management, and I hadn't chosen an opportune moment.

After the game, Mike congratulated us on the win. He told us he had done his best for Clare but if we didn't want him to remain in the job the following season he would walk away and return to fishing and his boat.

We had won. For the first time all year we had won a game, but the rug was pulled from beneath us. It was the end game, a meaningless, redundant fixture that was instantly buried in the big book of hurling results.

For us and for me, however, the game had served a function. My preparation had been right for the game. I wasn't drained, I wasn't tired. I was rested and fresh, and because of that I walked away from Wexford with confidence. Many of the frustrations that had lingered since Galway began to vanish. For the players, the week before had showed we could make our feelings known and we could make a difference.

Despite the game's lack of significance, the win brought a nourishing feeling and some collective belief – something we hadn't experienced for far too long. I wanted to carry that momentum into another game, to have just one more chance to express myself on the field.

It wasn't to be.

Once more, like all inter-county hurlers when their season ends, we went our separate ways. Back to the welcoming arms of our clubs and into another familiar routine. I looked forward to playing with Ballyea again.

The Clare Under-21s had won the All Ireland, and for the first time in a dozen years, Croke Park danced in saffron and blue beneath a September sun. Despite our own horrific season, hope grew for Clare hurling. We had some exceptional younger players on our own squad; we also had players from that Under-21 team ready to push the county forward.

As the summer began to shut down and when Clare players bumped into one another after club games or at funerals or in bars, we asked the same question: Do you think the management will stay around? Nobody expected the structure to remain. Almost everybody was on the same page. It seemed like a different kind of unity had been created because of the Wexford relegation game.

To most, it seemed a waste of a hurling year.

When autumn was edging towards winter and neither the county board nor management had made it clear who would be in charge for 2010, players became irritated. We began to meet to discuss the season, and very quickly it was plain there was still minimal faith in the management.

If I was looking for an indication that I had developed over the season, one major insight arrived, as most do, with no warning. My club, Ballyea, were taking on the battle-hardened Tulla once more. The stakes were high that morning because the loser would go on to compete in the relegation playoff.

Over the last four years with Ballyea we'd seemed to find ourselves perennially in relegation playoffs. Clare players had even joked that for the Wexford game it might be an idea to send out the Ballyea team to represent Clare because we had developed an instinct to keep our heads above water and in the senior ranks.

Once more, on this day, we overcame Tulla and avoided the possibility of relegation.

While there wasn't the intensity of the year before against Tulla when I had lost control and confronted that abusive supporter, the game had an inherent sour taste. I was having a good day and had nine or ten points on the scoreboard when one of their lads started up.

'You're useless, Griffin. The cycle ruined you. You've found your level here today, down at the lowest rung of competition. This is your future.'

On and on it went throughout the closing minutes of the game. As a younger player I had a tendency to lash out in these circumstances – I had done so on our club's biggest day in 2001 when we, the Davids of the Clare club scene, took on the

Goliaths of Clarecastle in the county final, the blue riband spectacle of club hurling. I caved into the goading of a Clarecastle player, threw a punch and received a red card.

But against Tulla that morning I held firm, and when the game was over I approached my tormentor.

In the days before this game, with thoughts of retirement on my mind, I had been dwelling a lot on my career. In my head I had gone over the ten years I had played with Clare and all those lingering doubts that I would never reach the goals I had first written in chalk on my bedroom door as a teenager. I thought about how I had answered my own questions and coped with demons that were no longer in my life.

I spoke to the Tulla player and must have sounded like some demented Baptist preacher. 'Look, my friend, I have faced myself. I know what is there. I am happy with what is there and I know myself.'

He probably thought I had watched too much *Oprah* and possibly ripped me to shreds in the dressing room afterwards, but the thing was, I felt another brick crashing to the ground that morning.

The Clare situation continued and word was seeping into the media that our team was unhappy with the management set-up, which had another year on their contract. Acres of column inches and hours of sports shows were given over to the issue.

We possibly could have handled things better from the start and organized ourselves into a stronger unit. We had no hard experience and could have tapped into templates used by other counties that had found themselves in a similar bind. We could have told our side of things to the press to garner public support, but we were operating in a vacuum of information ourselves. Meetings with the board had been cancelled, and on the one hand we were hearing the management was on the verge of resignation, but on the other there was no concrete sign that this was going to happen.

As the thing rolled on, we became unified.

One thing was clear: it was difficult to hold management entirely accountable. As players, we were the group of men chosen to lead our county back to glory and we had undoubtedly failed. On the field we did not perform to the levels we had come to expect of ourselves. More importantly, off the field we accepted mediocrity and by extension condoned it.

It was now clear that not only an overhaul in management was required but a complete examination of all the structures supporting Clare hurling.

In any company, success is measured by several quantifiable markers. If a business is not profitable then gradually it will move towards teetering on the edge of bankruptcy. If winning All Irelands was our county's marker of success, then we were in an unhealthy state and we too were facing bankruptcy. What we needed were strategic managers to come in and help improve our system, to help us identify where things had broken down.

Unfortunately, this climate doesn't exist in the world of hurling, so as players we ploughed on and vowed to stand up for what we felt was right for our team. A growing sense of knowing my own internal barometer for what was right and wrong resulted in me taking on a leading role in motivating players to demand more of themselves and the Clare set-up.

The saga spilled over into October and November. The administrators of the county board were now highly involved in trying to quench the fire, and I was fingered as the ring-leader of unrest.

Despite strong advice from members of the county board to step back from the stand-off, I forged on.

The younger members of the panel, the victorious Under-21s, became vocal in demanding a change of management. They did not want their futures hindered by a half-decent set-up. They wanted structures to mirror their ambitions, and in the end, in those player meetings, all I did was coordinate voices. With the other older players on the panel I encouraged guys to speak their minds, to remain fearless of the supposed ramifications to them or their careers.

After a few weeks, the whole thing became pedantic and taxing. Letters sent to the board, more and more phone calls. Devoting time to a new business was difficult.

In the back of my mind I knew I was retiring from Clare one way or the other and it became a balancing act of when to announce my intentions. I continued to believe the players needed new structures if they were to fulfil their potential, and as the chain of events unravelled, the younger guys began to lead. Considering my imminent retirement, I simply wanted to provide whatever direction I could.

Since that conversation in the Killaloe café, it had been clear I could not commit myself to Clare in 2010, and in mid-November, in a Sunday newspaper, I announced my departure from the game and outlined the reasons why I had made my decision. It was apparent that given the fallout from our unsuc-cessful season and the impasse that had arisen between players and management, my retirement would be interpreted as a statement against the set-up in 2009. Undoubtedly that had a large part to play, but I was eager to communicate that it wasn't the only reason why I had chosen to retire. The business and my ambitions to get involved in other aspects of life were all genuine factors. These elements may not grab the newspaper headlines like a player/management dispute, but they were just as significant for me.

In giving my final newspaper interview as a hurler, I was also eager that I wouldn't be remembered as the guy who left the game under the cloud created by the impasse. In the interview, I wanted to convey that in ten years of playing for Clare, this impasse was a mere footnote – an interesting, cathartic and slightly sad footnote, but a footnote nonetheless.

Before the article appeared I informed each of my team-mates of my intentions, and after that, I immediately withdrew from the negotiations between players, management and the board. I distanced myself and really had no desire to remain informed of the daily goings-on.

I would miss the banter, the lads, the feeling of driving from training on a summer's night with the radio playing and the window rolled down, satisfied after a hard session.

I was leaving the game at an early age but I was leaving happy and content. I considered my career as one of fulfilment: I had pushed my boundaries and the Canadian cycle came at the right time. It opened new experiences, it widened my horizons. If that meant it took time adjusting back to hurling, then such was my life.

A month after my retirement, the management resigned.

Shortly after this, a new set-up led by Ger 'The Sparrow' O'Loughlin was appointed.

The storm had passed, and whether the management or players were right or wrong didn't matter any more. Clare hurlers were on the training fields, inhaling the darkness of winter and once more dreaming of warmer days and Croke Park.

For me, for the first time since I was a young man, that search was over. Life had moved in a different direction.

Epilogue

The season ends high above the lush Kenyan landscape, in the hilltop town of Iten.

Before the Wexford relegation game I had visited Ger Hartmann's clinic for some pre-game psychology and last-minute tuning, and bumped into Lorna Kiplagat, an athlete Hartmann was working with.

Lorna had broken world records for the 5,000 metres, 10 miles, 20,000 metres and half-marathon. She comes from Kenya but now runs under the national flag of the Netherlands. We got to talking and she invited me to visit her high-altitude training centre in the Rift Valley of Kenya, 8,000 feet above sea level, where she and her team seek out to-morrow's champions from the ocean of young talented Kenyan runners.

Nine days of bunking down in Iten and running at altitude was the offer – a tough end to a tough season. But having heard Hartmann and Lorna speak of the Kenyan camp, where athletes grow their own food and focus on nothing but train-ing day after day, I had a desire to experience this first hand, so two weeks after announcing my retirement I flew to Africa with Keira.

Touching down at the small runway at Iten, one of the most bizarre welcome parties stood in wait. A group of thirty men, women and children had worn their Sunday best to see an aeroplane. It was a day out. Looking out on to the red clay roads and green countryside, I knew I was entering another world.

After a few days, the trip took on a steady rhythm. Three young athletes, Joanne, Dorchas and Nancy, had been given the task of taking us under their wing. All three are bound for the USA on running scholarships. This is the core philosophy of Lorna's camp. Athletes who show the greatest promise are matched with Ivy League schools across the US, and the wish of the camp leaders is that these athletes will one day return home and add to the economic and political development of Kenya.

Each morning, at six, we are woken from our restless altitude slumber and join Joanne, Dorchas and Nancy for a 10-kilometre loop in the half-light of early morning. The shortness of breath hits hard, but a few runs in, the lungs begin to burn less.

The body structure of the young athletes at this altitude camp allows them to glide across the ground. Each wants to grab the lottery ticket and make it out of Kenya and into the world of international athletics. These athletes look at us with vague curiosity and wonder what brings these white folk to Iten to run each morning.

Everywhere we go, local kids run with us. At 6.30, they are now making their way to school, many in bare feet, and they run shoulder to shoulder with us, sometimes for as many as 5 kilometres, at a breezy pace. They smile and point and shout 'mazungu', meaning 'white man'.

After each run, breakfast tastes like honey from the gods: fruit, pancakes with chocolate spread and freshly made coffee.

All week I have grown to really admire this girl Joanne. She is quietly driven to be the best, and on our morning runs I can see she is tough, that she refuses to give in to the pain. Her background is similar to the other athletes here. Her family is unable to pay for her education but she harbours genuine hopes of becoming a world-class athlete.

On our third day, she invites me to run alongside her for her interval session, which consists of ten runs as hard as possible for two minutes with one minute rest after each.

It is early afternoon, the sun is high and the red clay bubbles with heat.

We start fast, and the first run passes at a powerful pace. Joanne is strong and she knows it. She will push harder and harder as each two-minute interval passes. When the seconds tick down during our one-minute break, time becomes precious.

On our seventh interval, she begins to break me. She pulls away strongly as my oxygen levels deplete and my lungs burn once more. For the final three runs, once I catch up to her, it is time to go again. I finish the session panting, exhausted and beaten by a seventeen-year-old girl.

But I see things in Iten that I have not seen all season with Clare. Joy in the faces of those involved in their sport, delight in an environment that can actually help catapult you to your goal. When I leave, I am reminded of how I too once felt when I was on the cusp of my own sports dream.

A week later, I was back on the now familiar trail that leads through Ballycugguran Woods. A little over a year had passed since I first climbed this coarse, stony path.

Worries about the coming season came and went and were dealt with. For the first time in ten years I was no longer part of an inter-county hurling team, but for some reason I felt as though I was preparing for something unknown.

I knew it didn't bring fear or anxiety. I knew I was prepared for whatever may come.

Beneath the woods and in the silence of the valley, for the pure pleasure of it, for the pure pleasure of life, I found myself screaming at the sky.

Picture Acknowledgements

All photographs are kindly supplied by the author except for the following:

Page 1 – TG pointing: Ray McManus/Sportsfile.

Pages 2 and 3 – clockwise, starting top left: TG leaves the field, 28 May, 2006, Clare v. Cork: Ray McManus/Sportsfile; TG striking long: Matt Browne/Sportsfile; TG's side step, 13 August, 2006: © Inpho/Andrew Paton; TG and J. J. Delaney, 13 August, 2006: © Inpho/Andrew Paton; TG running at the Wexford defence, 23 July, 2006: © Inpho/Andrew Paton.

Pages 6 and 7 – clockwise, starting top left: ball boy and hurley carrier: © Eamon Ward; Sean Óg Ó hAilpín, TG and John Gardiner: ©Inpho/Donall Farmer; TG injured (both): ©Inpho/James Crombie; high fielding v. Waterford, 1 June, 2008: Brendan Moran/Sportsfile.

Index

Alberta, cycling through 145–7
All Ireland Championship 43–4
    see specific games
All Ireland medal 33, 39–40, 41–2,
    240
All Star awards 33, 49, 78
    2006, 96, 109–10, 123, 124, 229
    journey to 91, 92, 98, 109
All Stars game, New York 197
Armstrong, Lance 43, 63, 96
    endorsement for TG's ride 124,
    125
    foreword xi–xii
    It's not about the bike 96
    meeting with 112, 114, 126–32
    ride with 130–1
Ashton, Richard 15, 16, 20
Austin, Texas 128
    Ride for the Roses weekend
    188–90

Baker, Ollie 86–7, 199
    game analysis 45
Ballyea
    coping with questions 180–1, 185
    cycling return to 169, 172, 177,
    181
    family home 7, 15, 29, 36–7, 38–9,
    58, 180
    Christmas at 94, 190–1
    family settle at 18–19
    practice at 86
    weekly routine 38–9
Ballyea hurling team, playing for
    105
    2008 relegation playoff 215–17

Clarecastle, 2001 game against
    284
club championships 210–11,
    282–4
Ennis, 2008 relegation playoff
    against 215–17
Frankie [TG's brother], playing
    for 216–17
preferred to Clare 275–6
Tulla, games against
    2008 210–11
    2009 283–4
Ballyheigue 41
behaviour, healthy/obsessive
    227–30, 274–5
    breakthrough sensation 42–3
    competitiveness, inappropriate
    149–50
    compulsion, athletes 24
    control loss after Ballyea game
    210–12
    obsessive streak gone 274–5
    overcompensating, training
    alone 22–3
    performance analysis, obsessive
    8, 26–31, 33, 39
    perspective, maintaining 30–1,
    34–5
Bethune, Matt 132–3
    and news of JG's death 148
    and Ride for the Cure 98–9, 100,
    132, 135, 148, 171, 208–9
    bike crash on gravel 153–4
BFG, design/building 195, 196–7
Biddy Early, Curse of 46
bike crashes 153–5

bike, spare, and interaction 149
Bohan, Fr Harry (The Priest) 197
    and Clare management team
        59–61, 62
Book, Rob
    and Ride for the Cure 133, 149,
        156, 159
    and team interaction 149–50
    cures TG's knee 143–4
    sleeping problem 148
Boston Red Sox 46
boxing 20–1
    Dunne, Bernard 248–9, 259–60
    McDonough and 106, 107–8
    Muhammad Ali, visit to Ennis
        267–8
Brennan, Eddie 85
Brewer, Chris 128
Brooke, Zinzan 259
Bugler, Brendan 272

Cahercalla Hospice, funds for 186
Canadian Cascades, Coquihalla
    pass 142–3
Canadian plains 150–3
Canadian Shield 161
Canadian TV, backs Ride for the
    Cure 134
Canadians, and hurling 27
cancer
    fundraising for 93, 96, 124
    see also Ride for the Cure; Tony
        Griffin Foundation
cancer patients, wayside 158–9
cancer survivors, meet Ride at
    Halifax 168–9
Cape Split 195–6
Carey, D. J. 26, 48
Carmody, Tony 66, 70, 80, 83, 225
Cash, Johnny 152–3
Cheung, Dr Stephen 114–21
    on TG's physical condition 167,
        168
    on training into cycling 144
children, and hurling 25–6
Chinese emigrants (Canada), rail
    line construction 162
chiropractic, McDonough and
    101–4, 109

Chris [police officer] 141
Citadel Hill, Halifax 19–20
Clare hurling team
    2008 season 198, 199–202
    All Ireland 1995 win 46–8
    All Ireland 2002 23, 76–8
    All Ireland 2006, hopes 53–4, 62,
        76
    and Cork hurling team
        2005 championship semi-final
            against 9, 39, 50–2, 79
        2006 championship game
            against 53, 54, 55–9, 62
        2006 league game against
            45–6
        2007 championship game
            against 159–60
        2008 game against 208–9
        2009 league game against 248,
            249–50, 251, 252
    and Dublin hurling team
        2006 championship game
            against 62, 67
        2009 league game against
            254–5
    and Galway hurling team
        2006 challenge game against
            55
        2007 match against 181, 184
        2009 championship game
            against 221–27, 265, 270–5
    and Kilkenny hurling team 6
        2002 championship final
            against 53, 78–9
        2004 league final against 81
        2004 semi-final against 50,
            79–80
        2006 final against 80–7
        2009 league game against
            251–52
    and Limerick hurling team
        2006 championship game
            against 45–6, 64–7, 75
        2006 league semi-final against
            53
        2007 championship quarter-
            final against 184
        2008 championship game
            against 200–2

2009 league game against 242,
244
and Meath hurling team
2001 league game against
102–3
and Tipperary hurling team
2002 championship game
against 76–7
2005 championship game
against 51–2, 54
2008 championship final
against 205–7
2009 championship game
against 234–6, 265, 269–70
2009 league game against
245
2009 Waterford Crystal Cup
game against 239–40
and Waterford hurling team
2004 championship game
against 50
2005 league game against 22–3,
54
2006 game against 44–5
2008 championship game
against 199–200
2009 challenge game against
263–6
2009 league game against
242–4
and Wexford hurling team
2006 league game against 28–9,
31, 36
2006 quarter-final against 67,
69–76
2009 relegation semi-final
277–82
jerseys, respect for 247
management issues 233–4, 247,
288
and 2010 season planning
282–6
disrespect 257–8, 272–3
professionalism issues 254–61
managers see Daly, Anthony;
Loughnane, Ger; O'Loughlin,
Ger
TG and 7–10, 36–7, 217
commuting from Canada 7–8

debut 2002 season 76–9
management and 49–50, 202–3
retirement 232–3, 276, 277,
286–7
training, selected for 40
Under-14 squad 33
year out & return 122–3, 181–4,
190–1, 195
young players, helping 252
training 3–6, 9–10
McNamara and 238–9, 242–3,
243–4, 245–7, 254–63
overtraining 183
pre-Waterford 242–3, 243–4
objectivity 221, 260
Under-21s 257, 279–80, 282
demand management change
286
Clarecastle, 2001 Ballyea game
against 284
Collins, Michael (Gazzy) 61–2,
225–6
Conlon, John 222
Considine, Tony 161, 181, 183, 190,
199
and TG's year out 122–3
Coquihalla mountain pass 142–3
Cordoba, Ricardo 248, 260
Cork hurling team
2005 championship semi-final
against 9, 39, 50–2, 79
2006 championship game
against 53, 54, 55–9, 62
2006 league game against 45–6
2007 championship game
against 159–60
2008 game against 208–9
2009 league game against 248,
249–50, 251, 252
Cork, University College,
Waterford Crystal Cup match
39–40
Coyle, Dan, Tour de force 43, 155
Croke Park, Dublin 21, 46, 47, 57,
62, 86, 184, 205, 279, 282
Wexford match 69–70, 72, 74–5
Crusheen, training sessions 37–8
cryogenic therapy, Wexford 183
crystal meth effects 141

Cunningham, Alan, hurling coach 62
Curse of Biddy Early 46
Cusack Park 43, 49, 55, 62, 64–5, 184, 221, 223–5, 239, 244, 253, 271–73
cycling
  aftermath 177–80
  and identity 180–1
  effect on hurling fitness 182, 203–4
  effect on hurling mentality 204–5
  gear 111, 113
  fascination with 96–8
  training for 111, 113–21
  see also Ride for the Cure
cyclist, spiritual 146

Dalhousie University
  final exams completed 195
  final year, anxiety 177–80
  finance to study 11, 62–4, 82–3
  McDonough and 104
  study at 7–8, 10–11, 13–16
  track squad 21
Daly, Anthony 5, 8, 9, 28–9, 254
  1995 Clare captain 47
  and 2002 Tipperary game 76–7
  and 2006 loss to Cork 57–8, 59, 84, 86
  and Fr Bohan 61
  and Johnny Glynn 61
  as public figure 68
  Clare manager 48–50, 52
  game analysis 45
  TG and 49–50
Defiagbon, Dave 107–8
Delaney, J. J. 85
Donnellan, Michael, at Toronto fundraiser 165–6
Dorchas [Kenyan athlete] 290
Down, 2006 league game against 28
Dublin
  Croke Park 21, 46, 47, 57, 62, 86, 184, 205, 279, 282
  Wexford match 69–70, 72, 74–5
  cycle ride to Ennis 101, 125, 169–70

Keira 170, 184
LiveStrong Global Cancer Summit xii
Ride for the Cure launched 124
Dublin hurling team
  2006 championship game against 62, 67
  2009 league game against 254–5
Dunne, Bernard 248–9, 259–60
Dylan, Bob 230, 276

Ennis
  Clare team and 32, 65, 256, 263
  Cusack Park 43, 49, 55, 62, 64–5, 184, 221, 223–5, 239, 244, 253, 271–73
  cycle ride, last leg 101, 125–6, 169–72, 180, 208, 216, 249
  Fair Green 42
  life in 12, 31, 36, 122, 195, 231, 237, 240
  Muhammad Ali and 267–8
  school in 63
Ennis Abbey 55
Ennis hurling team, Ballyea 2008 relegation playoff against 215–17

Falkirk, TG's parents at 16–18
Farrell, Dessie 214
father/son relationships, and hurling 26
Field, The [movie] 52
fitness test, Clare team 32
Fitzgerald, Davy 41, 62, 71, 72, 161, 199, 252
Flynn, Colum 20
Forrest Gump [movie] 187
Fox, Terry, trans-Canada run 163–4
Francis, Stephen, walking preacher 156
François & Olivier, cycling east 157
Frasier Way, RV donation 125
full-time hurling, TG and 31, 37–9

GAA (Gaelic Athletic Association) 101, 185, 223, 279, 280

Gaelic football teams, training
  weekends 256
Gaelic Grounds 199, 206
Gaelic Players Association, and
  mental health issues 214
Galway
  boxing gym 20–1
  fundraising ball 186
Galway hurling team
  2006 challenge game against 55
  2007 match against 181, 184
  2009 championship game
    against 221–27, 265, 270–5
Galway University, studying
  economics 20
Gazzy (Michael Collins) 61–2,
  225–6
Gillen, Chick, boxing gym 20–1
Gilligan, Niall 71, 83, 84, 197, 240,
  252
Give to Live in Canada 215,
  215–17
Glynn, Johnny 4–5, 32, 57, 80, 231
  Daly and 61, 62
goalscoring, developing
  unpredictability 23–4
God, asking help from 147
golf 11
Gordon, Taylor 108
Grady, Abe 267
Grand-Pré 196
greetings, wayside 158–9
Grenoble, Tour de France 97–8
Griffin, Angela (TG's sister) 34
  visit to 192–4
Griffin, Frankie (TG's brother)
  playing for Ballyea 216–17
  wedding 190
Griffin, Jerome (TG's father)
    16–19, 26
  and cycling 96
  and hurling 96
  and TG's career 40, 41, 77–8
  asbestos exposure 17
  death 4, 7, 39, 54, 148–9
    coming to terms 92–1, 122, 152,
      192–4
    crying for 139
    goodbye statement 193–4, 228

guilt feelings about 94–5
his own man 34
spiritual support from 146, 170
Griffin, Liam, on TG's full-time
  hurling 31
Griffin, Maria (TG's mother) 16–19
  and JG's death 39
  and relegation semi–final 281
  on TG overworking 185–6, 187
Griffin, Rosaleen 94
  staying with 195
Griffin, Sean 121
Griffin family
  and TG's year out of hurling
    121–1
  home 7, 15, 18–19, 29, 36–7, 38–9,
    58, 180
  Christmas with 94, 190–1
  join TG at Nicolet 166–7
groin injury, osteitis pubis 67
Guevara, Che, The motorcycle
    diaries 63

Halifax
  break at 31
  Harbour 19–20
  Ride For The Cure arrives 167–8
  sense of freedom 12–13
  speaking commitments 187–8
  uncertainty 177–80
Halifax to Austin, charity cycle
    215, 217–18
Hall, Priscilla, at Toronto
  fundraiser 165
Hamilton, Tyler 155
hamstring injuries 191, 198–204,
  231–32, 237
Hartmann, Ger 24, 198–9, 231, 246,
  289
headwind, cycling into 151
Hemingway, Ernest, A farewell to
    arms 65
Hickey, Seamus 53
Hoey, David 56
Holtz, Lou, Winning every day 35
homesickness 13–14
Hope town, night in 141–2
Hoyt, Rick 98–100
human kinetics study 10, 104

hurling
and psychology 26–7
and self-worth 27–8
career
combining with Canada 11
full-time 31, 37–9
return to 181–4, 190–1
year out, criticisms 121–4
faster game 258
fitness, and cycling 182, 203–4
hating rivals, hurling and 204–5,
234–6, 237–8
Irish people and 24–7
McDonough and 106–7
stereotypes 12–13
year, components 44
see also Clare hurling team
Hurling All Stars game, New York
197

interval sessions, cycle training
119–20
Ireland Park, Toronto 165
Irish ambassador, at Ottawa 166
Irish Cancer Society, funds for 186
Irish community, and Ride for the
Cure 126, 147, 158, 164
Irish men, and emotion expression
212–13
Irish people and hurling 25–7
Iten, Kenya, high-altitude training
centre 289–92

Jacob, Michael 73
Joanne [Kenyan athlete] 290, 291

Keane, Michael 36
Keane, Roy 259
Keira 170, 178, 183, 209, 232
at Grand-Pré with 196
cycling with 184
in Kenya 290
visits in South Africa 191, 194
Kelly, Eoin 237, 275
Kennedy Park, late at 261–62
Kenny, Tom 55
Kenya, high-altitude training
centre 289–92
Kicking Horse Pass 161

Kilkenny hurling team 6
2002 championship final against
53, 78–9
2004 league final against 81
2004 semi-final against 50, 79–80
2006 final against 80–7
2009 league game against 251–52
and accountability 251–52
Killaloe Bridge 91
Killaloe, move to 230–1
Killarney, team training weekend
246–7, 255
Kimmage, Paul, on Armstrong
129, 130
kindness, wayside 158–9
kinesiology 10, 104
Kiplagat, Lorna 289, 290
Knaggs, Bart 129
knee trouble 143–4

Lahinch beach 68
Lake Superior, bike crash near
154–5
Lance Armstrong Foundation 112,
188
Landry, Hayden 232
Landry, Janice, PR for Ride for the
Cure 126
Larkin, Eoin 251
lateness issues 261–65
Layton, Jack, at Toronto fundraiser
165
Lee, John 222, 224, 272, 273
legs, quadriceps-dominant 203–4
Liam McCarthy Cup 47–8
Limerick hurling team
2006 championship game
against 45–6, 64–7, 75
2006 league semi-final against 53
2007 championship quarter-final
against 184
2008 championship game
against 200–2
2009 league game against 242,
244
LiveStrong organization 159
funds for 186
Lohan, Brian 5–7, 32, 41, 52–3, 57,
62, 70–1, 72, 73, 75, 76

Lohan, Frank 69–70, 123
Loughnane, Ger
  1995 Clare manager 47–8
  and weights training 103–4
  as referee 49–50
  training style 258
Lynch, Colin 6–7, 32, 41, 55, 56, 62,
  71, 72, 75, 77, 247, 248, 252
Lyng, Gizzy 278
Lyons, Cyril 40

Macken, Eddie, backs Ride for the
  Cure 134–6
Man of the Match award 66, 75
Manitoba flatlands 151–3
Mansour, Bruce 218
  and Armstrong meeting 128–32
  and Muhammad Ali visit 268
  and Ride for the Cure 110,
    111–12
  and TG's motivation 191
map-reading error, consquences
  138
Markham, Alan 252
  constructs BFG 196–7
Martin, Denise, performance
  analyst 61
Martinez, Kiko 248, 260
Mary [in Hope] 141–2
Mayo, Iban 43, 44
McCabe, Cathy 13
McCabe, John 10–11, 13–15, 31–2,
  165
  McDonough and 104
  on Cape Split 195
  on Halifax Harbour 19, 20
  on TG's fitness 198
McCormack, Eoin 84
McDonald, Todd
  and Armstrong meeting 127–32
  and relay cycle from Halifax to
    Austin 215
  and Ride for the Cure 110,
    112–13
McDonough, Alexa 108
  at Toronto fundraiser 165
McDonough, Margaret 160
McDonough, Travis 101–9
  2007 match reports 160

and McCabe 104
and Ride for the Cure planning
  91–2, 101, 124, 126
and TG's hamstring injury 203
and Tony Griffin Foundation 185
third child 160–1
McGarry, James 81, 84, 85
McGee (Canada), bike crash near
  153–4
McGee, Greg 159
McMahon, Conor, on attacking
  play 81
McMahon, Diarmuid 38–9, 53
  chooses wood 196
McMahon, Sean 32, 41, 52–3, 62,
  64–5, 75, 252
McNamara, Mike 190, 199, 238–41
  and lateness 261–66
  and planning 257
  and Quinn 240–1, 249–51
  and relegation semi-final 279,
    280
  and training 238–9, 242–3, 243–4,
    245–7, 254–63
  lost players' confidence 269–70
  on league Division Two games
    254
Meath hurling team
  2001 league game against 102–3
mental health issues,
  de-stigmatizing 214
Merritt, lost in dreams 144–5
Mexican riders, Ride for the Roses
  weekend 189–90
Michipicoten Bay, bike crash near
  154–5
mobile phone, on Ride 147
Moggan, Liam 61, 71, 231
Morrissey, Marty 109
motivation, speaking on 187, 188
Muhammad Ali, visit to Ennis
  267–8
Mullane, John 50
Mundy 268
Munster, provincial championship
  round against 53
Murphy, Brian 51

Nancy [Kenyan athlete] 290

Native Canadians
  poor 140–1
  reservations 162–3
New Forest, exploring 192–4, 195
New York, hurling All Stars game
  197
North Kerry
  2000 game against 41
note takers, games 232
Nugent, Barry 23, 57

O'Connell, Brian 50
  as fitness barometer 32
  designs BFG 196
O'Connor, Ben 55
O'Connor, Cian 66
O'Connor, Doc 70, 73–5
O'Connor, Jamesie 247
  coaching by 37
O'Connor, Jerry 56
Offaly, 2006 league game against
  43, 44–5
Óg Ó hAilpín, Seán 252
O'Loughlin, Ger 'The Sparrow',
  2010 manager 208
Ontario 159–64
opponents, winding-up 83
Ottawa, Parliament Hill reception
  166
Ovarian Cancer Canada, funds for
  186
over-the-shoulder shots 81

Patterson, Floyd 226
performance-enhancing drugs,
  Tour de France 129–30
Phelan, Brian 'Bull' 50
phone sponsorship 126
pie addiction 157
planning, teams and 247–8
Plunkett, Conor 56, 71
Plymouth, Jerome Griffin at 17
Postal Service team, Armstrong
  127
Pozzolo family, cycling east 156–7
prairies 151–3
pre-match strategy, personal 35
provisions, Ride for the Cure,
  finding 125, 126

psychology, and hurling 26–7
public figure, becoming 68–9
publicising Ride for the Cure
  133–6

Quebec City 166
Quinn, Gerry 51, 53, 56, 71, 74, 84,
  123, 240–1, 243, 249–51
  oversees BFG building 196

railway trains, prairies 151
relegation semi-final 2009 277–82
Ride for the Cure
  Bethune, Matt, and, 98–9, 100,
    132, 135, 148, 153–4, 171,
    208–9
  Book, Rob, and 133, 149, 156,
    159
  Canadian TV, backs Ride for the
    Cure 134
  donations 128, 147, 186–7
  Dublin launch 124
  Dublin to Ennis 101, 125–6,
    169–72, 180, 208, 216, 249
  Ennis to Ballyea 169, 172, 177,
    181
  Halifax arrival 167–8
  Hope, first day's ride to 136–41
  Irish community and 126, 147,
    158, 164
  Halifax arrival 167–8
  Landry, Janice and 126
  Macken, Eddie, backs 134–6
  Mansour, Bruce and 110, 111–12
  McDonald, Todd and 110, 112–13
  McDonough, Travis and 91–2,
    101, 124, 126
  planning 91–2, 98–101, 110–12,
    124, 125–7
  provisions, finding 125, 126
  publicising 126, 133–6
  RV, Fraserway donation 125
  sponsorship, finding 125–6
  Toronto arrival 164–6
  training for 111, 113–21
  Vancouver launch function
    124–5, 134–6
  volunteers team 125

Whidden, Ben, and 98, 100, 113, 132, 136, 148, 167, 171
see also Canadian provinces and cities
Ride for the Roses weekend 188–90
River Fergus 30
road team, Cheung and 118–19
road training, cycle 119
Rocky Mountains, overcome 142–6
routine, weekly, in Ballyea 38–9
running scholarships 290
RV (Ride for the Cure)
and traffic issues 137–8
Fraserway donation 125

sales work 11
Saskatoon, heading for 153, 159
self-belief 63–4
and self-doubt 8, 28–30, 31, 33–4, 85–8, 152–3
and cycle training 119, 120–1
anxiety/uncertainty 177–80
confidence loss in hurling game 206–7
emotion expression as weakness 212–13
Fr Bohan on 60
motivation loss 190, 191, 208–9
overcoming 70–1, 74, 75, 138–40
and self-worth 27–8
athlete, separating from man 221–30, 274
confidence from preparation 117, 198, 199
failure/defeat, overcoming 28–9, 138–40
freedom from hurler stereotype 12–13
negativity management 257–8
nothing to prove 189–90
others' opinions, freeing from 33–4, 44–5
Semple Stadium 55
Shannon, Sharon 268
Shefflin, Henry 48, 84–5
shoulder injury 154–5, 182, 183
sleep, during cycle training 120

sliotars
JG saves 41
old, effect on training 245–6, 254
snow, training in 21–2
South Africa, visits Keira 191, 194
Spanish Point 3–6, 9, 68
speaking commitments, continuing 185–8
speaking out, failure 260–1
sponsorship, Ride for the Cure, finding 125–6
sports psychology 24–5, 71
sports science 11
Sports Academy International 232, 256, 266–9
and Muhammad Ali visit 267–8
St Flannan's College 32, 37, 38
stationary bike, training 113–18
Stipe, Michael 106
striking movement, analysing 24
Summitt, Pat 270
support team, Clare 59–62
sustained power, developing 118

t'ai chi group, Citadel Hill 22
team development 251–53, 255–6
team players, and emotional issues 212–13
teenagers, cycling expedition 157–8
Temple Gate Hotel, Ennis 32
tennis, McDonough and 106–7
Terry Fox memorial 163
Thunder Bay 163–4
Thurles 55
championship game against Cork 2007 159–60
Tiernan, Tommy 66
Tipperary hurling team
2002 championship game against 76–7
2005 championship game against 51–2, 54
2008 championship final against 205–7
2009 championship game against 234–6, 265, 269–70
2009 league game against 245
2009 Waterford Crystal Cup game against 239–40

Tipperary hurling team (*cont.*)
rivalry 234–5
warm-up kit 245
Tony Griffin Foundation
7,000-Kilometre Ride for the
Cure, Dublin launch 124–5
becomes Give to Live in Canada
215
continuing work 185–8
in Canada 214–15, 215–17
Toronto, Ride for the Cure arrival
164–6
Tour de France 2005, watching
97–8
track squad, Dalhousie University
21
training, personal
background team 231–32
for cycling 111, 113–21
for All Stars game 197–8
hurling 19–22, 37, 182–3
obsessive 21–4, 30–1
with Dalhousie track squad 21
with Stephen Cheung 114–21
Trans-Canadian railway
construction 161–2
Trek bikes 128, 130
backup bike, crash 153–4
Tulla
Ballyea 2008 game against
210–11
Ballyea 2009 game against 283–4
Tuohy, Fergus 41
Tyrrell, Jackie 84

Under-21s 257, 279–80, 282
demand management change
286
University College Cork, game
against 39
Upsala, Ontario 159–61
USA, Kenyans on running
scholarships 290

Vancouver
Ride for the Cure launch
function 124–5, 134–6

first day's ride to Hope 136–41
video analysis 32
volunteers team, Ride for the Cure
125

Walk the line [movie] 152–3
Walsh, David, on Armstrong 129,
130
Walsh, Shane `Brick' 243
Walsh, Tommy 83
warm-up kit, Tipperary 245
Waterford hurling team
2004 championship game
against 50
2005 league game against 22–3,
54
2006 game against 44–5
2008 championship game
against 199–200
2009 challenge game against
263–6
2009 league game against 242–4
disarray 200
Waterford Crystal tournament 39,
190–1, 239–40
Wawa, bike crash near 154–5
weariness of the road 147–8
weather, prairies 151
weights training, McDonough and
103
Wexford
cryogenic therapy 183
training weekend 261–63
Wexford hurling team
2006 league game against 28–9,
31, 36
2006 quarter-final against 67,
69–76
2009 relegation semi-final 277–82
What's Important Now 35–6
Whidden, Ben
and news of JG's death 148–9
and Ride for the Cure 98, 100,
113, 132, 136, 148, 167, 171
white stone 192–4, 195, 228
Wilkinson, Jonny 228–9
Wood, Keith 259